FAMILIES AT WAR

VOICES FROM THE TROUBLES

To Emmeline and Bob

Peter Taylor has reported Northern Ireland for nearly twenty years, through the 1970s for *This Week* and *TV Eye*, and through the 1980s for *Panorama*, and has made over 30 documentaries on the conflict. He has also presented *Brass Tacks* and *Newsnight* on BBC 2. His Penguin special, *Beating the Terrorists?*, received the Cobden Trust Human Rights Award; *The Smoke Ring – Tobacco, Money and Multinational Politics* (Bodley Head and Sphere) won the WHO Commemorative Award for its contribution to public health; and *Stalker: The Search for the Truth* (Faber) was based on his Royal Television Society's award-winning *Panorama*

PETER TAYLOR

FAMILIES AT WAR

VOICES FROM THE TROUBLES

BBC BOOKS

Published by BBC Books,
A division of BBC Enterprises Ltd
Woodlands, 80 Wood Lane, London W12 0TT

First published 1989

ISBN 0 563 20787 6 (paperback)
ISBN 0 563 20788 4 (hardback)

Typset in 10/12pt Linotron Times
by Phoenix Photosetting, Chatham, Kent

Printed and bound in Great Britain by
Mackays of Chatham PLC, Chatham, Kent

Jacket/cover printed by Richard Clay Ltd, Norwich, Norfolk

CONTENTS

ACKNOWLEDGEMENTS

This book could not have been written without the help of all the families involved. They were patient, courageous and kind and gave me insights into Ireland I had never had before. They took me into their homes and into their confidence, sometimes reliving painful experiences most preferred to forget. All they asked was that I should treat them fairly. I hope they feel that I have. All of them, identified or otherwise, have my thanks and admiration.

I am also indebted to Sir James Glover, the Royal Green Jackets general, who first planted the seed of involving the Regiment as a 'family', from which the whole project grew, and to all those in the Green Jackets, in particular to Lt-Col. Jamie Daniell, and the Ministry of Defence who so tirelessly and effectively helped translate an idea into a television programme and a book. I also wish to thank the Press Office of the Royal Ulster Constabulary for giving me permission to interview members of the Force, and the Governor of Maghaberry Prison and the Press Office and Prisons Department of the Northern Ireland Office who gave me access to Shane Paul O'Doherty in gaol.

My thanks too to those who made it professionally possible: to George Carey and Michael Dutfield with whom I worked on the television trilogy, to Jonathan Powell who commissioned it, and to Tim Gardam who spared me from *Panorama* in order to do it; to Sheila Ableman of BBC Books who so enthusiastically commissioned the book, and to Tony Kingsford who so skilfully and patiently edited it.

And lastly my thanks and love to my own 'family at war', to Sue, Ben and Sam for putting up with me and supporting me throughout the long campaign.

INTRODUCTION

This book was meant to have fourteen chapters until I received a letter from one of the families I had interviewed. In the intervening period, one of its members had been murdered, adding yet further grief to that already suffered over the past twenty years. Over the months I had got to know them quite well and had been moved by their quiet dignity and strength in the face of a devastation that would have broken many families. They wrote and asked me not to use the chapter on their experience, hoping I would understand.

I mention this as a way of illustrating the sensitivity of the ground covered by the subject of this book and the accompanying television trilogy. Working in Northern Ireland over the past year, I found greater fear and suspicion than I'd ever encountered before in many years of reporting the Troubles – and they were fears expressed by all sides. Many families I met whose experiences would have illuminated the dramatic events of the period said they would have liked to help but felt the risks were too great. Time and again, people said they feared retaliation if they drew attention to themselves by taking part in a television programme or by being featured in a book. I couldn't blame them and never attempted to persuade them otherwise. Only people living in Northern Ireland, or soldiers serving there, can really understand the fear that holds a whole community in its grip. My gratitude is therefore all the deeper to those families and individuals who have made this book and the trilogy possible. In a few cases, names, dates and the detail of certain events have been modified to protect the identity of a particular family or members of it, and I hope that, with these considerations in mind, the occasional omission or blurring of the edges will be forgiven.

Roughly half the families in the book feature in the television documentaries and the other half do not: the reason is that two of the three programmes are based in Londonderry and I felt it important to extend the range of experience beyond the boundaries of that historic city. All the families are taken from the three traditions historically involved in the Irish conflict: the 'mainland' British, represented by soldiers from the 'family' of the Royal Green Jackets whose tours of duty span 1969 to the present day; the Roman Catholic Nationalist community, in its political shades from moderate to extreme; and the Protestant Unionist community, with its equivalent range of political views. I must stress, however, that many of the families are in no way 'political'. Although the historic twenty-year period begins in August 1969 with the intervention of the British Army, I have deliberately started the stories of most families well before that date as the events and climate that conditioned their attitudes did not suddenly begin when British soldiers marched into Londonderry and Belfast. In Northern Ireland, perhaps more than anywhere else, 1969 is not the Year Zero.

The reader may well ask the purpose of embarking upon such a venture if there are such risks involved. The answer is that all the participants, having given the matter a great deal of thought and family consultation, positively wanted their stories to be told, in the hope that others might better understand their experience and point of view. One mother, whom I call Mrs Marie Kelly in the book (Chapter 9), wrote to me in three simple lines and said:

> I would like to talk to you about how the Troubles here,
> and things that were done to my family and myself, affected
> my life.

My hope is that these experiences may help shed some light on the often bewildering complexities of the Irish conflict by involving the reader in the lives of 'families at war'. Some of them are combatants, be they British soldiers, police officers in the Royal Ulster Constabulary (RUC) or members or the Irish Republican Army (IRA). Some are ordinary families who've been caught up in the Troubles. Others have never been directly affected and carry on living 'normal' lives. But all these families share the common experience of the past twenty years.

As every word you use in Northern Ireland is open to scrutiny for signs of bias or favour or historical ignorance, I would like to be permitted to get my retaliation in first. Normally I would use the words Nationalist and Unionist, as opposed to Catholic and Protestant, to describe the two Northern Irish communities as it is the terminology that most accurately reflects the real issue that lies at the heart of the Anglo–Irish conflict, the political question of national identity:

Nationalists (who tend to be Roman Catholics) aspire to a United Ireland, and Unionists (who tend to be Protestants) wish to remain part of the United Kingdom. But in several parts of the book I must confess to a certain deviation in using the religious rather than the political terminology when I deemed it appropriate to do so: for example, one chapter (Chapter 9) is about a Roman Catholic who votes Unionist and another (Chapter 8) about a Protestant who would never dream of voting Unionist. Northern Ireland is not always as defiantly Orange and Green as many people might care to think. Some may be puzzled by my use of Londonderry and Derry to describe the same city: in Northern Ireland, most Catholics call it Derry and most Protestants call in Londonderry. When the question arises, I have called the city by the name that is generally used by the family that is the subject of the chapter.

History is the key to understanding Northern Ireland, and the eventual resolution of the conflict lies in unlocking that history, which, as the past twenty years have so dramatically shown, is far easier said than done. *Families at War* is not meant to be a history book or a key designed to open the historical lock: but in one way or another, history is a part of each family and to ignore the often bloody events that have shaped the attitudes of all three traditions over the past two decades – and for countless decades before – is to present an incomplete picture. Where appropriate in each chapter, I have tried to outline any relevant historical event which provides the backdrop to a family's particular experience at a particular time, in an attempt to illustrate the crucial interaction between individuals and the circumstances in which they find themselves – for example the impact that 'Bloody Sunday' had on Shane Paul O'Doherty (Chapters 4 and 5).

And what of the broader historical perspective? The following is the barest outline of the historical forces that drive the Irish conflict. To help readers find their way through the often bewildering maze of contemporary and historical events, I have added a chronology at the end of the book that is a necessarily inadequate attempt to summarise nearly four centuries of Anglo–Irish history in a few pages. I have also tried to weave some of the families featured in this book into the contemporary section of the chronology. Nevertheless, for those allergic to Irish history, I would hope that the human stories of *Families at War* will stand on their own.

At the risk of oversimplification, the reason why the families are 'at war' is that the problem presented by England's 'plantation' of Ulster nearly four centuries ago by 'loyal' colonists of the Protestant faith has never been fully resolved: to the Crown, the purpose of the 'plantation' was to consolidate its hold over the troublesome northern part of its Irish domain (England then ruled the whole of Ireland) and keep it safe from further rebellion by the native Roman Catholic Irish. The IRA's current campaign is a contemporary manifestation of that rebellion. The ancient hostility between two traditions living on the same island stems indirectly from that period (although some would say from long before), with one owing its allegiance to Britain and the other to the notion of a 'free' Ireland with the British political presence finally removed. Most Nationalists want to see this achieved peacefully, but the IRA is pledged to use violence in what it calls the 'armed struggle'. The 'war' arises because the Protestant Unionist majority in the North wants the British presence to stay, and successive British governments have declared their intention to abide by the will of that majority.

The partition of Ireland in 1921 was an unsuccessful attempt to solve the problem: the six counties in the North became Northern Ireland and remained under British control, and the twenty-six counties in the South eventually became a sovereign independent state, the Irish Republic. From the beginning, Northern Ireland was an unstable political entity because, although it had been deliberately partitioned to ensure a permanent Unionist majority, a third of its citizens were Roman Catholics. Many of them never accepted the state and some were actively committed to its destruction as members of the IRA.

For nearly fifty years, the province was run almost as a one-party state by the successive Unionist governments that controlled Northern Ireland's own parliament at Stormont, in the suburbs of Belfast. Roman Catholics were treated as second-class citizens because Unionists thought their loyalty was in doubt. These were the conditions that led to the emergence of the Civil Rights Movement in 1968 and, because of the violence that followed, to the introduction of British troops on 14 August 1969. Even when Edward Heath's Conservative government abolished the Stormont parliament in 1972 and introduced Direct Rule (the running of the province directly from Westminster), the security situation did not significantly improve. How the IRA grew from a virtually defunct organisation and turned the issue of civil rights into one of the British political presence is told through the eyes of some of the 'families at war' on opposite sides of the battle lines. The other families, on both sides of the Irish Sea, have had to live with the consequences.

CHAPTER ONE

LORD JIM

When James Roderick Campbell left Eton College in 1966, he had no clear ambition about what he wanted to do in life, not that such doubt would have unduly concerned any old Etonian about to set foot beyond the famous playing fields on which so many battles had been won. He probably went out into the world with the same jaunty steps that still cover the ground at an amazing rate of knots. I never knew that 'Jamie' was an old Etonian and I must admit it came as some surprise when he told me, although I had known him for several months. He could not have been farther removed from the stereotype. With his natural openness and ease of manner, Jamie could no doubt swop stories with the king in his castle and the poor man at his gate – and probably, I suspect, be just as happy at the gate. He reminded me of the man most admired by the ancient Roman poet Quintus Horatius Flaccus (Horace to generations of schoolboys) who would remain unmoved even if the sky fell in. In that unfortunate event, Jamie would no doubt shrug his shoulders, crack a joke and get his men to start picking up the pieces. Not that Colonel Campbell, as he went on to become, should be underestimated. Beneath the wit and the charm that threatens to disarm an enemy at a hundred paces lies a tough and shrewd mind.

Having fulfilled the urge to 'Go West, Young Man' – to Australia where he worked as a 'jackaroo' – he returned to England with his ambitions no more clearly defined. 'When casting about, I was programmed into talking to my cousin who was enthusing about the marvellous time he'd had with the army in Borneo serving with the Green Jackets* – where he'd been mentioned in dispatches. There was a tradition in the family: my father had served as a Green Jacket during the war, in the King's Royal Rifle Corps, and had remained a

---

* The Green Jackets Brigade was formed in 1958 – a fusion of the Oxfordshire and Buckinghamshire Light Infantry, the King's Royal Rifle Corps and the Rifle Brigade. On 1 January 1966 (in the closing months of the Borneo campaign), the Brigade was redesignated the Royal Green Jackets.

keen Regimental supporter. My cousin said I'd nothing to lose and everything to gain by applying for a three-year commission: it would give me a breathing space and a job if nothing else.' Jamie was persuaded and applied for a short-service commission but failed at the Regular Commissions Board. 'I was disappointed but not surprised. They said not to worry: I'd failed because I was too young; they told me to come back in a year and have another go. It was suggested that I come to Winchester, sign up for basic training as a Rifleman [the bottom rung of the Green Jackets ladder – an ordinary "squaddy"] and then I'd walk the Commissions Board.'

Jamie took the advice and the Queen's shilling. 'I think in those days we actually got a shilling. You probably get 5p now.' In May 1968 he presented himself at the gates of the Rifle Depot, Peninsula Barracks, Winchester, along with thirty other recruits to make up a platoon for fourteen weeks basic training. At the end, there were only Jamie and nine others left. 'They make you run around rather severely and you end up carrying more than you ever imagined you could. Some of the original intake were a bit "flash harry" until it came to being wet for the third night running and they found they couldn't cope. They and the rest couldn't hack it. Some went home to mum. There was a pretty high wastage rate.' I wondered how James Roderick Campbell had coped in such company. 'Yes, I did think, "What on earth am I doing here with this lot?" But they probably thought far more strongly what was I doing with them? As a public schoolboy I did receive a lot of special attention from the training corporal – in terms of discomfort – which was a good thing in many ways because it meant the other men felt sorry for me.'

Rifleman Campbell was known as a PO – a potential officer – which meant that although he was treated no differently from the rest of the men (except in the eyes of the training corporal) he was expected to absorb rather more about the art of soldiering than perhaps an ordinary Rifleman needed to know. 'It can only be a good thing to see your potential officers have service in the ranks. Until you wake up on a Saturday morning in a barrack room with thirty people who've all been out on the beer the night before, you've really no idea of the lives they live. And it's pretty eye-opening when you sit down and talk with the soldiers who, in the not too distant future, you'll actually be commanding. You find out that some of them can't write and they want you to write to their mum; that some of them don't know how to cope because their fathers are continually beating their mothers up; or they've got their girlfriend in the family way and don't know whether to believe her in case she's saying it to get him out of the army. So they sit down and talk to you as a mate because they know you have an education. And if you can relate to them and get them to talk to you, they'll open up. They used to come along, sit down and say, "Can I 'ave a talk?" They used to call me "Lord Jim".' Having seen Jamie talk to the lower ranks and having met and talked with some of the Riflemen he commanded in action in Northern Ireland, I can vouch for his rapport with his men. 'Jamie was one of the best, one of nature's real gentlemen,' one member of his former platoon told me, 'but Jamie was never a pushover.'

Almost without exception, the sergeants, corporals and junior officers who took the young Rifleman Campbell and his new mates in hand were veterans of the Borneo campaign in which all three battalions of the Royal Green Jackets had served. 'If you *hadn't* been a jungle soldier you weren't one of the lads – which was really quite a bore if you hadn't been a jungle soldier. It wasn't your fault and there really wasn't a lot you could do about it. They were all into hammocks and "bashas" [a Rifleman's jungle bivouac] and snakes and ambushes and that sort of thing.' I asked how soldiers fresh from the steaming jungles of Malaya had viewed the campaign they'd been involved in prior to Northern Ireland. 'This business of terrorism and counter-terrorism is a seventies' cry. In the perception of the people who were doing it in the sixties, they were fighting a war – against Chinese communists or Indonesian "irregulars" or the Indonesian army. To the Rifleman, they were all "choggies" – just guys in the jungle whom they had to go out and ambush and kill.' I enquired how you spelled "choggie". Jamie said he'd never tried.

In 1968, Northern Ireland never figured on Jamie's – or the army's – horizons. It wasn't even a blip on the screen. The world (and the other three-quarters of the United Kingdom) never became aware that there was a problem festering away in the province until TV cameras captured the 'B Specials'* wading into (mainly Catholic) civil rights demonstrators in Londonderry on 5 October 1968. That happened a month after Jamie had completed his Rifleman's training. But 1968 was the year of other people's

---

* The 'B Specials', the Ulster Special Constabulary, were formed with the assent of Prime Minister Lloyd George in 1920. They became an armed, paramilitary adjunct to the RUC, most recruits being drawn from the 'loyal' Protestant people of Northern Ireland. They were finally disbanded at the end of 1969, to the relief of Catholics who regarded them as the armed defenders of Unionist supremacy. Traditionally, their main purpose was to keep down the IRA and curb rebellious spirits.

revolutions, in Paris, in Prague, and in America's Deep South. 'At that time, Northern Ireland was irrelevant. It just wasn't there. For me it was the year of Czechoslovakia. I can remember being on battle camp in Wales and somebody appeared waving a newspaper saying that the Russians had invaded. Everyone suddenly felt very concerned: that we were in the wrong place at the wrong time and that we'd all have to go off and fight bloody World War Three. What a drag! It was a genuine concern to a young trainee Rifleman that it was to be kit on and next stop the central front in Europe. But it wasn't. It was next stop Northern Ireland.'

Whilst the civil rights movement marched through the autumn and winter of 1968–9, with most people outside the province preferring to remain deaf to the alarm bells, Rifleman Campbell renewed his efforts to become an officer. He applied for – and got – a short-service commission for three years, the result of a six-month crash course at Mons in Aldershot. 'Add water and there's an officer.' In April 1969 Jamie emerged as a platoon commander. 'Mons [compared with two years at Sandhurst] was always considered down market. It was bloody hard work but it produced very good junior officers because there was no "side" to it. It was just straight, hard graft. I had the edge on all that because I'd just had six months training as a Rifleman. I knew how a rifle worked and I knew how to clean my shoes – and I was fit.'

Second Lieutenant Campbell was looking forward to his first summer leave in his first year in the army and was off to enjoy some shooting in Scotland. No sooner had he unpacked his bags near Inverness when the telephone rang and he was told to get back to Battalion as quickly as possible. It was off to Ireland in three days time. Jamie jumped into his old car and drove furiously back to Battalion headquarters at Tidworth in Wiltshire. 'By then the papers were full of pictures of "B Specials" performing, so we knew there was a problem. We didn't quite appreciate that we were going to become part of it.' Few had any idea what the army was going over to do beyond helping the police, who were exhausted by a summer of street battles that had claimed such a heavy toll. The climax came in the wake of the Protestant Apprentice Boys parade on 12 August when the 'Battle of the Bogside' erupted, with the people of the Catholic enclave building barricades to keep the police out and the police trying to fight their way in. Police resources were finally stretched to their limit. When the rioting spread to Belfast, no doubt by design to relieve the pressure on the beleaguered Catholics of the Bogside, and Protestant mobs started to burn

Catholics out of their homes, the British government finally decided that enough was enough and the army was sent in. As the then Defence Secretary, Denis Healey, presciently observed at the time, it was easy enough to send the troops in, but getting them out might be more difficult.

Prior to departure, Jamie's Battalion was given a briefing by its commanding officer, then Lieutenant-Colonel Frank Kitson who was already the army's counter-insurgency guru – an expertise founded on his experience in Kenya fighting the Mau Mau in the fifties, and subsequently refined in other post-colonial campaigns. In the seventies Kitson was to become the 'bête noir' of the IRA and the British hard left, although much of the 'black propaganda' attributed to him by his enemies lay more in the realms of fantasy than fact. In August 1969 Lt-Col. Kitson told his men they should be ready for anything. Jamie's platoon took him at his word. 'We rushed around working out if we needed our anti-tank guns and someone said, "Bung 'em in, they might come in useful," so we did.' The old manuals on riot control that hadn't seen the light of day since the sun set on the Empire were exhumed and dusted down. The drills once designed to frighten the life out of recalcitrant natives were practised once again on the parade grounds of England. Soldiers fresh to the ancient geometry were drawn up in box form-ation and selected Riflemen given the real bullets – as opposed to blanks – that they were to fire at the crowd once they had ignored the final warning and crossed the line beyond which they had been warned not to go. 'Some Rifleman always complained and asked how come he'd been chosen as the bloke what did the shooting. He was told to shut up and do as he was told!' The warnings were traditionally spelled out on a banner which soldiers would run out and unfurl. (A story still persists that one veteran banner, presumably left over from Aden, was unfurled in Belfast and the crowd was warned to 'watch it' – in Arabic.) Traditionally, the demonstrator who gave his life in the cause of good order was 'the bloke in the red shirt' – invariably the soldiers' first target, although, one veteran told me, this could be extended to 'the bugger in the brown trousers – and if he didn't have brown trousers, he certainly would have by now!' But Jamie's platoon weren't hidebound by tradition on the parade ground at Tidworth. 'We soon binned the banners and got megaphones the size of a coffee table – and a huge box of batteries to go with it. You could hardly stand up with the thing!' Thus equipped, the British army marched off into the unknown twenty years ago. 'There was no fresh thinking. No knowledge of what we were trying to do. It was a case of "What are we

going to do when we get there?" The only answer was to remain flexible
– which is exactly what we did.'

I asked Jamie if he knew anything about Ireland at the time. He
shook his head. Or what the conflict was about? What about partition? Nothing. Had he heard about the IRA? Yes, but only in
Giles cartoons. 'They were some sort of jovial bunch of – I didn't
quite know what – of blokes who went around firing shots in the air,
with a few opinions related to the 1920s.' Jamie had nothing to be
ashamed of in his ignorance. In the summer of 1969 it was shared by
just about 99 per cent of the non-Irish population of the United
Kingdom, including myself. That was one of the reasons the problem had festered so long.

Jamie's platoon was sent to Armagh, the beautiful city whose
twin cathedrals, facing each other on opposite hills, mark the seat of
the two main religious denominations of Ireland, the Roman Catholic Church and the Protestant Church of Ireland. The local Territorial Army centre became the unit's headquarters. 'It was
dreadful. The whole company was living in one room with one basin
and one loo. And all those Riflemen's feet!' The platoon's role was
to be on stand-by to respond to any emergency. At three o'clock
one morning, they got a phone call from Forkhill RUC station,
which their map told them was a few miles from the border. 'A panicky voice on the end of the phone said something about "Could we
hear the shooting?"' Jamie and his men leaped into their four-ton
lorry and Ferret armoured car and roared off down the winding
country lanes that led to Forkhill. They arrived an hour later, frozen
stiff by the cold night air of South Armagh. 'I leaped out and ran up
to the police station. There was no sign of battle. No pair of boots
with smoke coming out of them. No smoking ruin.' He went up to
the door and banged and banged and banged. 'Eventually a peep-
hole opened, a chain dropped and a bloke shoved a Sterling
submachine-gun through it. "Identify yourself!" the voice said.'
Jamie had had enough. 'Here I was, an officer in the army, standing
there with a stupid tin-hat on, with my green uniform and a gun, and
this bloke wanted me to "identify" myself!' The man then disappeared. A few minutes later the door was flung open and Jamie's
men were welcomed inside like the Fifth Cavalry by the local
detachment of 'B Specials'. 'We went in and, because of the Irish
brogue, it was bloody hard to understand what any of them was saying. Eventually it emerged that a couple of hours earlier someone
had come along and fired a whole lot of shots at them. It all sounded
quite exciting. We asked them to show us where the shots were fired

from. One of them volunteered and we roared off towards the border. Then he suddenly became very concerned, warning us not to go any further or we'd be shot. I asked him who'd do the shooting as there was clearly no one there. By this time he'd got sweaty palms and had got his gun out. I told him to relax: that we'd got a Browning machine-gun mounted on our Ferret and nobody in his right mind was going to take a pot shot at us. He became even more agitated. Here was the border, with the hills possibly swarming with IRA men! I thought he was obviously very frightened of something – but it was nothing that I could identify around there. There was no tension at the time from across the border. The only problem was the police agitation. It surprised me that all the police stations were already equipped with steel shutters with rifle slits in them, as if they were always expecting something to happen. They must have been there for decades. It seemed much more a threat in the mind. It was nothing tangible.' In the end, their morale-boosting foray over, the platoon returned to base and had breakfast, putting the night's escapade down to experience. It was a good introduction to one side's set of ancient fears.

At the time, no one knew how long the military operation would take – least of all the soldiers on the ground for whom the burning question was whether they would be home by Christmas – Christmas 1969 that was. If anyone had suggested that they – or their sons – would still be there twenty years on, for Christmas 1989, the response would have been unprintable. Jamie's own horizons did not extend beyong the limit of his three-year short-service commission, and if anyone had suggested to him that there was a long haul ahead, he would have said they must have been joking – although he recognised at the time that it was unlikely to be a quick in and out job. 'We didn't know how long it would take. It was pretty obvious to us that the people who were there, supposedly in charge, weren't doing a particularly brilliant job. But having said that, nothing appeared to happen. So, apart from a few peculiar reactions from the custodians of the law at the time, where was the problem?'

Jamie had his rhetorical question answered for him to some extent when the Battalion was transferred to the heart of the Falls Road in November 1969, to the area around the Clonard monastery where the seeds of Republicanism had been sown decades earlier and had long laid dormant. Their base was an old mill in Cupar Street. 'Again we were all in one room, but at least this time they'd managed to partition it off. It was cripplingly cold and they had these giant blow heaters, that looked like jet engines. They ran on calor gas and they roared away twenty-four hours a day. It was absolutely unbelievable.' This home from home lay in the middle of a maze of Victorian terrace houses in streets whose names – ironically, given the political disposition of their inhabitants – recall the glories of the British Empire: Kashmir Road, Cawnpore Street, Lucknow Street, Benares Street and, most famous of all, Bombay Street. The whole area is the most sensitive interface between the Protestants of the Shankill and the Catholics of the Falls, and it was Bombay Street that was virtually burned out by Protestant mobs on 15 August 1969. This is where the 'Peace Line' was built – a temporary partition separating the two communities that later became solid brick, like a mini Berlin Wall. Arriving in the middle of the area where the spark had been lit, where the devastation was still clear for all to see, and where the bitterness and fear remained as deep as ever, gave the Green Jackets a clearer insight as to why they'd been called in – if not a deeper understanding of Irish history.

The welcome the Royal Green Jackets received in the Falls Road was ecstatic, as it had been when they first arrived in Armagh. 'People would rush up and say, "It's great to see the khaki on the street," and we used to wonder what they were on about. We were plied with endless cups of tea and you'd spend half the time looking for a loo. You'd just go and knock on people's doors, just to reassure them, and you'd be invited into these tiny terrace houses, barely one up and one down with a loo outside at the back. Some of them were spotless – and some were absolutely heaving. There was a very strong feeling of community. Yes, we did work out what it was all about. You could see what it was all about because Bombay Street wasn't there any more! But the fact that we were standing there meant that there weren't petrol bombs flying over from the Shankill. Occasionally someone would lob a stone over, but that was about it – and you didn't worry about it too much. It was quite clear what we had to do: we had to stop that lot [the Protestants] coming over and burning this lot [the Catholics] out. We also had to escort through the area Protestants who worked at Mackie's engineering factory up the Springfield Road, whose workforce was at the time almost exclusively Protestant although it was in the heart of a Catholic area. It was all very odd, and it wasn't in the least like home. And, in many ways, it still isn't,' he added.

In those unreal, faraway days, Jamie also met some of the IRA's leaders (such as they were at the time) over endless mugs of tea around braziers that burned at strategic points in the area. The men who manned them were the self-styled Citizens' Defence Committees whose purpose was to do exactly what their name suggests. They were to provide the nucleus of what was later to become the Provisional IRA. The 'old' IRA (Irish Republican Army), that traced its roots back to the Easter Rising in Dublin in 1916, split in December 1969 into the 'Officials' and the more militant 'Provisionals'. The split was both ideological and tactical. The Provisionals accused the Officials of 'selling out' the Republican ideal by recognising the parliamentary institutions that were the legacy of partition on both sides of the border, the Stormont parliament in the North and the Irish parliament, Dail Eireann, in the South. They also took issue with the Officials' Marxist-dominated political views. But in more down-to-earth terms they also accused the 'old' IRA leadership of failing to protect the Catholic enclaves in the North from Protestant attack, which traditionally, in the eyes of those who lived there, was the IRA's most important role. For army officers to swop yarns with those who later tried to kill them may seem bizarre twenty years on but it was the natural thing to do in the honeymoon period when the IRA was not illegal and the army was not the enemy. Keeping on good terms with these Citizens' Defence Committees was often the best way of gaining intelligence on what was going on in the area. But as the IRA was tearing itself apart in what was to be a momentous historical split that was to lead to the regeneration of the organisation, the Green Jackets were already packing their bags to be home in time for Christmas 1969. When they returned eighteen months later, bullets and bombs had replaced tea and biscuits.

In the intervening period, Jamie and his men were on much more familiar ground, the central front in Europe. 'We had a wonderful time with all the new equipment. We didn't really bother with what was going on elsewhere. And when you weren't busy, you'd be a young subaltern going off having fun, skiing and the like. But most of the time we were busy fighting the Russians. We weren't interested in anything else.' But the good times didn't last. 'All of a sudden, out of the blue came the order – "Up sticks, boys, we're off to Ireland again!" This time riot training went out of the window and urban warfare was in.'

In May 1971 the First Battalion of the Royal Green Jackets returned to Belfast. This time home was the Albert Street mill, at the bottom end of the Falls Road and a rifle shot away from the Divis Flats, without doubt the most awful and dangerous block of council flats in Europe (soon to be demolished and no tears will be shed). The Battalion's accommodation had still not achieved five-star status. 'It had the Blackwater River running next to it which was an open sewer. My platoon was all in one room and there were fleas everywhere. We lived with mountains of army flea powder and whenever you crawled into your sleeping bag, great clouds of the stuff would billow out of it.' The nearest the men had to home comforts was the little 'choggie' shop run by an Indian or Pakistani. 'He must have made a fortune out of us then. You'd come in off patrol and kick on his door to get him up. You were starving and he'd make you "egg banjos" – a fried egg with two bits of Mother's Pride either side of it. It's a great art. The consistency of the egg has to be just right so that when you roar off down the corridor and take your first bite, the whole lot doesn't splurt down your front!'

The First Battalion's four-month tour from May until September 1971 was the most memorable – and exciting – of all Jamie's seven tours during the twenty-year period, marking as it did the build-up to internment and the explosive consequences of it. 'There was now a pretty severe shortage of tea,' Jamie observed. 'The street vigilantes of 1969 had become the IRA quartermasters of 1971. At least it was much more simple when people were trying to kill you. In two years we'd gone from being peacekeepers to a threatened species.'

Nineteen seventy-one was the watershed year. On 6 February Gunner Robert Curtis was shot dead in a Provisional IRA machine-gun attack in the New Lodge Road, the first British soldier to be killed on service in Ireland since the War of Independence (the Anglo–Irish War) in 1920. The following day the Prime Minister of Northern Ireland, Major James Chichester-Clark (the province had its own government at Stormont until Direct Rule from Westminster was imposed in March 1972), declared on television, 'Northern Ireland is at war with the Irish Republican Army Provisionals.' In March the Provisionals lured three off-duty Scottish soldiers from a pub to their deaths in the hills above Belfast. They probably thought they were on their way to a party. Whilst they were relieving themselves by the roadside, the IRA shot them in the back of the head. Two of them were brothers aged seventeen and eighteen; the third was twenty-three. Events had started to career downhill and showed no sign of stopping. The army's task was to slow the momentum.

They were wild, wild days. At night – and daytime too – West Belfast would echo to the sound of ferocious gun battles between the army and the IRA. 'It was still the era of the cowboy, and a lot of the Falls was absolutely stuffed with guns. The Thompson [a Chicago-style submachine-gun] was still the favourite because it makes such a great noise. The Armalite was still the specialist weapon for the chosen few.' Jamie knew the sound of the Thompson well. 'We were shot at one time in a Landrover and the Rifleman on the back was hit through the elbow. We returned fire and put our standard procedure into operation – and we were pretty expert at it. We threw a cordon round the whole area and no one, but no one, got in or out. After about an hour the locals got bloody angry, and our continued presence really wound them up and then they got really aggravated. We didn't know whether the Rifleman was dead or alive. All we knew was that he had been rushed away to hospital. So it's not surprising we were all a bit hyped up about it. Eventually someone I knew from 1969, who'd been a prominent figure then and was now an IRA "godfather" figure, came to seek me out. He lived around the corner but had been caught up in the cordon. He came up to me as the officer in charge. I said, "How can I help you, Mr ——?" [Jamie called him by his name] and he knew I knew him. He said he wanted to go through the cordon. I said I was absolutely devastated but he wasn't allowed to do so – nor was anyone else. He said he had a sick mother and a dying cat and about eight other things. I said I was really sorry but rules were rules and that was that. He drew himself up, said with some contempt, "You call yourself an officer," summoned up as much spittle as he could and spat absolutely full in my face – which shook me slightly because I hadn't really expected him to do that. Whereupon one of my corporals appeared with a rubber-bullet gun, poked it straight up his nose and said, "Would you like me to smash him round the head with it, sir, or shall I fire it first!' The man in question just faded away. I wiped my face clean and made another mental note of how charming it all was.'

On another occasion the Green Jackets threw a cordon round the Long Bar, a pub in Leeson Street, one of the strongholds of the Official IRA. There were only a few people inside and the 'P' checks (personal checks radioed back to base – and in later years checked on computer) revealed nothing of interest. When Jamie had finished the search and went outside he realised the situation was getting quite nasty. 'All the old biddies came out and there was the clank, clank, clank of dustbin lids. One of my smaller Riflemen was confronted by a mob of women, yelling and screaming and spitting and dustbin-lidding. They started to move even closer until they were a matter of feet away – taunting him all the time. Then it all happened as if in slow motion,' he describes the scene with his hands and his face, 'as I watched him reach out, cock his rifle and put it into the aim position. I went up to him very slowly and gently put my hand on his shoulder as he was about to shoot about three women. I said, "Don't worry. It's OK. We'll sort this out." I thought he was about to shoot and the bullet would have gone through about five of them. Then my platoon sergeant intervened, rubber-bullet gun in hand, and said, "I don't care who you are, the first one who steps any further gets one of these!"' And that's the sanitised version. Jamie shakes his head and sighs. 'It was a lot to ask of a little Rifleman. He was only about 4′ 6″ tall – a little West Indian guy, all alone with twenty women yelling and spitting and coming towards him.' No wonder most Riflemen regarded any attempt to win hearts and minds as a joke.

For a young platoon commander, man-management skills could hardly have faced a more rigorous test. One of Jamie's men once refused to go out on patrol. Under the circumstances, to a non-soldier with a wife and family, his reluctance was understandable. The good news was that there was going to be an ambush. The bad news was that Jamie's platoon had been chosen to set it off. 'The company commander called the platoon commanders in and said that we were going out on patrol tonight and he'd been categorically informed, on very, very good information, that there'd been a "shoot" set up. Congratulations, my platoon was to be the one that was to go in and trigger it! We all made jokes about it, suggesting that it might be better to stay in and watch the late night movie instead. I then went off and briefed my blokes – I tended to brief them all together instead of just leaving it to the corporals, especially when there was something smelly. I told them what the score was but not to worry because it was never going to happen – and even if it did, we had plenty of our guys around. Afterwards, one of my Riflemen came up and said, "Look, I don't want to go on this bloody patrol. In fact, I'm *not* coming. I've got a wife and a young child. It's all very well saying that they've set up an ambush and we're going to get them – but they're going to get us first." I reasoned with him and he still said he wasn't going. But after an awful lot of talking, he came. I said that once he'd chosen to be a soldier, the fact that he had a young family didn't preclude him from going into any perceived danger.' Jamie apologised because he felt it all sounded rather pompous when it wasn't meant to. 'I told him he couldn't cop out. Why should any Rifleman, indeed I, go down that street rather than him? That was the argument I used rather than that he owed any honour to the Queen. Had he not come out on that patrol, he would have been disgraced and court-martialled.

22

He went – and nothing was ever said about it again.' I assumed it must have been a very testing moment. Jamie shrugged his shoulders and reflected that, looking back on it now, it hadn't seemed like that. And he wasn't being modest. I almost forgot to ask him if the ambush had been sprung. Needless to say, after all the drama, it had not. Then, obviously still thinking about my question, as an afterthought Jamie added, 'When I got back home on R and R [Rest and Recuperation], I was amazed at my family's reaction. They said I looked absolutely shattered – and I slept for about four days. You don't really appreciate how strung out you are.'

The next soldier to die in Northern Ireland was a Green Jacket, Corporal Robert Bankier. He was shot by the IRA on 22 May 1971 in the Markets area in the centre of the city and bled to death. Jamie knew him well as he was a member of a company he'd previously been in for two years. 'Corporal Bankier's death is the turning point for an awful lot of people in the Battalion. It's always the same when there's been an incident: you only get a bit of news at a time; people crowd into the "ops" room waiting to find out more. Word came that one of our men had been hurt; then news that it was Bankier; then that he'd been taken to hospital; then that he was dead. People couldn't believe it. "What do you mean, he's dead?" He's dead. He's not there any more. "He's one of our own – and they've killed him in an ambush. The IRA." In Borneo we'd ambushed and killed a lot. Now it had happened to us – in the United Kingdom. It took some time to sink in.' He pauses. 'Everyone said, "Right, that's it then. Never mind the tea and sympathy, let's go out shoot a few of the buggers!"' My raised eyebrows asked the next question. 'Absolutely. That's exactly what Riflemen are like and I wouldn't want them any other way.' But however understandable the human reaction, soldiers just can't go out and do that, so how do you stop them? 'Through discipline and care and knowledge and training. You'd know who was dodgy and you'd just keep an extra special eye on him.'

By the time of internment – carried out by 3000 troops at 4 a.m. on the morning of 9 August 1971 – the IRA had killed nine soldiers and the province had been shaken by nearly 300 explosions and over 300 shooting incidents. Nearly fifty other people had died violent deaths. A fortnight earlier, the Home Secretary, Reginald Maudling, had declared that he considered a state of 'open war' now existed between the IRA and the British army. Within hours of the raid, in which 337 men were arrested and detained without trial (97 were subsequently released), the Prime Minister of Northern

Ireland, Brian Faulkner, declared, 'We are, quite simply, at war with the terrorist, and in a state of war many sacrifices have to be made, and made in a co-operative and understanding spirit.' The swoop in the small hours of that morning took few by surprise – least of all the Provisional IRA, most of whose volunteers had 'got off-side' – across the border – their structure largely undamaged by the raids. Four days later the veteran Republican Joe Cahill, the commander of the Provisional IRA's Belfast Brigade, gave a press conference at a school in West Belfast where he claimed that only two IRA men had been shot in the post-internment gun battles and only thirty detained in the swoop because the IRA had been tipped off it was coming.

In the three-day explosion that followed the introduction of internment, twenty-two people were killed in the worst violence since 1969. Dozens more were injured and shot. One of them was Jamie. He subsequently received the award of a Mention in Dispatches. 'The build-up in the three weeks before internment was fantastically busy. We were permanently rushing round and dealing with incidents and getting shot at and bombed and God knows what. There was endless sniping. At 1 a.m. on 9 August we were given our orders: they were to be ready at 3.30 a.m. and to go in at 4 a.m. The whole platoon would have about ten blokes to pick up and about six houses to visit. We'd lift whoever was there. We would knock on the door discreetly for three seconds and then charge in. You'd get an awful lot of old blokes in dressing-gowns and an awful lot of serious abuse. It was pretty desperate really.' Other soldiers with similar sensitivities told me the same, some sharing the same feelings, if not of shame then of retrospective disgust or unease at what they'd been asked to do – no doubt triggered by their encounters with 'old men in dressing-gowns' instead of IRA men armed to the teeth. I said I wasn't surprised at the 'serious abuse'. 'Nor were we,' Jamie agreed. With 3000 soldiers giving discreet three-second taps on hundreds of doors at 4 a.m. in the morning – simultaneously – it wasn't surprising that the Catholic enclaves erupted. 'The place went completely berserk. There were burning cars and burning tyres and barricades everywhere. The place was solid with rioting people raining rocks and bottles down on us. We provided them with a lovely target in their angst. Our orders were to try and keep the main roads open – although God knows why on reflection.'

At the height of the rioting, Jamie's platoon was in Albert Street, trying to keep it open to traffic, at a point near St Peter's church which stands next-door to the Divis Flats. Suddenly, in the middle of the chaos, one of his men ran up and told him to train his 'binos' on the church, where he thought he'd spotted a sniper in the tower. But the sniper was elsewhere. 'I swung round and looked, and as I looked, I was hit by a shot from the Divis – and it was quite a good shot at about 200 yards. The bullet went through my right arm and then through my chest. All I knew was that I was flying through the air with the greatest of ease, completely winded – I couldn't breathe – and I landed with a great thump on the ground. I remember the bricks and dirt and stuff all around me. I remember thinking, "I've been shot – in the stomach, which can't be a good thing!" I can remember seeing things, like the sky, and hearing things, but nobody appeared to be doing anything: and I thought, "Why isn't everybody helping? Perhaps they've all been shot!" And then someone appeared and there were lots of other faces and things started happening. They got my flak jacket open and tried to staunch what was obviously a very serious wound – the bullet had gone in one side and out the other. Then more anxious faces started appearing and they all had those little morphine things and I remember thinking, "I hope they're not going to fill me full of all that stuff!" I heard what was quite obviously fire being returned and thought, "They'll be enjoying that!" It turned out that one of my men thought I'd been shot from behind the crowd at the top of Albert Street, where the crowd was whooping and jeering anyway at seeing me hitting the ground. He thought he spotted a gunman and let fly at him. Whether he hit the target history doesn't relate.' Seventeen field dressings were used on Jamie. 'There was no pain. Everything just shuts down, a complete blank. My hand was twitching uncontrollably, opening and closing like that.' He demonstrates, opening and shutting his fist in fast, panicky movements. 'It was a nerve reaction. The bullet took out a couple of ribs.'

Jamie had been shot, he and his men believed, by an IRA sniper whom they knew as 'The Rifleman'. The same day he was also thought to have shot and wounded one of Jamie's men, Corporal Dave Fairhurst, who was fortifying a sangar (a concrete observation post) with sandbags. The bullet travelled through the observation slit and hit Corporal Fairhurst in the chest, the bullet going in one side and out the other. It then ricocheted and wounded another Rifleman in the elbow. Corporal Fairhurst, a gentle, soft-spoken Lancastrian, remembers being hit and screaming, 'Get the bastard!' Nobody did. He is also thought to have shot another Green Jacket through the neck as he was manning an observation post on top of Albert Street mill. The soldier lived but never fully recovered from his injuries. I asked Jamie what he knew about 'The Rifleman'. 'I have no particular feelings about him except I would very much have liked someone to have shot him. That would have given me an enormous amount of pleasure. I'd have been equally happy if he'd been bundled in gaol for doing it, but I don't think either of those things have happened. In hearsay terms we knew who he was. He was a good shot and he was the guy who was doing the business that day from the Divis.'

Jamie was rushed in an ambulance to the Royal Victoria Hospital a few hundred yards up the road, where the doctors and nurses saved his life. He remains eternally grateful to them. 'They stuck about fifteen tubes in me. They rather suspected that I'd given up wanting to live and produced padres and all sorts of people. That's what happens. It's the logical consequence of assuming that you're about to go. Therefore you do. I don't think I fought to stay alive – it just hadn't occurred to me not to.' Whilst Jamie was recovering, members of his platoon came to visit him. In the bed next door was another patient who'd been wounded in the gun battles that had raged outside. Jamie clearly remembers his neighbour. 'He had a lot of bullet holes in him and very long hair. He was clearly not a member of Her Majesty's Forces. When my platoon came to visit me, there was a bit of overspill into the next bed space where this chap's wife or fiancée and parents were mournfully looking at him. There was some aggravation when one of my Riflemen probably rested his gun [with a notable lack of tact] on the end of this chap's bed. The family started to give him a hard time, taunting him with some remark like, "Youse all right there with yer gun!" to which my Rifleman replied, "Yes, I'm all right with my gun and another word out of you lot and I'll rip his tubes out!"' I asked Jamie if that was clearly his recollection of his Rifleman's bedside manner. 'Oh yes, it was great. It made me laugh a lot and within a fairly short space of time, I found myself down on the women's ward.'

The Battalion's second-in-command, who was a friend of the family, broke the news to Jamie's parents and then held the receiver out of the window so they could hear the sound of that night for themselves. 'I remember my parents telling me it sounded like World War Three.' I assumed that the news that their son was going to live preceded the relay of the sound effects. Jamie's mother was then rung up by the local newspaper and asked the time-honoured 'How does it feel?' question. 'And she said, "One must expect this sort of thing to happen if one is in the army." Marvellous quote! I've still got the cutting at home.'

I asked how his platoon had reacted to their commander being shot – and seeing other colleagues hit too. It was the one area during the whole of our many conversations on which Jamie wasn't too keen to elaborate. Clearly there'd been problems and a degree of overreaction. What it was and what had happened was never fully ventured, but clearly it caused some embarrassment. 'They were pretty unhappy about it really and needed to be curbed in their enthusiasm. That's about as much as I would dare – or care – to say about it really. I think they needed very careful management, which I'm delighted to say they had in the shape of my very excellent platoon sergeant, who assumed command until I was fit again. Feelings were running pretty high, and I suspect he had to wield the rod of iron pretty carefully to stop them running out of control. They were very angry.' Whatever the 'enthusiasm' that needed to be curbed, it was abundantly clear that it did not affect Jamie's loyalty and affection for his men, nor theirs for him.

Although Jamie recovered and returned to Northern Ireland for a further five tours – three of them 'emergency' tours (each of four months) and two 'resident' tours (each of two years) – the summer of 1971 remains the highlight in both military and personal terms. By the end of his next tour in 1972, 'I think we'd had Northern Ireland. We were fed up. It was dirty and it was horrid and we were fed up. All we seemed to do was observe endless, endless funerals.'

I concluded by asking Jamie about the IRA, knowing that he'd seen the organisation develop from a handful of men warming their hands round braziers in 1969 to one of the more sophisticated and deadly organisations of its kind in the world. I must admit the strength and colour of his language surprised me – even though I expected any soldier who'd been shot by the IRA and seen the mutilated remains of their unsparing campaign to have strong feelings on the subject. Perhaps it was unreasonable to expect any degree of detachment from a serving soldier under such circumstances. And it wasn't surprising when you consider that, where Northern Ireland is concerned, detachment is a luxury even journalists are not supposed to afford. Jamie offered an assessment of the IRA on a very personal level. 'The IRA has changed and grown better at its business over the years. It's by and large carefully and well directed by its own godfathers. It's well equipped and its techniques improve consistently well. But the 200 or so who are in their active service units are not IRA activists' – he now speaks slowly, with firm, deliberate emphasis: the jokes are over – 'they are professional thugs who are very well skilled in the art of killing, and probably revel in it and justify it with some spurious claim that it's done "for the cause". But basically they get their kicks out of killing people. They seek to justify their murderous deeds by claiming that we're an "occupying force": how ridiculous can you get! I mean, so what? I mean, so nothing!' Listening to the anger and contempt he so clearly felt for the enemy was almost like hearing the words of another man. 'If you analyse "the cause", frankly it's pathetic. It doesn't fit any remotely successful – or even potentially successful – political template that could work in Ireland.' He concluded with a fierce attack on IRA fund-raising. 'There's a fantastic amount of money floating around that they get through extortion and terror-ising the people – mafia style – and the godfathers will say it's for the cause as they rattle the cans in America for "the boys behind wire". Absolute crap. They all drive Mercedes and they've probably got Swiss bank accounts to go with it. If they really think that they're going to create a wonderful new society by killing endless soldiers and policemen and anyone else who incidentally happens to get in the way, they've got to be out of their minds, because the goal posts aren't even on the same planet.'

So what was Jamie's prognosis? 'If they stop now – and everyone knows who they are – they just lose all face – a recognition that they've failed. So they keep going. They go on and kill some more.' What about taking the gloves off, going in and sorting the IRA out? 'I've never heard anyone with any common sense ever say that. They must want their heads seeing to! What are we supposed to do, go storming round Dundalk [just across the border] shooting every man over the age of ten?' What about 'taking out' well-known figures? 'I'm afraid they've been reading the wrong comics. I'm just relieved to think that they aren't in charge and that someone with more sense is.'

Jamie told me how Northern Ireland had, for twenty years, domi-nated his military career and how his wife sometimes cautioned him to tread carefully when the inevitable subject arises at dinner parties. I felt some sympathy. So I finally asked him whether he saw his successors still leading Riflemen through the streets and ditches of Northern Ireland in another twenty years time. 'Lord Jim' smiled, and with the practised diplomacy of the Old Etonian replied that if that were the wish of the government, they would.

CHAPTER TWO

A MOTHER'S ONLY DAUGHTER

To most people not from Northern Ireland, the name Belfast probably conjures up the same kind of images as does Beirut – a city of horrible, irrational and incomprehensible violence – where killing is done in the name of causes that appear irretrievably damaged by what is done in their name, be they the unification of Ireland or the preservation of the status quo.

What most killings have in common is the geography of death: Andersonstown and Ballymurphy, the Shankill and the Newtownards Road, Turf Lodge and Ardoyne. Perhaps outsiders may not recollect or care which are Catholic and which are Protestant but the names, through long and gruesome repetition, stay firm in the mind long after the atrocity and its perpetrator are forgotten. The face of these areas is what you would expect after twenty years of street violence. Most are scared, grim and unlovely except in places where the Housing Executive has razed whole streets to the ground and started all over again. But even in areas like Andersonstown, there are things you don't expect like a wonderful leisure centre and a florist where you can buy the best, and cheapest, freesias any side of the water. There are other surprises too: middle-class houses with Volvos in the drive at the fringe of the council-house estates. Their presence seems to excite little envy or animosity as it might do in other parts of the United Kingdom, where class not religion is the divider. In Andersonstown and most other areas like it – and in their Protestant equivalents too – the sense of community still remains defiantly strong. Although such enclaves throughout Northern Ireland have long enjoyed this sense of community, the bonds have been strengthened over the twenty years because each feels itself under threat from outside.

Mairead Farrell was brought up in this part of Andersonstown by middle-class parents in a middle-class house. She died on the streets of Gibraltar, shot dead by the SAS. The IRA admitted that she was an IRA volunteer on active service. The controversy over how

Mairead Farrell and the two other members of the IRA unit, Sean Savage and Daniel McCann, met their deaths – in particular the controversy over the ultimately vindicated Thames Television *This Week* programme – has understandably overshadowed any curiosity as to what a middle-class daughter from a good family was doing with an IRA unit in Gibraltar. When the world saw her photograph – an attractive, smiling young woman with long brown hair and striking eyes – and learned that she was at university studying politics and economics (*The Economist* still falls through the Farrells' letterbox every week as subscription computers don't heed the news), many may have wondered how someone with apparently everything to live for ended up dead in a Gibraltar street. I remember my wife shaking her head incredulously when she saw the photograph of Mairead, who bore a striking resemblance to her sister, and heard of the home she'd come from.

Mrs Farrell is a woman still shattered by the experience, still scarcely able to believe that her daughter is gone. She often watches a videotape of a programme in which Mairead featured some time before her death. 'I like to watch it,' she reflects, 'it makes me feel she's still near. It makes me feel she's not too far away, just listening to her.'

One branch of Mairead's family was staunchly Republican. Her mother's father, John Gaffney, had been an active Republican from 1916 onwards, the year Patrick Pearse proclaimed the Irish Republic from the Post Office in Dublin before it became a smouldering ruin and his handful of rebels were battered into submission by British troops. The leaders of the Easter uprising, intended as a call to arms to free all thirty-two counties of Ireland from British rule, were executed for their treason. Their martyrdom fuelled the cause that had been laughed at when Pearse had read his proclamation declaring the Irish Republic barely a week before outside the GPO in O'Connell Street. Thus was Yeats's 'terrible beauty' born, and the IRA was raised in its shadow. Thousands of young men like John Gaffney joined the Irish Republican Army and took up arms to finish the job that Pearse and his tiny band of dreamers had started. In 1920, Gaffney was arrested and imprisoned, first in Athlone gaol and then the Curragh. Mairead's mother was eight weeks old at the time. 'He was in gaol because he was a Republican,' she states without equivocation. 'When we were growing up, he used to tell us how prisoners were taken out every morning to be shot. No one knew who was going to be next. Everyone wondered if it was going to be them.' John Gaffney was never called out. His crime, as the family remembers it, scarcely amounted to a capital offence: he had refused to carry the notorious Black and Tans (the name given to the 7000 men recruited in England to supplement the Royal Irish Constabulary) on the Leitrim narrow-gauge railway, on which he'd worked since the age of thirteen. John was released after a year and returned to the railway where he worked until his retirement in the 1950s. But politics were always part of his life. 'He was always in the union, always a man that looked after people and always writing letters to different people for different things. He was very active on the political scene – for De Valera's party [Fianna Fail].' In 1937 he was elected a senator with a narrow majority.

But his political career was short-lived. De Valera enacted a new Constitution which recognised Eire's claim to the six partitioned counties of the North whilst accepting that the claim could not be implemented for the foreseeable future. Such a recognition of political reality was anathema to many traditional Republicans – John Gaffney included. 'My father was very dogmatic and wouldn't toe the party line. The next election came pretty quickly and he wasn't put up again. He was too independent-minded – just like Mairead.' That was the beginning of the parting of the ways for Gaffney and De Valera. When De Valera finally turned his guns on those members of the IRA who wouldn't accept his constitutional politics and eliminated all remaining opposition through gaol, execution and letting hunger strikers die, John Gaffney saw it as the final act of betrayal by the man whose cause he had once championed. By the end of 1945 the IRA was pronounced dead.

Mairead's grandfather died in 1974, having lived long enough to see its resurrection. He never moved from his beloved County Leitrim but since his daughter had long since gone North with her aunt and married a local man, Dan Farrell, he had a regular first-hand account of what was happening in Belfast. He'd make trips too, 'down' to Belfast to see the family (the journey is regarded as 'down' not 'up') and would bemoan the fact he wasn't 'thirty years younger'. Surprisingly, although he would have joined the fight he regarded as 'unfinished business' had he the energy and youth, he did not wish to see his grandchildren involved. 'I remember him being worried about my boys here, in case they would be involved. He told me to see that they didn't get caught up.' I expressed surprise at the contradiction. 'I told my father he didn't have to worry. My children weren't interested – which was quite true. Two of my boys had been through university, and apart from perhaps having dabbled in civil rights and CND, they had their minds on other things.' Danny, for example, Mairead's eldest brother and a former 'Mr Ireland', was more interested in body-building than building a new Ireland. I asked Mrs Farrell if she'd ever specifically told her children never to get involved. 'It wasn't necessary,' she said.

The other branch of the family could not have been more different. Mrs Farrell's grandfather on her mother's side had been an officer in the Royal Irish Constabulary (RIC) – the all-Ireland police force that predated partition and the formation of the Royal Ulster Constabulary (RUC) in the North. Her aunts too were both married to RIC men. 'They never had much call for my father. They weren't too keen on him. If you joined the RIC, your family would be divided about it. Some of them would join and others would never dream of it. That's the way it was then and it's exactly the same now. I know a whole lot of RIC and RUC men. If a policeman came to my door now, I would treat him with courtesy and wouldn't offend him.' (It's difficult to imagine Mrs Farrell treating anyone with anything other than courtesy.) Would she make him a cup of tea? 'I might offer them a cup, but I might not rush to make it!' she laughs.

But it was in the Republican footsteps that Mairead chose to follow. She adored meeting her grandfather on holidays at the family's little cottage in Ballynamore, County Leitrim, a dozen miles across the border, where they'd go every summer, Easter and most weekends. She would love talking with John Gaffney and swimming in the ice-cold Atlantic pools whilst her brothers stood shivering on the shore. 'After having four boys, having a girl was terrific,' reminisces her mother. 'There was great rejoicing when she was born. She was always smiling, a very placid, very good child. And she learned to look after herself. She took no nonsense from the boys. When they used to ask her to do things for them, she used to ask them why they couldn't do it for themselves. She was determined to let them get used to looking after themselves.'

When the Troubles began in 1968 Mairead was eleven and the family had just moved to their new home in Andersonstown where her parents still live. It's a neat, comfortable house with garage and drive around a well-kept garden. The hall floor sparkles and the tables are heavy with well-kept plants. It's the kind of house that looks as if it's always ready to receive visitors, not in any prissy way, but as if it were the natural thing to do. Mr Farrell's pride is his cocktail bar in the billiard room which can meet just about any request the visitor may, on invitation, make. But wine is kept upstairs 'lest it put temptation in the children's way'. The walls of the parlour are now hung with pictures of Mairead, and IRA memorabilia crafted in the prisons of the North now adorn the tables. Mr Farrell normally does most of the talking, although both prefer to shun the publicity that Gibraltar has forced their way. They do not bask in the martyrdom and fame that is now attached to their daughter's name in Republican circles the world over. Mrs Farrell is a reluctant interviewee not least because the pain so visibly returns whenever she is asked to talk about her daughter. You can see it in her face and eyes and hear it in a voice which at times drifts and fades.

I asked if Mairead had any Protestant friends. Mrs Farrell seemed surprised that I should even ask. 'Yes, there was absolutely no distinction in our house between Catholic and Protestant. There was no sectarianism – no, no, no,' she said, emphasising each syllable with a shake of the head. Nor was there any hostility towards the police – Catholic or Protestant. 'After Mairead's death, the wife of a Catholic policeman we'd known many years was on the phone in tears and invited me to come down and stay with her for a few days.' The policeman's two children had been Mairead's best friends when all were too young to understand what the Troubles were about. 'They were bosom pals.' But growing up together and going to the same school, they soon found out.

When Mairead passed her eleven plus she, like thousands of children on both sides of the Irish Sea, got a bicycle on which she rode to her new grammar school, Rathmore Convent, every morning. But the journey was hazardous as it entailed crossing a Protestant area where the local youths would pull them off their bikes because they were wearing the uniform of the Catholic college. Mairead and her friends were forced to switch to the bus which Protestant gangs then stoned. The bus was forced to divert and the journey to school got longer and longer. In the summer of 1969, when she was twelve, Mairead would come home and hear stories of how Catholics her parents knew well had been burned out of their homes by Protestant mobs. Her mother and father had a drapery and a hardware shop in the Grosvenor Road, the artery that runs from the city centre into the heart of the Falls. Many of the victims of these arson attacks were their friends and customers. 'We'd just moved up here to our new house, but we still knew everybody down there. It was dreadful, really terrible. I knew so many people who'd been burned out of their houses. Hearing those stories must have had a terrible effect on the children.'

So presumably Mrs Farrell, like most Catholics, was relieved and overjoyed when the troops came in? Surprisingly she was not. 'A whole lot of people did welcome them, but I had reservations about it. Maybe I was just the odd man out. I didn't feel any great elation. To be honest, I didn't really think much about it. When you're working and you've a family, you've other concerns. But I wondered just what they would do. As it turned out I was right. As time passed they changed.'

The process whereby the army 'changed' in the perception of the Catholics is one of the most intriguing questions of the past twenty years. Why was it that those who had welcomed the soldiers with open arms and endless cups of tea in the summer of 1969 were shooting them dead less than two years later? The answer is a potent mix of history and the circumstances of the time. Obviously the IRA made the most of the opportunity of turning the presence of British soldiers on the streets to its advantage, but that took some time. Nor is there any evidence that the leadership of the IRA (such as it was in August 1969) thought that its hour had come. At that time those who were about to become the leaders of the regenerated organisation were drinking tea and swapping yarns with the soldiers. The IRA was probably as pleased as anybody to see the army come in to keep the Protestant mobs at bay, seemingly in 'defence' of the Catholic enclaves, the job that historically had been its responsibility. In August 1969 the IRA had failed in a spectacular way to live up to that responsibility and was taunted from the walls with the slogan, 'IRA – I RAN AWAY'. Stung by its failure, the IRA was determined to reassert itself in its traditional role as defender of the Catholic community in order to restore its battered credibility. The search for weapons and recruits began.

This IRA build-up inevitably outraged the Unionist government at Stormont that had ruled Northern Ireland for fifty years, and to whom the RUC and 'B Specials' were an instrument of political control. The army too, which had been sent in to 'aid the civil power', inevitably found itself doing the bidding of that civil power. So when there was intelligence that guns were being stockpiled in the Catholic enclaves, the army had the job of rooting them out. Soldiers looking for weapons and ammunition don't carry out house-to-house searches in carpet slippers. By the summer of 1970 many Catholics in the affected areas began to see the army in a different light, a change in perception now openly encouraged by the Provisional IRA which was beginning to organise in its traditional strongholds.

For many Catholics, and perhaps for the impressionable thirteen-year-old Mairead Farrell, the turning point was the Falls Road curfew in July 1970. There had been 'aggro' following an arms search in Balkan Street, with the soldiers coming under missile attack from an increasingly angry crowd. More troops came to their rescue and canisters of CS gas were fired to try and disperse the rioters. But the gas dispersed as well as the rioters, drifting into the small terraced houses that criss-cross the Falls Road, most of whose occupants had no inclination to get involved in the rioting. The all-pervasive, choking and sickening gas made many have second thoughts about the soldiers they had seen as their saviours only twelve months earlier. The situation got worse. To restore order, the army's General Officer Commanding (GOC) Northern Ireland, General Sir Ian Freeland (who once told me he had been looking forward to Northern Ireland, as his last posting, for the shooting and fishing), imposed a curfew on the Falls. The whole area was sealed off for thirty-five hours whilst the army conducted a house-to-house search. Apart from a two-hour shopping break at tea-time on Saturday, everyone was confined to their homes. Five civilians were killed during the operation, one of them run down by an armoured car. From the army's point of view, the search wasn't fruitless, with a haul of 52 pistols, 35 rifles, 250 lb of explosives and a staggering (for the times) 21 000 rounds of ammunition. But the effect on the Catholic population was catastrophic, and their anger was intensified when they saw the army driving two obviously satisfied Unionist ministers of the Stormont government on a tour of the subjugated Falls.

The curfew made an indelible impression on the mind of the young Mairead Farrell who went down to the shop to help her mother during the two-hour 'break' on the Saturday afternoon. 'We'd heard over the radio and TV that the shops were going to be allowed open between four and five and that all shopkeepers had to be at their premises by 2 p.m. I was worried because one person had arranged to come in and collect some baby clothes from our draper's shop and I thought she might need them urgently. So we decided to go down and to take some bread and milk for our relatives at the same time. When we got to Springfield Road corner, a soldier stopped us and asked us where we were going. He said we couldn't go any further. Dan had an argument with him. In the end he let us through but insisted on coming down in the car with us. When we reached the shop he put us in and closed the door. Everyone was peering through the windows. One girl put her head right out to see what was going on. The soldier turned and shouted, "If you don't take your head in, I'll blow it off." And she was even a married woman with children. Mairead was horrified. She always talked about that – how horrible it was the way they spoke to the people. When four o'clock came, everyone poured out. The place was swarming. Everyone was carrying on telling us what the soldiers did and what they said.' The army's honeymoon was over, although Mrs Farrell had never felt particularly wedded to it.

As the months and then the years passed, the gulf grew wider. The more estranged the Catholics became, the more support they gave to the IRA: and the more menacing and effective the IRA became, the harder the troops cracked down on the people in the areas that supported them. Alienation inexorably grew.

Living in Andersonstown, Mairead Farrell witnessed it all happen from the inside and was angered by what she saw and heard going on around her. She was never affected directly but many of her friends and neighbours were. When Mairead was fourteen, the mother of one of her schoolfriends was blinded by a rubber bullet. Mrs Emma Groves lived in Tullymore Gardens, a few streets away from the Farrells. On 4 November 1971 paratroopers were reported to have placed the street under house arrest. Mrs Groves, whose house had been raided earlier that morning, is said to have told her daughter to play a rebel song in protest. The sound of 'Four Green Fields' drifted across the gardens – hardly the most strident of Republican songs. A soldier is reported to have fired a rubber bullet through her open window at about eight yards range, hitting Mrs Groves in the face. The 51-year-old mother of eleven was blinded for life. She is subsequently reported to have received £35 000 compensation for injuries; no soldier was ever charged. According to Mrs Farrell, that may have been the point of no return for her daughter. 'That would have been something that didn't leave her mind. She was determined to make her contribution to getting the troops out of Ireland.'

Mairead Farrell joined the IRA. Her mother insists she knew nothing about it. I suggested she must have had some suspicion. 'Well, people would call I wasn't familiar with or people I didn't know would leave a message. I remember saying to Mairead, "How do you know her?" or "Where does she live?" You would have asked questions about these things.' She sighs and pauses. 'I suppose that deep down I was always worried that, with all the things that were happening then, she'd just get involved without knowing. It was very easy to happen. You've just got to do one thing and that's you involved. Then you think it's easy, and you go on to something else.' Although quite clearly Mrs Farrell would have been desolated had she found out that any of her children were contemplating joining the IRA, I wondered whether that meant that she herself did not support them. I asked her whether she did support the IRA. 'I support Sinn Fein's political viewpoint,' she said. (Sinn Fein is the political wing of the IRA.) Did she support them because of her father? 'No.' The answer came with equal firmness. 'It's because of the way things are here. I always did support them, and I still would. England would never give up anything without a fight, no matter what the politicians tell you. I feel that most families around here, with few exceptions, would have the same feeling.' And that's why they elect Sinn Fein President, Gerry Adams, to Westminster, I reflected without giving words to the thought. 'There's no way you'd ever get freedom here without shedding blood,' she continued, adding 'unfortunately' as an afterthought. 'Or having your blood shed,' I added. 'Yes, that's right.'

When Mrs Farrell found out that Mairead was involved, it was already too late. On 5 April 1976 the IRA blitzed Belfast, planting four bombs around the city shopping centre and several in two of the area's biggest hotels, the Conway and the Wellington Park. All exploded within fifty minutes. Three bombs destroyed the Conway and the Wellington Park was badly damaged. The traffic in Belfast was reduced to chaos. Mrs Farrell had been into town, but finding it impossible because of the diversions, had driven back to the shop. As she was pulling up outside, one of her sons ran out and said his brother Niall had just rung and said the house was being searched. 'The house had only been searched once before, along with many others in the area. I went back and tried to open the door but I couldn't because the catch had been dropped from the inside. A soldier opened it and said, "What do you want?" I said, "I live here!" He let us in, put us in the dining-room and placed us under house arrest. I kept on asking why they were here.' She never got a reply. The house was searched and the soldiers left. It was only when they had gone that somebody rang with the news that Mairead had been arrested. She was eighteen at the time. 'It was the end of the world. I couldn't believe it. I couldn't believe it. I *could not believe* it,' she said, pausing between each syllable to emphasise the point.

Mairead Farrell had been a member of an IRA unit that had planted the three bombs that destroyed the Conway Hotel at Dunmurry, just outside Belfast. The others with her were Kieran

Doherty, later one of the ten men to die on hunger strike in 1981, and Sean McDermott, who had been released from The Maze prison (Long Kesh) the year before. Mairead Farrell was arrested in the hotel grounds, Kieran Doherty got away and Sean McDermott did not. Mairead later admitted she was lucky not to have been shot on the spot. Whilst trying to make good his escape, McDermott entered a house and demanded the keys to a car. He followed the owner upstairs who made as if to get them. McDermott didn't know he had picked the home of an RUC reservist. There was a struggle and McDermott was shot dead with his own gun; the policeman was wounded. Kieran Doherty attended McDermott's funeral despite orders to lie low. In the graveside oration McDermott was hailed as a man of simple and rare qualities, of great integrity and high-mindedness, whose every act was guided by the fact that he was striving for a socialist, united Ireland.

Hearing that Mairead had been arrested was shock enough for Mrs Farrell. When she heard what her daughter had been involved in she was devastated. 'I couldn't understand why she'd let herself be involved at that stage. I didn't expect it – never, never. It was dreadful, it was dreadful.' I asked her again whether she really had no idea of her involvement. 'No, not to that extent. I never thought she'd have been on a mission like that, never. If I had, I wouldn't have slept. I would't have rested. As far as I was concerned, that was the first time she'd ever been involved – and I still don't know to this day because Mairead wouldn't talk about it.' I asked what she would have said if she had found out. 'I would have said to her not to have been involved but I know that probably wouldn't have made much difference because Mairead was very determined. She probably wouldn't have listened to me anyhow. And I would say that once they're involved, that's it. They just go ahead and do it. I couldn't talk her out of anything, let alone something like this.' But would she have tried? She nodded her head sadly, knowing the futility of such an attempt. Because she disagreed? 'No, not because I disagreed but because of the consequences, because of what would happen to her if she was caught or blown up.' The worry of a mother for her daughter? 'Yes. People say Mairead was terrific, she was strong, but these kind of things didn't matter to me. I just wanted Mairead to be here and not to be involved with anything. I admire others that can do things, but I couldn't do them. It was the same I felt about her. I'd rather she'd been different and not involved in anything.' The obvious pain of the memory made it clear that she meant it.

Mairead spent the next ten years in Armagh gaol. Her mother's first visit was traumatic. 'I didn't know how we'd ever survive. The first time I ever went to the gaol, I cried all the way home from Armagh. But it's amazing how you have to adjust to these things because you've no choice in the matter.' Mairead adjusted too and became the IRA officer commanding the women in the prison. As for most Republican prisoners – although not all – prison life served to strengthen her commitment and deepen the bitterness against the British government. Prison became the IRA's Sandhurst – 'the University of Terrorism' – with endless hours on hand to read the tracts of revolutionary socialism and plan strategy and tactics for the years ahead. The seeds of the revolutionary politics of the Republican Movement of today (that's Sinn Fein and the IRA) were planted in the prisons of the seventies by those who now control and direct both wings of the Movement. For Mairead Farrell there was no turning back. She was one of the three women in Armagh who went on hunger strike in 1980. After nineteen days without food and drink, she was assured that concessions had been won – most importantly, the right of IRA prisoners to wear their own clothes instead of the prison uniform which they believe branded them as criminals instead of the prisoners of war they claimed to be. Mairead and the others came off the hunger strike. But the concession they wanted was not to be. A second hunger strike was called to force the issue once and for all. A year later, ten men were dead.

The hunger strike of 1981 effectively won the prisoners what they had been fighting for – the right to wear their own clothes – which was the most potent symbol of what they called 'political status'. In fact the women in Armagh gaol had always been allowed to wear their own clothes: they were fighting for the other demands, including free association and the right not to do prison work, which in the eyes of the Republican Movement added up to 'political status'. The OC of the women in Armagh was choosy about what she wore. 'The social worker at the gaol use to ring me up and say that Mairead would want this or that by Saturday. I was only too happy to do it. I had to buy all the clothes. I'd send them up and she'd send them back. I used to ask what was wrong with it – or why she didn't like it. She never worried that I might be annoyed that she might not like the things I'd picked. There was no way she'd keep something she didn't like.' She smiled. 'It didn't bother me. It happened all the time.'

Like any mother, she counted the days to her daughter's release.

Mairead had received a fourteen-year sentence for her part in the bomb attack on the Conway Hotel, and under the 50 per cent remission scheme operating at the time would have been out after seven had she not lost three years through her hunger strike and part in other prison protests. But perhaps still unaware of the depth of her daughter's commitment, Mrs Farrell was determined to see that once Mairead was released she never got involved again. She partly blamed herself for her involvement in the first place. 'It's the biggest regret of my life that in the early days I was never around when Mairead came home from school. I was always at work and a relative used to be at home to get their tea. You never realised you were leaving them for hours on their own. I always think that if I'd been there, I'd have been able to supervise who came and who went. I'd have been there to go out with her, to take her places – instead of me always being at work. It might have made a difference to her getting involved. When she was arrested, that was one of the things that bothered me.' Did she blame herself? 'Well, you do, you know.' Mrs Farrell was determined to see it didn't happen again through any fault of hers, although the young girl who went into Armagh at nineteen was coming out of gaol on 19 September 1986 as a woman of twenty-nine. 'When she came out, I didn't go back to the shop for a lot of weeks. I stayed home all the time. After her being away for ten years, I just wanted to be with her again. We'd go out together. We'd go shopping. She had a place at Queen's University for that October and we tried to get her to go then. But she wanted to take a year off. She said she wanted to adjust. You know, I just keep thinking, if only she'd went right away. . .' Her voice trailed off in the distance although words weren't necessary to read her thoughts.

Mairead took her year off, going to Tenerife with friends, Germany with her brother Niall, and helping Sinn Fein in Cork in the Republic's 1987 general election. 'She worked like mad in those elections and I was very happy about it because she was going to read politics at Queen's. I thought it was good because she wouldn't get involved in anything else. But she had other interests we didn't know about. I know people say "Och, I don't believe that" – but it's the truth. Things can be happening under your eyes and you don't notice them. You don't want to, maybe. Perhaps you don't want to see them.'

There were signs of Mairead's caution. She would slip into a doorway whilst out shopping with her mother, saying she thought they were being followed. She would stand in the hall at home and point at the telephone saying not to say anything because it was bugged. 'She always imagined that if the TV was plugged in but not switched on, people [possibly army or MI5 technical surveillance] could pick up conversations that were heard in the house.' Mrs Farrell probably dismissed such caution as the natural sensitivity of a daughter who had just spent ten years in gaol. With hindsight, her sensitivity may well have been right.

In the autumn of 1987 Mairead enrolled at Queen's University, Belfast. She was, by accounts, a good student and apparently worked hard. By the beginning of 1988 she was beginning to prepare for one of her first exams. 29 January was her father's birthday; an informal birthday tea had been arranged but Mairead was late back from college. When her mother asked what had kept her, she said some friends had got engaged and they'd gone to the students' union for a drink. She joked because she said there wasn't any wine on the dining-room table. Her father sent her upstairs for a bottle. Mairead poured it out, raised her glass and wished Dan a happy birthday. She then went round the table, put her arms round him and told him that she loved him. 'You know, Daddy,' she said, 'I could be shot dead.' The remark came out of the blue. 'It was the way she said it,' remembers Mrs Farrell. 'Dan didn't want to be too serious about it and warned her not to go getting shot dead because funerals were so expensive. "You needn't worry," she said, "if I'm shot dead the IRA will bury me." Although Dan tried to pass it off as a joke, it worried me. I asked her what she meant when she said she could be shot dead. "They all know who I am," she replied. "It could happen but don't you go worrying about it."' But her parents misinterpreted their daughter's remark. They thought she was talking about being shot dead by Loyalist assassins.

On Wednesday morning, 2 March, Mairead went over to Queen's – at least that's where she said she was going. She returned sooner than expected and told her mother that they were off for a three-week break. She said she was going down to Dublin for a few days. When would she be back? She didn't know. 'Whenever she went down to Dublin where all her old schoolfriends were, she always used to say if she wasn't back on Saturday night, she'd be back for her dinner on Sunday – at midday. It was a family occasion – and Mairead loved her Sunday dinner.' Her mother, as usual, asked her if she'd be back for the meal. She said she didn't know but didn't want any keeping for her. Mairead never returned. On Sunday afternoon, 6 March 1988, she and her two IRA colleagues, Daniel McCann and Sean Savage, were shot dead by the SAS in Gibraltar. None of the three was armed.

Belfast heard the news on the radio that Sunday afternoon, although the detail was scant: three IRA terrorists had been shot dead – two men and a woman; no names were given. The Farrells' doorbell rang at about seven o'clock. Mrs Farrell thought it was Mairead home a last. Then she saw the expression on the faces of the man and the woman in the hall. 'What is it?' she said. 'It's Mairead,' the man replied. Mrs Farrell broke down uncontrollably.

Farrell, McCann and Savage were three of the IRA's most experienced volunteers – the name the IRA gives to its activists. There was intelligence that they were in Gibraltar to place a massive car bomb designed to massacre a British military band who played at the weekly parade in front of the Governor-General's residence. Had the bomb been planted and gone off, it was virtually inconceivable that watching tourists and civilians would not have been injured or killed – although Mrs Farrell, remembering her daughter's reaction to the Enniskillen Remembrance Day bomb, insists that Mairead would never have been involved in an operation that jeopardised civilians' lives. The three were shot having apparently reserved a parking space for the parade with an empty car. The explosives – 140 lb of deadly Semtex – were later found in a car park across the border in Spain, presumably waiting to be transferred to Gibraltar. Although the coroner's inquest returned a verdict of lawful killing, the controversy still rages: did the SAS really believe their victims were armed or about to trigger a bomb by remote control, or were they shot down in cold blood? Certainly the Farrells have no doubts and are in the process of taking the case to the European Court of Human Rights in Strasbourg. The controversy refuses to die.

Mrs Farrell vehemently rejects the charge that her daughter was a terrorist – which is how most of Britain would see her. 'No, never. No. No,' she insists, almost as a plea for understanding, 'Her ideal was the freedom of Ireland. She was dedicated to one thing, putting an end to all this. It was the only way she knew how to do anything about it. She thought she was doing the right thing.' I asked if she thought Mairead's death had helped free Ireland. There was a long pause and a long sigh before she answered. 'When it happened, everybody said, "This will be what it has taken" – and I hoped then that it was. But now I can't see it having made any difference.' She pauses sadly. 'I'd be very surprised if it does. I don't know how many is going to have to die.'

CHAPTER THREE

PRODS, TAIGS AND POLICEMEN

Michael O'Connell always wanted to be a policeman, although that may seem strange to some in the current political climate in Northern Ireland, given such an obviously Catholic name. Even when he joined the RUC eighteen years ago in 1971, some local Nationalist eyebrows were no doubt raised. In the eyes of most of their politicians, joining the RUC has never been encouraged on the grounds that the political institutions of the state have never fully reflected the interests of the minority Catholic community. Whatever weight that argument had twenty years ago, when Northern Ireland was run by, and essentially for, the Protestant majority, it is far less convincing today given the workings of the Anglo–Irish Agreement, in which Nationalist interests are directly represented to the British government by the government of the Irish Republic. The Royal Ulster Constabulary too has changed almost beyond all recognition. But ancient prejudices die hard. The fact, however, remains that the composition of the RUC remains primarily Protestant, largely as an accident of history, despite all the efforts made to attract Catholics into its ranks. To date the leaders of the Social and Democratic Labour Party (SDLP), which represents two-thirds of Nationalist voters (with the IRA's political wing, Sinn Fein, representing the rest), have shrunk from openly encouraging its supporters to join the RUC. When, and if, they ever do so, it would represent a major breakthrough in the battle against the IRA, which can only survive with the support of a good percentage of the people in the areas from which it comes. For Catholics to join the police in any significant numbers would pose a threat to the IRA which would increase in direct proportion to the numbers who joined. That's why *Catholic* policemen may run double the risk.

This was not something that worried the young Michael O'Connell in 1971, one of four brothers in a family of six who were brought up on a mixed estate of Catholics and Protestants in the beautiful 'Orchard Country' of County Armagh. One of his brothers, Kevin, had already been in the force since 1964 and policemen were always in and out of the house. 'My father was a tailor and there was a constant stream of policemen who came to get their uniforms shortened or lengthened or taken in or let out or whatever.' The O'Connells also had a neighbour who was a policeman; he lived a hundred yards down the road and had done more years on the beat than most would care to imagine. Michael used to watch and admire him walking up and down the street and envy the younger men in their panda cars driving round the estate. 'Ever since I was a little boy, I thought, "That's the life for me!" People say, "If you don't want to work, join the police!" I soon found out how wrong they were.'

Michael now lives on one of the hundreds of new private housing estates that have sprung up across Northern Ireland in recent years, with neat rows of streets whose names evoke flowers, trees and birds instead of the glories of the British Empire. Each lawn is trimmed. Each car is washed. Sunday mornings are no doubt a frenzy of domestic activity. You might guess that Michael, now in his mid-thirties, was a policeman, with his hair well trimmed and a frame that promises to keep middle age well at bay. You can imagine him in the pub with his mates on a Sunday lunchtime, with sports shirt and slacks and a good one for the 'crack' (the Irish antithesis of being boring and dull). Michael and his home, with his wife and two children, give the impression of a happy family, comfortably off.

For policemen the only 'up side' of the Troubles are pay-packets fat with overtime, assuming they live to enjoy it. I asked Michael if he'd considered the dangers when he decided to join the police. He said he really hadn't thought much about it, coming from a country area where what happened in Belfast seemed a million miles away. 'Where we lived, the Troubles didn't affect us. Life was still normal. And even in Belfast things weren't too bad. Policemen weren't getting killed. I thought it was safe enough.' Michael joined in June 1971. Two months later internment was introduced and Catholic areas in the North erupted. Michael was a recruit at the RUC's training depot in Enniskillen when it happened. But it all still seemed far away – until, because of the pressure on manpower, his class was sent out on to the streets. 'Although we were still in training, we were standing out there with the uniformed men and none of us had a clue what was happening.' Michael soon found out. His first posting in September 1971 was to Londonderry, which was still boiling away after internment and getting worse by the month as the following January and 'Bloody Sunday' approached (when paratroopers shot dead thirteen civilians after a civil rights march).

'We soon saw things happening there that made our eyes stick out of our heads like saucers. We kept saying, "They didn't teach us this in the damn book!" We couldn't believe it was really happening. What we were taught in the depot was completely detached from what we were experiencing out there on the streets. When the shooting and rioting were still going on, and the petrol bombs were flying, we were still going about in ordinary police cars. We had no armoured vehicles or anything like that. It was one hell of a shock to the system!'

The initiation started quietly enough. Michael and two other recruits, with a total of three months service between them, were dispatched on a routine patrol of the town centre, with the usual brief to keep an eye open for shoplifters and drunks. 'It just happened out of the blue. A crowd appeared from the direction of the Bogside and began to shout "Black Bastards", and "RUC–SS" and all the usual stuff – and they're still shouting the same twenty years on, they've no originality. It started off with bricks and bottles – and there we were, three recruits fresh out of the factory. A bottle took my hat off. And then the petrol bombs started to come. I'd never seen a riot before, except on television, and suddenly to be on the receiving end of it was a hell of a frightening experience. When we saw the petrol bombs, we knew it was time to go. We weren't armed. We had no protection. No shields. So we just ran for it. We were only a month out of the depot. People would say afterwards, "Were you scared?" I'd say, "No. Somebody else wet themselves down the inside of my trousers."'

Michael's first riot did have a lighter moment, although it hardly seemed like it at the time. In the tirade of abuse Michael was called a 'Protestant bastard'. 'Everybody automatically thinks that because you're a policeman, you're a Protestant.' In the middle of the riot Michael had neither the opportunity nor the inclination to correct his verbal abuser. I wondered if the misconception often arose. Clearly over the years it had caused him more amusement than embarrassment. He once had to go and interview an old farmer over an accident and went to see him with another officer who was also a Catholic. It was shortly after the Ulster Workers Council strike in 1974 when Loyalist action had brought about the collapse of the new Northern Ireland government at Stormont in which, for the first time in history, Protestants had shared power with Catholics. The opposition to this 'sell out' was led most vociferously by the Rev. Ian Paisley who, in the wake of this dramatically successful challenge to government authority, was the hero of every died-in-the-red (and white and blue) Protestant in the province, not least the old farmer whom Michael and his fellow Catholic went to visit. 'As we were in his house, taking the statement from him, he started to go on about his Protestant heritage and how he would never let a Catholic set foot across his doorstep. I looked at my colleague and he looked at me. We both smiled at each other and agreed that "bloody Catholics were destroying the country". I must admit, we egged him on. He went on about how he'd never employ a Catholic worker on his farm and what he wouldn't do to Catholics if he could get his hands on them. Paisley was the greatest thing in the world and he thought we were the greatest two policemen in it! Ulster was proud of us! Of course, we never let on. When we got outside we agreed he was a stupid old bastard and had a good laugh about it.'

Michael's religion from time to time also offered light relief at difficult moments. In the two years that followed the signing of the Anglo–Irish Agreement on 15 November 1985, Unionist politicians and their supporters tried to bring the Agreement down, originally through strikes and street protests, the weapons so successfully used in 1974. To them, the Agreement marked a betrayal of their heritage and the first step on the road to a United Ireland. But this time there was no tangible target to hit and the campaign failed to attract the same kind of mass support. Furthermore, the political mood of the time was different and the protesters were faced with a Prime Minister who, with the scalps of Arthur Scargill and General Galtieri to her credit, was unlikely to budge. The RUC, who were still regarded (albeit erroneously) by many of the Protestant people as 'their' force, was tasked with policing the demonstrations. There were ugly clashes with demonstrators. In one nasty confrontation in Portadown, television cameras captured the memorable image of a 'Loyalist' demonstrator attacking a policeman with a Union Jack. Loyalist fury and frustration intensified as gangs burned policemen out of their homes in unprecedented attacks. Despite intense provocation the police stood firm. Had they not done so, the infant Agreement might well have been consigned to the dustbin of history, like the short-lived power-sharing executive in 1974. In the verbal skirmishes that inevitably preceded the demonstrations, the Loyalist protesters would hurl abuse at the RUC, calling them 'Fenian lovers' (a Fenian being a Catholic rebel from the nineteenth century and now a term a abuse) or, even worse, straight 'Fenians'. Michael remembers his mates shouting across to him, in voices intended to be heard, 'Hey, Patrick!' – at which point the crowd would roar with anger, 'They're all Fenians, they've been and brought in Catholic peelers!' One demonstrator even came over to Michael (or, as he thought, 'Patrick') and asked him if he *was* a Fenian. Michael said he wasn't: he was a policeman.

But there were moments, although according to Michael they were few and brief, when being a Catholic in the RUC wasn't a joke. On 27 January 1972, three days before 'Bloody Sunday', five policemen were ambushed in their car by the IRA in Londonderry. Two were shot dead. One was Michael's sergeant, also a Roman Catholic; the other was his best mate. In the month that followed, other policemen lost their lives, although it touched Michael less directly. In the aftermath feelings among the police ran high and there was the inevitable canteen gossip that police officers in Londonderry were being set up by one of their own – the putative person, of course, being a Catholic. Most of the police knew that Michael was a Catholic because his brother, Kevin, had been stationed in the city for several years. Michael was having a drink in a pub shortly afterwards, with the shock of the shooting still fresh, when a policeman in his early twenties came over to Michael's table and called him a 'Fenian bastard'. He'd obviously been drinking. He said Fenians were only on the job (working as policemen) as plants for the IRA. Michael, who might have been forgiven any desire to rearrange his features, did not rise to the insult. His friends, most of them Protestant officers, intervened and escorted the man away, telling him to 'catch himself on'. 'My mates told me he was only an arsehole and not to take any notice of him. I would say that he's about the only one in my eighteen years in the force who's ever come out with that.'

I asked Michael if he ever felt that that kind of attitude lay just beneath the surface in the RUC, though it would seldom be voiced. He smiled and said, 'Sometimes my men would say, "Oh Jesus, a bloody Catholic!' but it's only meant as a joke. My crew in West Belfast [to where he was subsequently posted] were 100 per cent Protestant and they would have done anything for me. If I said we were going here, they'd be right behind me. They used to take the mickey at times, but there was never any malice in it. I must say, there were times when I didn't blame them when we all saw what so-called "Catholics" could do.' He elaborated by describing his reactions when he and his crew were first to arrive on the scene of the shooting of three soldiers of the Royal Green Jackets on 25 March 1982. I was familiar with the incident as several members of the Regiment whom I'd interviewed for the Green Jackets programme in the television series had spoken of it with anger and distress. The shooting happened two days before the Battalion was due to leave the province. The Provisionals had taken over a house commanding a view of Crocus Street, which runs into the Springfield Road in West Belfast. As a patrol was leaving Springfield Road RUC station, they opened fire with an M60 heavy machine-gun and high-velocity rifles at the two Landrovers in which the Green Jackets were travelling, killing three. Michael and his crew were only about 200 yards away when they heard the shots ring out. The M60 sounded like thunder. 'We were first on the scene. I saw a soldier lying in the road. I jumped out of my Landrover and tried to put a field-dressing on his head but the dressing just went into the skull. We tried another one, and all we were doing was packing a large hole with field-dressings. I even said it myself then, that they were Fenian bastards for getting three soldiers.'

No one was ever charged with the killing of the three Royal Green Jackets. People were arrested but there was no evidence on which to charge them. Michael and his crew had very strong suspicions as to who was responsible, but intelligence is not evidence. 'We basically knew who the IRA teams were that were operating and the favourite weapons they used. We had a fair idea who was involved.' We discussed the frustrations of the job and the difficulty of getting evidence that would stand the test of a court of law and ensure a conviction. Michael told me of one occasion when some of his colleagues came across a group of men coming away from Divis Flats and noticed spots of blood on their clothing. They were searched and nothing was found. Special Branch were contacted to see if the individuals were wanted for questioning in connection with any particular incident. They were not, so they were allowed to go on their way. Around ten minutes later, Michael and his crew were told by some of the locals that there was a body in one of the housings for the rubbish chutes in the flats. They said they'd heard shots. 'We were very cagey in case we were being led into a booby-trap, but if the locals came with us we reckoned that it was pretty safe. Although it was broad daylight outside, the ante-room to the rubbish chute was in total darkness. You couldn't see your finger in front of your face. That's where we found the body. It was still warm. There were all the usual signs of an IRA "execution": hands tied behind the back, eyes taped and a bullet through the back of the head. There was no doubt that before the boy was killed his interrogation consisted mainly of a good beating. I can't remember his name, but we knew he was a member of PIRA [the Provisional IRA]. We put two and two together and realised that the men who'd been stopped by the other crew a matter of minutes earlier were those who dished out the punishments – the sort of internal security unit within the Provisionals. Now we had a body, we knew – I knew – that they'd done it.' More officers were sent off to find the men who'd been stopped, but by the time they were located all their clothes had been washed and all the bloodstains had gone. I said I was surprised that they'd been allowed to go in the first place if they had bloodstains on their clothes. Michael shrugged his shoulders as if it was nothing new and said it wasn't surprising at all: their clothes weren't saturated; there were just a few spots; they probably said they'd been in a fight.

The frustration of seeing men and women walking the streets who they know are almost certainly responsible for the death or maiming of their friends is something that policemen and soldiers learn to live with in Northern Ireland. What often makes it even more frustrat-ing is that, however deadly and bloody the game, it's one which, by and large, has to be played by the legal rules – at least as far as the security forces are concerned. They are rules in which the enemy is well versed and which it uses to its advantage. 'In places like West Belfast, you see and stop well-known Republicans every day. Sometimes you kind of kid them along a bit under the emergency legislation,' Michael laughs. 'We ask them if they know anything about any acts of terrorism that have been committed and enquire if they have any information they'd care to give us.' I presumed they invariably declined. 'They're quite agreeable to deal with and you know you're not going to get any hassle. They'll state who they are, where they're coming from and where they're going to. They'll do everything in accordance with the law. And they are very civil.' He made it all sound like customs officers asking holidaymakers if they had anything to declare. 'I'm not saying there was a rapport between us and the top Provos, but they never gave us any problem when we stopped them on the streets. They never had anything incriminating on them, and they knew they weren't going to get themselves arrested for any minor offence like disorderly conduct. On the street, they would chat away with you as if you were old friends. But, given the opportunity, they would blow you away as quick as look at you.'

During his time with the RUC's Mobile Support Unit in West Belfast Michael had more traditional encounters with some of the Provisionals' top men, like Danny McCann who met his end with Mairead Farrell in Gibraltar. Whilst on patrol around the Clonard monastery, shots were fired from a house at a police Landrover.

The sound suggested a handgun and not a high-powered rifle. Michael and his men, who were close by, responded immediately and saw a man and a woman running away. The woman was caught but the man, Danny McCann, made off with Michael in hot pursuit. McCann ran into the monastery, a huge friendless building of grey stone, no doubt with escape not sanctuary in mind. Michael drew his revolver and followed him into the vast, gloomy chapel, dimly illuminated by rows of giant candles. The chapel was empty apart from the occasinal kneeling devotee. McCann was nowhere to be seen. 'I didn't know where he had gone but there was an old priest three or four pews from the back. I was very cagey because of all the confessional boxes and I knew there was a gun somewhere around. I asked the priest if he'd seen anybody. He never looked up, and never looked at me, but he obviously knew I was a policeman and said with barely an interruption in his prayers, "The third door on the right down the side." I heard a scuffling, burst in through the door, and there was Danny McCann trying to get out through the window. He wasn't armed. I grabbed him and put him down on the floor with my gun to the back of his head. I searched him, found nothing, called the crew on the radio, and brought him out of the chapel at gunpoint. One of the local priests arrived and saw me with McCann on the ground and a gun at the back of his head. He went on about it being "scandalous" that I was in the house of God with my gun drawn and all that sort of thing. I told him to f— off out of my sight. The adrenalin was running pretty high at the time.'

McCann was 'bagged' – his hands and arms sealed in thick paper bags to preserve any trace of powder or explosives – and taken to Springfield Road police station. No traces were found on him although detonating wire was found on the woman. 'We knew McCann was "a worker" [an explosives expert] and we were suspicious. We'd sealed off the house where the shots had been fired from and called in the army bomb disposal unit. They found what we'd expected. The house had been booby-trapped to catch us when we did the follow-up.' McCann was taken to Castlereagh for questioning and held for several days. Predictably, he exercised his right to silence. At the end he was released for lack of evidence. 'He walked.' McCann remained active for several more years until he was shot dead in Gibraltar by the SAS along with Sean Savage and Mairead Farrell.

Unlike most of the families I interviewed for this book, I only met Michael on one occasion. I'd heard that he was a mature, experienced RUC sergeant but didn't know he was a Catholic until I met him. Nor did I know that his family had suffered. His mood and his expression changed as he relived what he'd tried to forget. Kevin (the policeman) was Michael's eldest brother and David was the next in line.

David had no connection with the security forces. After university he'd gone to work for the DHSS and spent much of his time in some of the most depressed areas of the province on both sides of the religious divide. He was doing very well and was due for promotion. Late one afternoon, in the early seventies, as he was leaving a house in a Catholic area, a man got out of a beige-coloured Austin 1800 and shot him five times in the head and chest at point-blank range. David died in hospital the following day. He left a wife and four sons, the youngest a six-month-old baby. The finger seemed to point at the Provisional IRA who had declared that all agents of the Crown were 'legitimate' targets. The killing caused great resentment in an area where most people were unemployed and relied on the DHSS for their livelihood. But shortly after the killing a telephone call was made to the BBC in Belfast in which Loyalist paramilitaries claimed responsibility. The caller said the attack was in retaliation for the IRA's killing of a UDR corporal, two days earlier. Later that day a further call was made and a man who simply identified himself as 'George' said:

> There was a shooting incident today. Our organisation, which carried it out, is a very extreme Loyalist group. We were responsible for most of the assassinations last summer [by the end of that year seventy Catholics had been murdered]. This attack today was carried out in retaliation for the murder of the UDR corporal.
>
> We are issuing a warning to the IRA that if they keep on murdering members of the security forces and harassing loyal citizens of Ulster, we will take very stern action against Roman Catholics.

The murder of Michael's brother appears to have been the first officially claimed by the Ulster Freedom Fighters (UFF), the extreme Loyalist group responsible for most of the sectarian killings in the province. The UFF is a flag of convenience for the still legal Loyalist paramilitary group, the Ulster Defence Association (UDA).

The death of his brother devastated Michael and his family. 'Why was he singled out? He wasn't a local and travelled to his job every day from outside. It was a case of him being in the wrong place at the

wrong time. The fact that he happened to be a Catholic was justi-
fication in Loyalist eyes, but he could just as easily have been a Protestant worker from the DHSS. It was a tragedy for all of us. I had
lost very good friends who were killed, but when it comes to your
own family, it's very, very hard to take. The day he died was his
thirtieth birthday . . .' Michael pauses and composes himself.

Throughout his years in the RUC Michael had been very close to
his eldest brother, Kevin, who had joined the force seven years
earlier, in 1964. They served in Londonderry together, in the
Bangor area together and in West Belfast together, with Michael in
the Springfield Road and Kevin next door in Andersonstown. They
sat and passed their sergeant's exams together. 'Kevin and I were
especially close in a way that brothers who are policemen only can
be. We'd served with each other and he taught me a lot of things I'd
have stamped headlong into had he not shown me how to avoid
them. He had all the experience.' But the inseparable brothers were
separated in West Belfast when the new Divisional Superintendent
decided that it wasn't a good idea to have two brothers serving in two
dangerous areas so close together. He thought that if one brother
was summoned to an incident and found his other brother dead, the
trauma would be too great; it was a risk the new commander was not
prepared to take. So Kevin was advised to apply for a transfer. He'd
always wanted to go to one of the country areas where he could
enjoy some of the wonderful fishing that many parts of Northern
Ireland have to offer. His wish was granted and he ended up with a
desk job in a beautiful part of the province, in charge of legal
training. He didn't miss charging around in Landrovers, reacting to
the latest incident, and the legal work was fresh and stimulating. He
had plenty of time for fishing (one of his old fishing pals from
Londonderry had also got a transfer to the same area), and for one
of his other pleasures, singing in the church choir. Kevin was welcomed with open arms by the local Catholic population because he
was a wonderful soloist and had sung in the RUC choir. For once, at
least one of the RUC brothers seemed to be leading a normal life.

Kevin and his family went to mass every Sunday morning. He followed the same routine: driving to the church, locking the car, and
walking into church to take his place in the choir. One Sunday
morning, he'd just locked the car when a man walked up and shot
him with a high-powered rifle. Another man ran up and shot him six
more times as he lay dying on the ground in front of his wife and
three children. Neither gunman was masked and there were
witnesses to the shooting. No one was ever charged. Michael heard

the news with horror as he was attending the funeral of a friend who'd been killed in an IRA mortar attack. Anger and bitterness followed. 'You never think that if you're going to mass, there's someone waiting there to murder you. You start to wonder who did point the finger at him? Who let them know that he went there every Sunday morning to sing in the choir? Who knew he was a policeman? He didn't have a high-profile job out on the streets but spent most of his time behind a desk. I believe that someone within that congregation would have passed the word on. I think it happened at the time when people were trying to encourage Catholics to join the police service. There are quite a few people I know who would like to join but are afraid to because of the threat of assassination and the fear that they can't go home to see their families in Catholic areas because of the danger.' I asked him about the men who shot his brother. He said he knew who one of them was. 'When I was at the mortuary, identifying Kevin's body, if that man had walked past the door I would have shot him. I would have killed him. Why did they do it? Why did it have to be Kevin? And you began to get feeling guilt. Why him, when he wasn't harming a soul, sitting behind a desk all day? Anyone who says they wouldn't seek revenge isn't human. Some part of them is bound to want to do so. If I'd known where the killer was there and then, I would have probably gone after him and shot him. But I didn't. You'd like to do it but I don't think I could. I couldn't go along, plan a murder and just go and shoot him – although I did feel like it at the time.'

The death of his second brother finished Michael. He'd had enough of the killing ground that Northern Ireland had become. 'I was sick, sick and tired of the whole thing. My eight-year-old son kept saying, "Daddy, are they going to come and kill you next?" I said to my wife, Angela, "Why don't we get the hell out of here and bring the children up in a place free from all this hatred and bigotry?"' His wife, a former policewoman, was ready to follow Michael wherever he wanted to go.

The day before Kevin was shot, Michael's brother Sean had arrived home for a visit from Adelaide. They hadn't seen each other for over twelve years. Michael decided to join him on the other side of the world, as far away from Northern Ireland as possible. By the end of the year the family had emigrated to Australia. 'I suppose what went through my head was, "To hell with this bloody lot. I'm not going to put my own family through this again. My mother has broken her heart completely with two sons murdered, one by Loyalists and the other by the Provisional IRA."' I asked Michael what his mates in the police said when he broke the news that he was off to Australia. 'They all said I was doing the right thing after Kevin's death. Many were saying to themselves that they wished they could take the same decision, because they too were totally fed up with the situation here. They didn't want to get killed either and leave widows and children with no fathers. They supported me 100 per cent and were glad to see me getting out of it.'

But Michael was determined to stay a policeman, the job he loved, despite all the tragedies in Northern Ireland. 'I enjoy every minute of it. It's a job I would never give up.' The South Australia Police were delighted to welcome an officer with such unique, although unenviable, experience. Soon he was training their special operations team, the STAR force (Special Tasks and Rescue). It sounded more like one of those children's television programmes whose side effect is to get little boys into toy shops to buy the figures from the series. I was also puzzled that an apparently quiet, sleepy Australian city like Adelaide needed a STAR force or officers with Michael's particular experience and talents. Michael told me I could not have been more wrong. 'The murders that are occurring out there are quite incredible and the crime rate is quite incredible compared to here.' I must have looked taken aback. 'Yes, it is a beautiful city. The standard of living is good but the *way* of life is totally different to here. The drug scene is terrible. When I used to go out on patrol in a police car, we used to see youngsters of ten, eleven and twelve – boys and girls – selling themselves as prostitutes to buy money for drugs. And the schools aren't as good as here anyway. And the family unit really doesn't exist in the way it does here. The weather's good but that's about the height of it.' All the family felt the same. 'Angela was terribly homesick, so much so that it was affecting her health. I was homesick and the children were homesick. We were so far away from home and we all wanted to get back. So, after eighteen months, we decided to pack our bags and come back and face it all again.' Michael laughs at what must have been my look of incredulity. 'But I'm glad I went away. I'm glad I did it.'

But before he left he had a telephone call from a friend in the RUC who told him that the 'Alphabet Regiment' (the SAS) had shot dead the man who, Michael believed, had killed his brother Kevin. 'I wasn't elated and I didn't jump for joy. I just thought the bastard got his end the way he should have done. As a matter of fact, when I thought about it and told Angela, I felt rather strange. It wasn't sadness, but I was sorry that another boy was dead. I wasn't overjoyed, nor was I over-sad. I just thought, "There goes another killing."'

Not only did Michael return to Northern Ireland, he rejoined the RUC. What did his mates say when they saw their suntanned colleague back in uniform again? 'They said I was "bloody mad" coming back to this place.' But why had he gone back to the RUC and all its dangers? Why hadn't he joined an English force instead, like the 'Met' or Greater Manchester? 'Oh no, not the English police!' he said with a look of mock horror. 'A lot of guys who do leave the RUC for another force end up coming back. There's this sort of pulling back to the RUC.' I asked whether it was Northern Ireland or the Force that did the pulling. He said it was the Force. 'It's a way of life, like nowhere else. You see, we've all been affected the same way. I can't think of one policeman who hasn't been affected either by losing very good friends or having some relative murdered.' I wondered whether that bond of common suffering had brought the Force closer together. He said it wasn't that that bound it together: it was something else – a something he'd been told about when he was a probationary policeman eighteen years before. 'I'll always remember an old policeman said to me there were three religions in this country – prods, taigs [a derogatory term for a Catholic] and policemen – and you know that the majority of policemen are prods. That still holds good. Whether a policeman is a Catholic or a Protestant, he's a policeman first. At the end of the day, that's his job and he has to be professional about it. That's what binds us together.'

I said that when he returned to Northern Ireland, I supposed he glimpsed no more light at the end of the proverbial tunnel than there had been when he'd gone away. 'None whatsoever. In fact it appears to have got darker. The IRA are still doing what they do, the Loyalist equivalent doing what they do, and the politicians not doing anything. But then we all have a job to do and I do my little bit the way everyone else would do theirs. We all hope it will stop. We might be asking far too much for it to stop but we would all like to see a bit of peace in the country.' I asked Michael if he saw another twenty years of Troubles. 'I can see no end to it at the moment,' he said. 'I can see no end. Certainly they're not going to achieve peace by a military campaign.' Looking back, I should have asked Michael to specify whom he meant by 'they', although I was pretty sure he was talking about the Provisional IRA. But perhaps he really meant everybody.

CHAPTER FOUR

TOO LONG A SACRIFICE:

THE VOLUNTEER

Too long a sacrifice
Can make a stone of the heart.
O when may it suffice?
William Butler Yeats, 'Easter 1916'

Clarendon Street in Derry must be one of the most beautiful Georgian streets in Ireland. Dublin has its fine eighteenth-century avenues and squares but, not least because Dublin is flat, has nothing to compare with the magnificent street that sweeps down from the hill on the fringe of the Bogside to the harbour in what is still regarded as Ireland's second city. The elegant three-storey houses, built by and for the rich merchants from London who gave the city the prefix to its name, are now occupied by accountants and solicitors, estate agents and insurance brokers, architects, doctors and dentists – and the Samaritans. The fact that Clarendon Street stands in the shadow of the mortar-proof fortress that is Strand Road RUC station makes one marvel all the more that it has survived the ravages of the past twenty years.

For years one of those houses with the wide-panelled front doors was home to the O'Doherty family, where Sadie and Bernard O'Doherty (known as 'Barney') raised their six sons – Eamonn, Bernard, Cahir, Muredach, Shane and Fergal. Sadie, a gentle, caring mother, sad that her children have gone but proud of them, now lives by herself in the town. She's cheerful and friendly and remarkably resilient. Only occasionally do you glimpse the lonely widow and see the sadness in her eyes. Warming herself by the blazing coal fire and surrounded by pictures of her family, she sighs and smiles when she remembers the days that are gone. 'They were happy days in Clarendon Street. I wish the children were all back

once more. The boys were very close. They didn't need any outside
company as they used to make all their own fun. We had a huge attic
where they used to play on wet days. Little Fergal, the youngest,
used to have problems. He and Shane weren't particularly close in
those days because there was five years between them and Fergal
used to feel totally out of it. He always wanted to play too, but
whenever he went into a room it was "Out! Out! Out!" So I used to
take him along to the pictures and we'd go off and have a treat of
chips.'

Traditionally, Clarendon Street had always been mixed, with
Catholics and Protestants living side by side or across the road from
one another, most of them middle-class business or professional
people. 'Barney' O'Doherty was a well-respected figure in the community, becoming Principal of the Christian Brothers primary
school, Brow-of-the-Hill, overlooking the Bogside, and raising six
children, most of whom seemed destined for greater things – even if
those things could only be achieved outside the confines of Derry
where, in the fifties and sixties, employment opportunities for
bright children, of either religion, were strictly limited. Barney was
determined to see that his children had the best opportunity possible. 'He was very strict on their education, it always came first. He
was firm but he was fair,' Sadie recalls. The house became known as
'O'Doherty's Academy' as every evening Barney insisted that
homework was completed before the children went out and, in
schoolmasterly manner, would do the rounds of the various rooms
to ensure that his orders were carried out. They invariably were as
Barney was an awesome figure and few of his children were inclined
to disobey or contradict him. Fergal lived in permanent fear of his
father. 'He was not an easy man to get on with, especially when we
reached adolescence. He was really strict about everything and
really headmasterly at home. He was a respectable member of the
community but he didn't want us to reflect badly on him – the image
of having perfect children. I think that was probably one of the
pressures that kept me out of trouble more than anything. I was
dreadfully afraid of my father. I was terrified of getting into trouble
and getting on his bad side. So I was really a "goodie two shoes" –
and at school too. And so was Shane.'

The family, like most Catholics in Derry, had always been
Nationalists, aspiring to the ultimate reunification of Ireland by
peaceful means. Republicans, on the other hand, from whom the
IRA draws its traditional support, believe that the country can only
be united by physical force. Neither tradition, however, is anti-

Protestant, despite what many Protestants feel. It is often forgotten that Wolfe Tone, the first Irish Republican who in 1798, nine years after the French Revolution, led the United Irishmen in rebellion against the Crown, was a Protestant. He set out his Republican ideal and its purpose in words that have been dusted down and polished over the centuries – perhaps seldom more so than during the past twenty years:

> To subvert the tyranny of our execrable government, to break the connection with England, the never-failing source of all our political evils, and to assert the independence of my country – these were my objects. To unite the whole people of Ireland, to abolish the memory of all past dissensions and to substitute the common name of Irishman in place of the denominations of Protestant, Catholic and Dissenter – these were my means.

To the O'Doherty children, there was never any question of there being differences between Catholics and Protestants apart from the obvious fact that they went to different churches and celebrated different anniversaries. To Fergal, Protestants were the friends in the street he played with. 'I remember becoming aware that they were Protestants, but I couldn't define in my child's mind what the difference was. It was something mysterious, something different. I knew they didn't go to mass but it didn't make a lot of difference at the time. It didn't become embarrassing to be around them until the Troubles really got going. There was a Protestant family across the street who were in business in the town and when they became targets [of the IRA's "economic" bombing campaign], we became aware that we were really on the other side. Within a couple of years, all the Protestants in Clarendon Street had moved out and the street ended up becoming entirely Catholic. So that ended the relationships I had with Protestants.'

By the time the Troubles began, the O'Dohertys had effectively become two separate families, with the older boys growing up, leaving home for their further education and then going out into the world to look for work. That inevitably meant leaving Derry. Eamonn took a degree at Maynooth, part of the Natinal University of Ireland, and then went to work in a Catholic mission in Tanzania; Bernard studied to be a Jesuit priest, decided it wasn't for him and emigrated to America; Cahir, having been 'frogmarched' into the RAF, where he served for five years, went to work for Bank Saderat Iran (the Shah's Bank) in London, and then emigrated to Australia where he took a degree, taught and became an active supporter of the Aborigines' cause whom he saw as another oppressed minority; and Muredach graduated from University College, Dublin, taught briefly and then became a town planner for Southwark Borough Council in London. The two youngest O'Doherty brothers, Shane and Fergal, were left at home with their parents, where Shane attended the local Catholic grammar school, St Columb's College, and Fergal the Christian Brothers Brow-of-the-Hill primary school where their father taught. Mrs O'Doherty doesn't remember discussing the Troubles with either Shane or Fergal, who were fifteen and ten in 1969. 'We didn't tell them anything about the Troubles. Of course, living on the edge of the Bogside, we all saw what was going on. Barney had to go through the barricades every day to get to school and those manning them used to let him through because he had to go and teach. I remember Barney having to send the children home when the tear gas got so bad and drifted up to the school. He'd call their parents in the middle of the riots, and ask them to come and pick their children up. It was dreadful. There were days when the school didn't open.' Although Sadie may not have said anything to her children, her husband was quite categoric: he told them that under no circumstances did he want any of his boys mixed up in any Republican activities.

Unlike many of their middle-class contemporaries, Barney and Sadie O'Doherty did not become actively involved in the protests and demonstrations of the civil rights movement. Taking to the streets would not have been in Sadie's nature, nor perhaps in keeping with the dignity of Barney's position. They would, of course, have supported its aims as did just about every Catholic in Northern Ireland. It was the newly emergent Catholic middle classes, led by the first generation of Catholic graduates like John Hume from Derry, that provided the movement with much of its driving force and many of its most articulate spokesmen. The grievances of the Catholic minority were real: they suffered discrimination in housing and employment; they were disadvantaged by a 'gerrymandered' electoral system that, in Derry for example, ensured that a city with a Catholic majority was run by a Protestant local authority; and they were on the receiving end of the Special Powers Act which, since 1922, had enabled the Northern Ireland Minister for Home Affairs to enact whatever security measures he thought fit – an Act whose scope the South African government reputedly envied. But whilst his mother and father sat at home and watched these momentous events on the TV, the young Fergal, barely into long trousers, was eager to be involved. He used to sneak off with his aunt and cousin next door and take part in the demonstrations. 'I got involved secretly. Mother didn't know. But then I'd come home late with tears in my eyes from the CS gas or my clothes covered in dye from the water cannon, and mother would be furious and attack her sister for leading her boy astray.' Eamonn, too, had a brief flirtation with the civil rights movement. After his five years in Tanzania, he returned to Belfast to study for a teaching qualification at Queen's University. Intrigued by the civil rights protest, he took part – for a day only – in the march from Belfast to Derry which ended in the Loyalist ambush at Burntollet Bridge. Eamonn pulled out the day before Burntollet. He'd only gone along out of curiosity, not out of any sense of political commitment. For Eamonn one day was enough. Muredach too took a week's leave from his planner's job in London to return to witness at first hand the 'Battle of the Bogside' in August 1969, but arrived too late and found no rioters but soldiers being hailed as heroes.

But Shane Paul O'Doherty's thoughts were set in a different direction. Long before the outbreak of the Troubles, he would spend hours upstairs in the attic where he had his 'den' and in the local library immersed in books. Whereas other boys his age may have been obsessed with Manchester United and John, George, Paul and Ringo, Shane's romantic heroes were Patrick Pearse and the small band of rebels who seized the GPO in Dublin in 1916 and held out briefly against the might of the British Empire. Shane Paul became fascinated at how the blood of their martyrdom – as Pearse would have put it – watered the seed of Irish nationhood. Martyrdom became a childhood fantasy at a child's most impressionable age. 'I used to read history books and recognised that what measure of freedom or independence or nationhood Ireland had achieved had been fought for in 1916 and in the War of Independence,' he told me. 'We regard them as patriots, the founding fathers of the Irish nation, and the Irish government and the Church pay tribute to them every Easter. They're written about in history books and sung about in songs. I was caught up in the romance of it all. Although I had other dreams as well at that age, at one particular period I thought that nothing could be more glorious or exciting or beautiful or fulfilling than to be involved in that fight for Irish freedom. The whole meaning of life, you might say, would be contained in it. I dreamed of a re-creation of an Easter Rising, perhaps in Northern Ireland, and of death as a martyr and a hero, with an eternal place in the memory of the Irish people. That impressed me a lot.'

I asked Shane if he was sure he'd read and imbibed all this *before* 1968–9. He said it was quite some time before, and ever since then he'd wanted to join the IRA. 'When I read books about how the Irish Republic achieved its freedom from Britain, I realised it was through violence, through IRA violence and through the self-sacrifice of patriots. I admired these people and those days and wanted to be part of it.' Whilst other children his age, or perhaps slightly younger, might write a letter to Santa Claus, Shane Paul O'Doherty wrote a letter to posterity. Many years later it was found under the floorboards in the attic, dated and signed and written in Shane's young hand. 'I think I must have been about ten or eleven at the time. I'd written that I would join the IRA, become a hero and a martyr and would die for Ireland. When I heard about it all those years later, I was very embarrassed and amused and horrified to think that at that age I could have been so dedicated to the sacrifice idea.'

When I first heard the story from Fergal I found it difficult to believe, until Sadie and then Shane himself confirmed it. I certainly knew it was possible in the climate of Northern Ireland, remembering an eight- or nine-year-old boy called Sean whom I'd interviewed in the Divis Flats in Belfast at the end of 1973. He had a chilling maturity and the letters IRA tattooed in ball-point on the back of his hand. He told me he wanted to fight and die for Ireland. I often wonder if he did.

I expressed surprise at Shane's childhood obsession, given that such ideas could not have been further removed from his parents' values and the quality of life in Clarendon Street. They were clearly a secret obsession. I was also surprised that there appeared to be so many history books lying around, but then Shane's father was a teacher and such reading would not have been considered likely to have had such a profound and dangerous effect on the mind of a child. Shane agreed that such notions would have been utterly foreign to his parents but he had studied his family tree and told me, with some pride, that his father's two uncles had been involved in Republican activities in the twenties, and that the O'Doherty house in Waterloo Street, where his father's parents had lived, was a contact house for the IRA in the twenties – and that, he said, was the only reference to the IRA in Derry at that time. Shane's brother, Muredach, has no doubt where these romantic dreams came from, placing the blame fairly and squarely on the excessively nationalistic tone of the history books in the Christian Brothers Brow-of-the-Hill school and on the emphasis the teachers placed on it.

Shane's romantic fantasy grew. On 7 March 1966, just before the fiftieth anniversary of the Easter Rising, the IRA blew up Nelson's pillar in O'Connell Street in Dublin where the rebuilt GPO still stands. For aesthetic and historical reasons there were few tears shed at the removal of the towering symbol of British rule in the street where the shackles had been broken. The IRA's demolition job gave the twelve-year-old Shane new hope. 'I was brilliantly impressed by the use of gelignite, and lots of students came back to Derry with alleged pieces of the statue. It was an insight into the possibility that the IRA still existed and could be active.' According to Eamonn, his Lordship's head is said to have found its way back to Derry, but was disposed of when it became too 'hot'. Shane said he was also profoundly impressed when 'the IRA's recruiting sergeant' came to Derry in the mid-sixties to hold a public meeting. I was slightly puzzled as his words conjured up a vision of a man with a beret and dark glasses handing out membership forms. I thought such an event was unlikely, in particular at a public meeting. I'd completely missed the point. The 'recruiting sergeant' was the Rev. Ian Paisley. 'There was quite a lot of rabble-rousing going on at the time. I was quite young and quite frightened when I heard that this monster figure was coming to Derry to attack Catholics and burn Catholics – at least that is what I was told on the street by guys my age. There was a lot of trouble at the meeting and it seemed like it might be a good idea to have an IRA even if it didn't exist.'

Given Shane's disposition, it was never a question of if he joined the IRA but when. His ideas were formed at the most impressionable stage of a young person's life – at a time when no one could have imagined how events were going to evolve. It was almost as if they were waiting for their hour to come. The historical moment came at four o'clock on 14 August 1969 in London when the Labour government's Home Secretary, James Callaghan, agreed to the request from the Northern Ireland government for British troops to come to the aid of the civil power and take the pressure off the beleaguered RUC. An hour later a company of the Prince of Wales's Own Regiment took over security duties in Derry city centre and, to the delight of the Catholics, the police were drawn back behind army lines. The soldiers were seen as the saviours. At that time the enemies of the Catholics of the Bogside and Creggan were the Loyalist mobs, and the police and 'B Specials' whom they saw as their supporters. Historically, in the eyes of veteran Republicans, the wrong enemy was being identified.

Such nuances of history were lost on Shane Paul O'Doherty

despite his commitment to a then non-existent IRA cause. 'Initially, of course, the whole Catholic community was delighted to see the army come in. They barricaded the streets off with wire and seemed to take over security. They were British – or English – and seemed to be non-sectarian and independent. They produced security on the streets overnight. I remember on frequent occasions making banana sandwiches for them and taking flasks of coffee down to the troops at the bottom of Clarendon Street – and running "messages" for them, for cigarettes. This was when I was fourteen.'

The change in attitude towards the army happened more slowly in Derry than it did in Belfast. There was no Falls Road curfew to hurry it along. Although, with the benefit of hindsight, the change seems as inevitable as day follows night, that was not how it appeared at the time. The change in Derry may have been slower and less dramatic but the reasons for it were essentially the same: the IRA armed to ensure it would not leave the Nationalist areas undefended again, and demands from Unionist politicians grew for the army to go in and root out the weapons before the IRA grew too strong. The inevitable clashes developed between soldiers not trained to knock politely on doors and families who regarded the IRA as their last line of defence against Protestant mobs and a police force they still distrusted. It was not difficult for a resurgent IRA to turn the situation to its advantage, assisted by incidents for which the army was inevitably given the blame.

The turning point in Derry came on 8 July 1971, when soldiers shot two men dead in two separate incidents. There had been rioting for four consecutive nights, and in the early hours of the fourth morning, the army said, a man was seen to raise a rifle against the troops of the Royal Anglian Regiment. The army shot him dead. He was called Seamus Cusack and he came from the Creggan. Later that day, in the mourning parades and demonstrations that followed, the army shot dead another man, Desmond Beattie. A police statement said he was about to throw a nail bomb. Neither official account of the shooting of Cusack and Beattie was believed by most Nationalists in the area. The Derry Sinn Fein leader and Republican activist at the time, Martin McGuinness, subsequently observed that it was that incident that marked 'the rejection of the British army and the establishment of the Republican base in Derry'.

By this time Shane Paul O'Doherty had already joined the IRA. He felt that at long last his hour had come, but didn't know how to go about becoming involved. He travelled across the Bogside four times a day on his way to school and back but didn't know who the IRA were or where they lived. He didn't even know a single leading Republican, which perhaps indicates the extent to which Shane's fantasies were limited to his mind and the pages of his books. Not knowing where to start, he bought the newspaper of the Official Republican movement, noted down a contact address in the Creggan (the huge Catholic estate on the hill above the Bogside), and went off and knocked on the door. It was opened by an Englishman who laughed when Shane told him he wanted to join the IRA. Questions were asked about his family and the fact that his father taught at the Christian Brothers school appeared to be a good enough Nationalist credential for a potential recruit. Shane was told to come back at a later date and ended up fund-raising on the fringes of the organisation. The money was supposed to be used to buy weapons but no one ever saw them. Someone said that they'd seen the houses of some of the big men in the movement full of new carpets and new furniture. Disillusioned, Shane drifted away from the Officials. His experience gives some impression of how unstructured and haphazard the IRA's organisation was barely two years into the Troubles.

Having flirted with the Officials, Shane then almost literally bumped into the Provisionals. He was walking along Rossville Street one day – the main arterial road that runs through the Bogside and has a dreadful block of flats named after it – when he met a couple of school friends who said they were going off to join the Provisionals that evening. Did he want to come along? Shane made it sound as if he was going off to join the boy scouts. 'At the end of 1970, the Provisionals were looked upon as the saviours of the Catholic community, especially in Belfast where there were tales of two or three men with ancient, clapped-out rifles taking up positions around churches to hold off mobs attacking Catholic areas.' He was clearly referring to an incident on 27 June 1970 that became famous in Republican legend when the Belfast Provisional leader, Billy McKee, and a handful of others held off a Protestant mob intent on burning down Short Strand, the enclave of 6000 Catholics in the east of the city. Three Protestants were killed and McKee was wounded. This was the stuff that fired the imagination of young men, although sectarian gun battles between Catholics and Protestants were hardly in keeping with the lofty principles of Irish Republicanism. But this was the reality on the ground. 'I'd grown up with one of the boys I met that day and I was delighted at last to have discovered the real Provisional IRA. The Provos were the people who didn't just talk about action, they produced it. Whereas the "Stickies"* just seemed to do a lot of talking. In a flat that evening we were asked about our backgrounds and sworn in on the spot. That's where we took the oath of allegiance to the IRA. The other two had to leave the room so they could never give evidence that they'd actually seen me being sworn in. Two members of the IRA administered the oath and I stood with my right hand up and swore to God – and anyone else who was listening – that I would take orders from the IRA and dedicate myself to the IRA, and that was it. It was probably the most brilliant moment of my existence up till then because I'd found the terrible beauty, and from that day forth my whole life and existence changed. I was no longer an insignificant teenager, I was a fully-fledged member of the IRA.'

Shane was now a 'volunteer'. I asked him whether he realised that this meant he was liable to be ordered to go out and kill people. He said that such an idea didn't really occur to him at the time. 'There hadn't really been an active IRA in Derry and this was the first budding of the Provisional IRA and it was a sort of romantic thing. I thought it was going to be about blowing up statues and installations. At that stage it didn't seem to mean shooting at army patrols and ambushes. But the thought that the rattle of the Thompson could be re-created in Derry was extremely attractive. I never looked back from that day on. I wasn't an ordinary fifteen-year-old schoolboy. I was a secret agent of the IRA.' During this period, Shane was still at school and he found the uniform a convenient cover for his clandestine IRA activities. He used to look out for suitable bombing targets in the town centre or good places for an ambush where army patrols would regularly stop and rest. 'I felt centrally involved and that, if there were any more attacks on the Bogside, I would be part of its defence, this time using real weapons as opposed to stones and petrol bombs. It made me feel great. It was like having a television camera going on in my own imagination. I was a central player.'

Early on, Shane made a decision that he was going to become an explosives expert, an area in which there wasn't a great deal of competition for obvious reasons. He had long had an interest in fireworks and would take them apart to see how they worked. Making bombs, he felt, was a natural progression. Whilst others during the rioting were learning how to make petrol bombs and

---

* The 'Stickies' are the Official IRA, so called after the paper lilies that 'stick' on jacket lapels at Easter.

Molotov cocktails, Shane was in reference libraries learning about explosives. 'I knew the difference between detonators and gelignite long before I saw them. I think I first proved myself to the IRA Brigade staff in Derry when they'd been unable to plant a bomb and had left me to dump it. I didn't know how that particular bomb worked. All I saw was a duffle bag with a black piece of cord coming out of it with matches attached to the end. They told me to strike a matchbox against them, check that the fuse had taken, and then get the hell out after I'd planted it. That's what I did. Nobody was hurt. It was against a place not a person but it did a fair bit of damage. That gave me points, that gave me some pull. Then I planted another one, with a much older guy, against an electricity pylon. It seemed very adventurous and very exciting. It was making the news – headlines in the press – and I couldn't get enough of it.' Shane became expert in the art of deception to keep his secret. 'You deceive family, friends, school, you name it. Everybody's deceived and everybody's used. You make decisions for other people – it's not a very democratic process. If you get shot or imprisoned, that's when your family find out and you're automatically involving them in circumstances and situations over which they have no choice.'

Shane's parents found out before he was shot or imprisoned. It was only a matter of time before they did, and their suspicions had already been aroused by a visit from the President of St Columb's College who told them that Shane hadn't been attending school. Shane says his family discovered his IRA connections whilst he was away for the weekend at an IRA training camp, on the pretext of being away in Dublin for some student activity. He knew he'd left a bag of bullets at home under his pillow in bed and thought, naively, that they would be safe there as his room was at the top of the house and few people ever went in. He was wrong. 'When I got home from the training camp and walked into the house, I found my mother in some state. I didn't realise at first what it was. Then I denied everything. My mother said it was no use. Bullets had been found behind my pillow and my father had got rid of them by dropping them in the Foyle. She wanted to know what I was involved in. The tragic part of it – or the amusing part of it – is that in the argument that ensued, my mother said she would go to the Bishop – and of course it didn't matter a damn to me then if she went to the Pope: the element of tragedy was that she was dealing with the complete unknown. My main worry at the time was explaining to the IRA how the bullets had been lost.'

But it wasn't just around a hundred rounds of ammunition that were discovered in Shane's attic bedroom. His father also uncovered, to his amazement, a considerable number of condoms and the necessary chemicals and acid to make 'condom bombs', so called because the explosion is triggered once the acid has eaten through the condom. The result is a huge ball of fire. The bullets and firebomb-making equipment were hurriedly placed in two carrier bags, taken past the soldiers at the bottom of Clarendon Street, and dumped in the harbour a few hundred yards further on, with the bearer saying rosaries all the way. When Shane came home that afternoon, his father took him into the kitchen and there was a showdown. Fergal was in the living-room with his mother. 'I knew for some reason that something was going on in the kitchen and that I shouldn't go in. I heard my father's voice being raised, very characteristically, and Shane's voice raising itself for the first time in his life against my father. When he came out, Shane had his head down and was very quiet. He put his coat on and left and never came back to that house. That evening, one of his friends came round and said that Shane wasn't going to be staying at home any more and could we pack his clothes.' After the row in the kitchen, Barney told Sadie that he was going to go and see the leaders of the organisation, most of whom he thought he'd taught at school at some time or other: he was going to ask them to release his son until he'd finished his education, 'and then they can have him,' he said.

The realisation that Shane was in the IRA devastated his family, and particularly his mother. 'I just couldn't believe it. I just could not believe it that one of my boys was in the IRA. He'd just moved into the A-level class and I thought he was studying and going to go on to do a degree like his brothers. I hadn't the slightest idea. There was nothing to make me suspicious. He used to come home from the College and do his work: his friends used to call for him and he used to go off to the football or whatever. He was just like the other lads.' I asked Sadie how a boy from a good family, with a good education, living in a middle-class area, came to be involved in the IRA. She looked at me and said softly and sadly, 'You tell me, Peter, you tell me. That's a question I still want answered. It was my son and I knew the consequences . . .' she added as her voice tailed off.

Fergal's reaction to his brother's involvement was one of confusion, as might be expected in a young brother of eleven or twelve. Shane was his hero. 'He was my big brother. He showed me the ropes. He was like my guardian, and what he would do I naturally did. When I discovered he was in the IRA I felt this sudden pressure to join as well. I was also very idealistic but I was realistic too. I was afraid for Shane – I didn't want him to get shot or blown up – but I didn't want to get shot myself. I thought, "If he wants to get involved, he can do it. But I don't want to get involved. I don't want to die." So I made a conscious decision not to join, although I felt guilty about it at the time – and still do.'

Shane didn't move far away, spending much of his time in the Creggan estate which, after internment on 9 August 1971, became a huge 'No Go' area, blocked off by monster barricades. The Bogside and Creggan became known as 'Free Derry' – 'No Go' to the army and police. The gable end on which the famous words were originally painted still stands alone on a traffic island in the middle of the Bogside, the slogan touched up from time to time, unvandalised and graffiti-free. Any youth rash enough to attempt modification would do so at his peril. Those were the days when men with masks and guns would parade openly for the television crews of the world who flocked to the farthest outpost of the United Kingdom to record this defiant challenge to the authority of the government. Those days gave Shane a real 'high'. 'It was commonplace to see cars floating about with six or seven men packed into them holding rifles and machine-guns and not wearing masks. Naturally I wanted to be part of that scene because, although in theory you're a member of a secret organisation, it's nice if some people knew because that would give you status. Yes, it was an ego trip, if you like, and it was very fulfilling. You could almost be a "live" hero or a "live" martyr if they realised you were in the IRA before you were a dead one.' Such contemporary recognition was obviously preferable to any posthumous respect. Shane made it all sound like a glorious game, all the more exciting because it was so dangerous.

No doubt that's how many young men felt at the time, but not all of them lived to tell the tale. One of the Provisionals Shane spent much of his time with during the summer of 1971 was a man from the Creggan called Eamonn Lafferty. Nine days after internment, he was shot dead in a gun battle with the army. Eamonn Lafferty merits a paragraph in the Republican Movement's chronicle of IRA dead from 1916 to 1985, *The Last Post*:

> On 18 August 1971, British soldiers tried to enter the
> Creggan area of Derry in order to carry out a reign of terror
> and rampage. The area and its hard-pressed inhabitants
> were defended by a number of young men – among them
> Eamonn Lafferty, and for his trouble he was shot dead.

Eamonn's attitude on that morning was related to a priest by a British officer who took part in the engagement: 'The fearlessness and bravery of Eamonn on the fateful morning made my blood run cold.'

Although it may be difficult to imagine any British officer referring to a 'fateful morning' – or to the deceased as 'Eamonn' – that is how Eamonn Lafferty is remembered by his comrades. Shane was with him just before he died. 'I was going round checking the barricades in the Creggan that night in a car with a number of others because we'd heard that the army was going to try and come into the area. Eamonn was sleeping in a safe house at the time. I went and gave him the car keys and he took over the patrol. I fell asleep in the chair and then, after about an hour, a close friend who was then a leading bomber woke me up and told me that Eamonn had just been shot dead in a gun battle with the army.' Shortly afterwards, Shane drifted away from the Provisionals. He says it was because the organisation was becoming flooded with recruits – which was no doubt true in the charged atmosphere of the summer of 1971 – and as a result his own central role was diminished. It was not in Shane's nature to be on the periphery of things. It may also be that he realised that he'd had a close brush with death.

It was 'Bloody Sunday' that prompted Shane to become rein-volved in the Provisional IRA. On Sunday 30 January 1972 the Northern Ireland Civil Rights Association had organised an anti-internment march in Derry, which the acting Minister for Home Affairs, Brian Faulkner, had banned under the Special Powers Act. Thousands of marchers ignored the order. The army, under increasing political pressure from the Stormont government to get tough, had decided to use the opportunity – if, indeed, it arose – to teach the 'young hooligans' of Derry, who had already caused around £4 million worth of damage in the town, a lesson. The soldiers brought in to do the teaching were men of the Parachute Regiment who already enjoyed the reputation of having 'tamed' some of the toughest areas in Belfast. The plan was for their 'snatch squads' to go out and arrest the hooligans when the stone-throwing started – but only after their targets were well separated from the majority of peaceable marchers. Certainly there was no intention expressed or order given to 'flush out the IRA', despite what some may like to think. The IRA are reported to have given an assurance to the organisers of the march that there would be no operation whilst it was under way.

When the marchers came up against a line of the Royal Green Jackets in William Street at the entrance to the Bogside, the stoning started. The Paras went in – and the rest, as they say, is history. The versions of what happened next are diametrically opposed. The paratroopers say that, about four o'clock, a machine-gun opened up on them from the direction of Rossville Flats in the Bogside. Marchers and eyewitnesses say that there was no gunfire and that the soldiers opened up indiscriminately. What is not in dispute is the end result. Thirteen civilians were dead, seven of them under nineteen, and thirteen others were wounded. The paratroopers fired 108 rounds of 7.62mm bullets into the crowd. It was, in the eyes of those taking part in the march, unadulterated murder.

The trauma of that day, which perhaps more than any other single event in the twenty years drove young people into the arms of the IRA, is most vividly illustrated by Father Edward Daly, who is now the Bishop of Derry but at the time had been a Bogside priest for nearly ten years.

> We heard the sound of heavy engines revving up . . . and I saw three or four Saracen armoured cars come dashing in our direction with soldiers on foot behind them. I'd had experience of this on many occasions before, so I decided to get out of the area because it doesn't matter whether you have a Roman collar or a dog collar . . . Everybody was running and some people were laughing, there was terrible good humour about it, there was no panic . . . they thought the soldiers would come into the area and stop. Suddenly alarm grew when the armoured car kept coming on. It suddenly dawned on people that this was something different. I remember a young boy laughing at me. I'm not an athlete and I'm not a very graceful runner. That was the only reason I could think he was laughing. He was very cheery . . . the next thing, he suddenly gasped and threw his hands up in the air and fell on his face . . . There was a terrible lot of blood. We pulled up his jersey and there was a massive bloody hole . . . He asked me, 'Am I going to die?' and I said, 'No,' but I administered the last rites . . . I remember trying to talk to the wounded lad and calm him. He was getting confused and upset and I can remember him holding my hand and squeezing it . . . We seemed to be just holding on to one another . . . We all wept . . . We got to the top of the street, turned and got the little fellow down

. . . I kneeled beside him and told him, 'Look son, we've got you out.' But he was dead. He was just in his seventeenth year, but only looked about twelve . . . Jackie Duddy was his name.

The television pictures of the stooping Father Daly, waving a white, bloodstained handkerchief in front of the men carrying Jackie Duddy's body, is an image forever associated with the events of that day. In the wake of the public outcry, the government set up an inquiry under Lord Widgery to investigate what had happened. His report, published on 19 April 1972, concluded:

There would have been no deaths . . . if those who organised the illegal march had not thereby created a highly dangerous situation in which a clash between demonstrators and the security forces was almost inevitable.

Soldiers who identified armed gunmen fired upon them in accordance with the standing orders in the Yellow Card [the instructions which detail the circumstances under which a soldier may open fire]. Each soldier was his own judge of whether he had identified a gunman . . . At one end of the scale some soldiers showed a high degree of responsibility; at the other . . . firing bordered on the reckless. These distinctions reflect differences in the character and temperament of the soldiers concerned.

None of the deceased or wounded is proved to have been shot whilst handling a firearm or bomb. Some are wholly acquitted of complicity in such action; but there is a strong suspicion that some others had been firing weapons or handling bombs in the course of the afternoon and that yet others had ben closely supporting them.

There was no general breakdown in discipline. For the most part the soldiers acted as they did because they thought that their orders required it.*

The Catholics of Derry regarded the Widgery Report as a 'whitewash'. Their young men queued up to join the IRA and Shane Paul O'Doherty decided to become active again. He'd been on the march and then gone up to Altnagelvin hospital with a priest to see if he could find a friend who he feared might have been shot.

* The Widgery Report: Summary of Conclusions (H.L. 101/H.C. 220) London, 1972.

'Because he was a priest, we got right to the door of the morgue. He went in to look at the bodies but I would not go in. There were top army officers and policemen standing outside the morgue, smiling happily, obviously under the impression that they had shot dead terrorists or IRA men – whereas they hadn't. They'd shot civilians. I saw families being brought in by their sons and daughters and I watched wives and mothers walk past me into the morgue to check the bodies of people who an hour before had been alive. And I saw them come out.' That's when Shane made up his mind to become an active IRA volunteer once again. 'Bloody Sunday had that effect.'

CHAPTER FIVE

TOO LONG A SACRIFICE:
THE PRISONER

Shane Paul O'Doherty returned to what he knew best: bomb-making. But by the early summer of 1973 he'd been put out of action – and almost killed – by an 'own goal'. 'I made up bombs that were maybe 500 pounds to go in vans to be smuggled into the city centre. There would only be three or four of us working on bombs of this scale in the city because it was a job no one else wanted. When you're setting up a 500-pound bomb, you're quite nervous – and there tended not to be too many people around, for obvious reasons. You're also maybe suffering from a severe gelignite head-ache and you know that you're the most expendable of all.' But by the middle of 1973 he was also refining the art of making up letter-bombs, small but potentially lethal explosive devices that could be sent through the post concealed in a book and detonated when the package or envelope was opened. As he was demonstrating the technique, one bomb went off. 'I saw a rainbow of light coming towards me, and the next thing I was blown across the room. I ended up with metal in my chest and face, severe pain, and injuries to my eye and hand.' He was taken to a hospital across the border where he made a gradual recovery. But his second brush with death, which he had ample time to contemplate lying in a hospital bed, still didn't make him think about leaving the IRA: instead it led him to reappraise the tactics of what the organisation calls 'the armed struggle'. 'By then I was eighteen years of age. I had seen three years of rioting and three years of IRA activity. I'd known friends shot dead and had friends blown up – and I'd seen Bloody Sunday. I had become quite immunised to the idea of violence, the idea of death and the idea of me sacrificing my life – and others theirs. And I thought these three years of IRA activity in Derry hadn't really made an impact.'

The IRA's Army Council reached the same conclusion early in 1973 and decided to extend the bombing campaign to mainland Britain, on the largely correct assumption that, as far as headlines were concerned, a bomb in London was worth ten in Belfast. The leadership had declined to take the step earlier because it had mistakenly believed that the British government might be amenable to doing a deal with the Provisionals. On 17 July 1972, during the first IRA ceasefire, members of the IRA's ruling body, the Army Council, were flown to London for talks with the then Northern Ireland Secretary, William Whitelaw, at the elegant Chelsea home of his junior minister, Paul Channon. The IRA delegation consisted of two men from the South, Sean MacStiofain and David O'Connell, and four from the North, Gerry Adams, Seamus Twomey and Ivor Bell from Belfast, and Martin McGuinness from Derry. The talks proved fruitless and the IRA decided to hit Britain where it thought it would hurt.

The first mission was undertaken by a unit which planted two bombs in London which exploded in Whitehall and outside the Old Bailey on 8 March 1973. One man was killed and 180 were injured. Among those arrested were Dolours and Marion Price – the Price sisters; they were convicted on 15 November of that year. Although two other bombs were discovered and defused, the Provisionals' first strike on the mainland commanded huge headlines, a fact not lost on Shane Paul O'Doherty. Letter-bombs, he reasoned, could have an even greater impact – and a continuous one – if they were sent to specially selected targets, like Reginald Maudling, Home Secretary at the time of 'Bloody Sunday'. 'The IRA knew letter-bombs were good for publicity – world publicity – for no outlay whatsoever. The Price sisters had been arrested in London after one bombing operation – and that was it. Letter-bombs could run for months, with no arrests and major publicity and propaganda.'

For the next eighteen months, from the summer of 1973 until the end of 1974, Shane Paul O'Doherty became the mastermind of the IRA's letter-bomb campaign. None of the family knew. They were, of course, aware of his involvement but had no knowledge of precisely what he was doing: nor was it a knowledge they wished to possess. At weekends they would join dozens of families who were making the forty-minute trip across the border from Derry to visit their sons, brothers and husbands who were on the run in Buncrana or Moville in the Irish Republic. Fergal often made the trip with his mother. 'When we went to see Shane, everything was unspoken. It was all unacknowledged. I'm sure mother felt like saying, "What the hell are you doing! Get out of this. Come home." I'm sure she was feeling all these things but I never heard her express them. We didn't really talk about it although we obviously knew he was still involved. He wasn't living across the border just because he liked the climate better. Or perhaps he did. I always remember crossing the border and feeling that now we were in "our" Ireland, not "their" Ireland. Going back to Derry was like going back to prison.' The only time that Sadie saw her son in the North was when he arrived out of the blue for the funeral of his father, who had died in 1973 of a terminal illness. 'He came into the cathedral and sat beside me. I couldn't believe it. I heard that he'd wept all the way there and back.' Shane came and went in disguise, with his distinctive red hair dyed black.

On 20 December 1974 Shane Paul O'Doherty and hundreds of IRA volunteers heaved sighs of relief when the IRA's Army Council announced a temporary ceasefire in which they would suspend operations over an eleven-day Christmas period. The IRA leadership had voted five to two in favour, with the two Northern representatives on the Army Council voting against. The move followed a secret meeting ten days earlier between a group of nine senior Protestant clergymen, with the Rev. William Arlow as spokesman, and the leaders of the Provisional IRA and Sinn Fein in a small hotel in Feakle, County Clare. Within days, Labour's Northern Ireland Secretary, Merlyn Rees, announced that if 'a genuine and sustained cessation of violence' were forthcoming, the government 'would not be found wanting in its response'. On 2 January 1975 the Provisionals announced they would extend their Christmas ceasefire, and a month later, on 5 February, Merlyn Rees told the House of Commons at least the beginnings of what the IRA wanted to hear: if the IRA ended all offensive operations, the army would slowly be reduced to peacetime levels and ultimately withdrawn to barracks; internment would be phased out; and there would be no action by the security forces which could be construed by the civilian population as harassment. But there was never at any stage any hint of the precondition the IRA has always insisted upon for what it calls 'a lasting peace' – a declaration by the British government that it intends to withdraw not just militarily but politically from Northern Ireland. Four days later, the Provisionals' Army Council announced that 'hostilities against the Crown forces' would be suspended as from the following day, 10 February. In the hope of weaning the Provisionals from the armalite to the ballot-box, Merlyn Rees legalised the IRA's political party, Sinn Fein, and established 'incident centres' through which the Provisionals and officials from the Northern Ireland Office could monitor the ceasefire and investigate any violations – by either side.

The lull in hostilities suited both parties. The Provisionals wanted time to rest and regroup and the government the opportunity to change to a new political tack – which was to have far-reaching implications. Britain had made a decision to 'criminalise' the conflict by removing the special category status (which the Provisionals regarded as 'political' status) and special privileges the IRA's prisoners had enjoyed, and to use the non-jury Diplock courts to convict the IRA's volunteers as common criminals under a much-amended criminal law. On the face of it, the government seemed to win hands down. The Provisionals accept that the ceasefire of 1975, which lasted into the summer, was the closest they have come to defeat. Restarting a war machine which had been switched off for many months proved far more difficult than they had ever imagined. But that analysis does not take into account the long-term gains the Provisionals made from the government's decision to criminalise the conflict – a decision that was to lead to six years of prison protest and the hunger strike that dramatically changed the IRA's political fortunes.

Ironically, it was Shane Paul O'Doherty's arrest on 8 May 1975 that effectively marked the beginning of the end of the ceasefire. He may well have been arrested earlier had the ceasefire not been in place. On 2 December 1974, a woman was killed in an explosion in a flat at 23 Crawford Square in Derry, barely a few hundred yards from Clarendon Street. She was a 22-year-old IRA volunteer called Ethel Lynch who, according to IRA death notices in the *Derry Journal*, was a 'Brigade Officer, killed in action, who gave her life so that future generations might live in a free Ireland'. The flat in which she died was Shane Paul O'Doherty's bomb factory. In the ruins of the flat, the police subsequently found twenty-seven pounds of explosive, a quantity of bomb-making equipment and four ready-made letter-bombs addressed to different people in England. They also discovered several documents on which the mysterious initials 'S.P.' appeared. It was these initials that gave the RUC the breakthrough they needed in a remarkable piece of detective work. They also came across a reference to 'S.P.' being injured as a civilian by shrapnel from a car bomb in Clarendon Street in 1972 that had been intended for an army patrol. Detectives sifted through every conceivable piece of paperwork on the explosion and discovered that one Shane Paul O'Doherty had received £300 compensation from the

British taxpayer for his injuries. Shane appears to have been sitting at home in the front room when the bomb went off in the street. The compensation claim form was signed in his name S. P. O'Doherty and the handwriting matched those on the letter-bombs. When the forensic experts got to work, they also discovered that Shane's fingerprints were identical to those on the bombs. All the O'Doherty family had volunteered their fingerprints some time earlier when the police asked people in Derry to allow themselves to be fingerprinted to assist in the battle against terrorism. For Shane to have refused would immediately have aroused suspicion, not only amongst the police but amongst his own family. Eventually, to complete the case against him, it was established that his saliva matched traces of saliva found on some of the envelopes in which the bombs had been sent. Such painstaking detective work would have taken considerable time and, perhaps as an additional consideration, the authorities would have had to proceed with some care given the delicate nature of the ceasefire. But no doubt, whilst the case was being built up against him, Shane was being carefully watched as he, like a great many volunteers, had returned home once the ceasefire was established.

Following the death of her husband, Sadie had moved and bought a bungalow in another part of Derry. Fergal was still living at home and there was great rejoicing when Shane came back. 'That's it,' he told his mother, 'the truce is on. There'll be peace now.' That's what Sadie, and no doubt hundreds of anxious mothers, thought too. But Shane didn't return until the truce had been well established, perhaps because he wanted to ensure that he would be safe, knowing that the debris in his bomb factory would have been minutely analysed during the intervening months. Sadie remembers only having one brief exchange with him about his IRA activities: the only one, she says, she ever had. She may not remember how it arose, but she remembers what was said. 'No one, Shane,' she said, 'has the right in this world to put anyone into Kingdom come, to kill anyone. I don't know how anyone can kill anyone.' 'Oh, I agree with you, mammy,' he said, 'all the way. I agree with you.' Shane insisted that all his bombs, with the notable exception of his letter-bombs, had always been accompanied by a warning: no one had ever been killed.

Shane was arrested on a glorious May morning. He was out in the garden mowing the lawn, wearing only his jeans and no shoes. Two police Landrovers drew up and the house was surrounded. The place seemed bristling with guns. An RUC detective with tweed jacket and leather elbow-patches stopped Fergal, who was just about to leave the house. 'You're not Shane,' he said. The police were firm but not hostile. There was a shout from the back, 'We've got him!' Sadie became very upset and asked what was the meaning of the intrusion as there was supposed to be a ceasefire. She remembers the detective trying to comfort her. 'He sat me down on the couch and said, "I know you, I know all your people and I knew your husband. They're just taking Shane in for questioning. If he's not back by six o'clock, just give us a ring." When I phoned at six o'clock, Shane wasn't getting out.'

Shane was twenty when he was arrested. The IRA lost little time in making its response. Two days later the Provisionals shot dead Constable Paul Gray who was on patrol along the city walls. Two bullets from a rifle slammed into his back. He was the same age as Shane and had only been in the force for eighteen months. Shane's arrest effectively marked the beginning of the end of the ceasefire, which was already under increasing strain. When politicians and clergymen condemned the killing, the IRA asked why, under the terms of the ceasefire, they had not condemned the arrest of 'a well-known republican' – Shane Paul O'Doherty? The IRA issued a statement:

> A member of the Republican Movement was arrested, subjected to severe mental torture in Victoria Barracks [in Derry], and charged. He is now remanded in Crumlin Road gaol. This last breach was the most serious, therefore retaliatory action was directed against the RUC.

Shane was initially charged with sending a letter-bomb to a Derry solicitor, F. H. Babington, and remanded in custody pending further enquiries that were immediately extended to England. When his case came to court in Belfast on 25 September 1975, the prosecution offered no evidence after a deal had been done between the Northern Ireland Director of Public Prosecutions and his opposite number in London. He was immediately rearrested by Scotland Yard bomb squad officers who had flown over from London to take him back to stand trial in England. The following day, Shane was charged at Bow Street Magistrates Court with bomb offences in England. In court he declared:

> I refuse to accept any jurisdiction in these proceedings. I am being treated like a criminal when I am an Irish Republican prisoner, a political hostage.

He demanded to be returned to Ireland from where, he said, he'd been 'kidnapped' the day before. He was remanded in custody again and then charged with a total of thirty terrorist offences committed between May 1973 and November 1974. Twenty-three of the charges involved letter-bombs and five involved parcel-bombs.

What Shane calls 'the letter-bomb conspiracy' evolved during the time he spent in the hospital across the border recovering from his self-inflicted injuries during the first half of 1973. He selected his targets mainly, but not entirely, from what he would have regarded as the upper echelons of the British establishment. They included: the former Home Secretary, Reginald Maudling, who received injuries to his left thumb and fingers from a book on horoscopes; Edward Heath's secretary at Number Ten Downing Street, who threw a BBC paperback on music she thought was a prank from a girls' school into a waste-paper bin; an Old Bailey judge, Judge John Buzzard, who received injuries to both hands; the Secretary General to the Stock Exchange, whose secretary, Miss Joanna Knight, received injuries to her face, neck, hands and foot; Sir Max Aitken, the proprietor of the *Daily Express*, whose security officer, Andrew Meikle, had most of the fingers of one hand blown off; the Roman Catholic bishop to the armed services, the Rt Rev. Gerard Tickle, who received a 'Presentation Bible' with a hollowed-out centre packed with explosives and large steel nails; Brigadier Michael O'Cock, who lost part of his right thumb as he tried to push the packet under the settee on which he was sitting, having realised what it was; and the Military Attaché at the British Embassy in Washington, where a secretary, Mrs Nora Murray, lost her left hand. In the words of the prosecution, all were 'ingenious, diabolical and horrifically lethal devices'. Shane's other targets, for reasons best known to him, included the tobacco company W.D. & H.O. Wills in Bristol and Pilkington's Glass in St Helens. Miraculously, no one was killed in any of the attacks.

But Shane wasn't just charged with letter-bomb offences. He had also left his imprint on three time-bombs which had been placed in London. Two had been left in shops, a three-pound bomb in Etam's in Oxford Street and a six-pound bomb in Brighter Homes in Kilburn High Road; and one had been planted in the main hall of Baker Street underground station where it was discovered in a black plastic bag by a cleaner. The Baker Street bomb, which contained nearly three pounds of explosive, the equivalent of sixteen hand grenades, was defused sixteen minutes before it was timed to go off, after a coded warning had been received by the Press Association.

Shane's fingerprints were on the Baker Street bomb and most of the other devices.

At the time of his arrest the architect of the campaign showed no remorse. He told his interrogators he had no regrets and would do it all again: he said he could meet his God with a clear conscience; he stressed that none of the letter-bombs had been intended to kill and the other bombs had always been accompanied by a warning. His purpose, he said, had been to make people aware of the situation in Ireland. According to the police, he allegedly claimed that the bombs had made six to eight million people in London aware of the Irish situation, and thirty million throughout the whole of the country.

When his trial began at the Old Bailey on 6 September 1976, Shane Paul O'Doherty refused to recognise the court – the traditional Republican denial of the right of a British court to try an Irishman – and made a brief statement from the dock:

> I refuse to plead in respect of what I consider are political charges in a court where politics masquerade as justice.

The judge, Mr Justice Thesiger, directed a plea of not guilty to be entered on Shane Paul O'Doherty's behalf. The evidence from most of the victims was read out in previously prepared statements but several of them came to give evidence in person. One, Derek Woodward, a security officer from the Bank of England, had to be helped into court. He was badly scarred and hardly able to see. He described what happened:

> There was a tremendous flash. It was a bang like the crack of a pistol. I was thrown back on my right side. I could feel something hanging from my right hand, which afterwards I found to be my thumb. There was this tremendous pain in my left side and I couldn't see.

Mr Woodward lost the sight of his right eye and can only see partially with his left. His left arm had been badly injured and an artificial limb had been fitted which he showed to the jury. He also showed them the remains of his right thumb, half of which doctors had managed to stitch back. For the first time, Shane was brought face to face with his victims and forced to see and hear the consequences of his commitment to the Republican ideal. Most of them were not, as the Provisionals might say, 'manipulators of the British war machine' or 'agents of British repression in Ireland' but innocent civilians who had just opened a letter or parcel. Shane was deeply moved by their testimony and apologised to his civilian victims in court. Reginald Maudling did not merit an apology because he was regarded as a 'legitimate' target.

Before he was sentenced, Shane made a second statement to the court, the classic 'speech from the dock' that Republican prisoners have made since Robert Emmet's famous last remarks in 1803:

> When my country takes her place among the nations of the earth, then and not till then, let my epitaph be written.

He took the opportunity to justify 'the armed struggle', waged to try and force Britain to withdraw from Northern Ireland:

> Like many Irishmen, I believe that there is ample moral justification for the armed struggle in Ireland. Like them, I would like to see a just and enduring peace established there . . . I wish only to say I regret any injuries accidentally caused to members of the British working class which may have been caused by my acts. I was kidnapped in Northern Ireland by members of the British Army and brought forcibly to England. I am a political hostage. Justice means England getting out of Ireland and I shall never consider any of the verdicts of your courts binding on me.

Mr Justice Thesiger was not impressed and before passing sentence told Shane that his crimes were more cold-blooded than murder, designed to inflict fearful injuries:

> What you have said comes very near to treason. It is war on the community, which is treason and which still carries the capital penalty.

On 10 September 1976 Mr Justice Thesiger sentenced Shane Paul O'Doherty to thirty life sentences, one for each count, and twenty years for the bomb at Baker Street station. The following morning, *The Sun* declared with satisfaction:

LETTER BLITZ KID GETS LIFE

Provo master bomber Shane O'Doherty had his evil reign of terror ended yesterday when an Old Bailey judge jailed him for life 30 times.

At last, Shane Paul O'Doherty had the martyrdom he'd sought.

There is little doubt that seeing his victims before him in court and hearing the testimony of those absent had a profound effect on

Shane. It marked the beginning of what was to become a remarkable transformation in which the 'Provo master bomber' underwent
a religious conversion that led to his rejection of the IRA and of the
'armed struggle' as a means of securing Irish unity. Although the
sincerity of his conversion was accepted early on by the clergymen
who visited him, and by the other eminent people who took up his
case, the prison authorities and the Home Office remained sceptical
for almost a decade because, from the very beginning, Shane Paul
O'Doherty was considered a highly subversive prisoner. The
description was not without foundation. No sooner had the gates of
Wormwood Scrubs closed behind him than he presented the prison
authorities with their first problem: he refused to conform and wear
prison uniform, following the example of an IRA prisoner in
Northern Ireland.

On 16 September 1976, less than a week after Shane's conviction,
an IRA man in the Maze prison near Belfast, Ciaran Nugent,
refused to put on a prison uniform and opted to stay wrapped in the
blanket the prison authorities provided. The gesture marked the
beginning of what became known as the 'blanket protest'. To put on
the prison uniform, Nugent declared, would be to accept that he
was a common criminal. This first act of defiance against the
government's new policy of 'criminalisation' was to escalate to the
'dirty protest' – in which IRA prisoners refused to wash and 'slop
out', smearing the walls of their cells with their own excreta – and
eventually to the hunger strike of 1981. Shane Paul O'Doherty, as a
Republican prisoner in an English gaol, immediately joined the
'blanket' protest and spent fourteen months, with a towel and a
blanket, in solitary confinement at Wormwood Scrubs. His mother
and his brother Eamonn, allowed special permission to visit, finally
talked him out of it.

Shane's fourteen months 'on the blanket' was the period when he
first began to reassess his life, reading, thinking and immersing
himself in the study of human rights and, in particular, Quaker philosophy. It was this experience that led to his religious conversion
and the desire to apologise to his victims in a more meaningful way
than he had done from the dock of the court. In this respect, the
biblical text that made most impression upon him was Chapter Five
of St Matthew's gospel:

> You have heard that it was said to the men of old, 'You
> shall not kill; and whoever kills will be liable to judgement.'
> But I say to you that every one who is angry with his

brother shall be liable to judgement . . . So if you are
offering your gift at the altar, and there remember that your
brother has something against you, leave your gift there
before the altar and go; first be reconciled with your
brother, and then come and offer your gift.

According to Shane, St Matthew made it clear what he had to do. 'I
felt a total hypocrite trying to re-enter the Christian fold and be
associated with Christian ideals once more, without first having
apologised to my victims.'

But the process wasn't as straightforward as he thought. In the
autumn of 1977, after a year in gaol, he wrote in the newsletter of
the Howard League for Penal Reform:

Since my trial, I have come up against problems in regard to
my continuing attempt to conciliate my victims. I know I
cannot right injuries I caused. I know I cannot give them
money. But how do I find out if my victims would be
prepared even to 'hear' a mere apology? Through whom do
I begin to contact them?

It took another two years before 'an unwilling Home Office' finally
granted him permission to get in touch with his victims, but even
then, only indirectly. By the end of 1979 an agreement had been
reached whereby Father Gerald Ennis, the Roman Catholic
Chaplain at Wormwood Scrubs, was allowed to write to those who
had been injured by Shane's bombs to ask if they would be prepared
to receive such an apology from Shane himself. One of the victims
to whom Father Ennis wrote was Brigadier Michael O'Cock. At the
time he received the letter-bomb Brigadier O'Cock had been Chief
of Staff, Headquarters, London District. He had given evidence in
person at Shane's trial. He told me he was convinced that Shane had
got his name from an article in the *Sunday Times* colour supplement
about Princess Anne's wedding, in which he had featured as the
officer responsible for the military parade. He believes that
O'Doherty found his home address by the simple expedient of looking it up in the telephone directory. Shane recalls he got his name
from *Who's Who* but Brigadier O'Cock says he's never been listed
in the publication.

In his letter to the Brigadier, Father Ennis outlined the position:

The law has now taken its course and the offender is
securely locked up. He has, however, had much time and
opportunity for reflection during the four and a half years

since his arrest in May 1975. I have seen him every day for over three years and I feel I know him very well. We have often disagreed, but I could never accuse him of dishonesty. His views have dramatically changed since his arrest and trial, and he now recognises the terrible nature of his offences. He has publicly renounced the violence of his youth and has become a Christian in more than name only. For a considerable time he has been expressing a desire to write to each of his victims expressing his sorrow . . . The purpose of this letter is to find out if you would be agreeable to receiving such an apology from him.

Brigadier O'Cock replied:

I wouldn't object if O'Doherty likes to write and apologise for his past deeds, although I am afraid I would take a little convincing that he really does regret his actions. If he genuinely does want to make amends, I would have thought that he could have done so much more efficiently by starting a crusade to convince his fellow terrorists, who continue to perpetrate their evil deeds, of the wickedness and folly of their activities.

A public repudiation of violence would mean much more to me than a mere letter of apology from a repentant terrorist. Perhaps O'Doherty feels this too, in which case, I hope you may be able to help by obtaining permission to give such a renunciation the widest possible publicity.

I asked Shane if many of his victims had accepted his apologies. 'Well, some did and some didn't. I think the Chaplain wrote to about fourteen of them for me and about eight replied. Some of them went to the press. I remember a *News of the World*-type headline, "Anger as IRA Bomber Says Sorry". You can't win, can you? There's anger when you don't say sorry and anger when you do.'

By the time Father Ennis wrote these letters, Shane had also rejected the IRA and severed all connections with the organisation. 'There's nothing to be ashamed of in leaving the IRA,' he told me. 'It's quite a common fact. There are many people in Northern Ireland – and Irish – society who are ex-UDA, ex-UVF and ex-IRA. There've been many prominent people too in Irish political life who are ex-IRA – like Eamonn De Valera and Sean Mac-Bride, the Nobel Peace Prize winner. People are thrown out too. It really didn't concern me if people unknown to me didn't believe it. I made my decision to volunteer my services to the IRA and I made the decision to cease to volunteer my services to the IRA.'

In February 1978 Shane decided it was time to make his change of heart public. He wrote a letter to the Republican Movement's newspaper *An Phoblacht*, which, not surprisingly, it refused to publish. He then wrote to his local paper, *The Derry Journal*, which obliged. Leaving the IRA is one thing. Going public on the reasons requires some courage. Those who may remain sceptical about his conversion may care to reflect why he should store up trouble for himself by making public views he didn't really hold. The letter is worth quoting in full as it gives an insight into his thinking over a decade ago, a few weeks after his twenty-second birthday:

> When I was sixteen, nothing seemed so romantically self-sacrificial as a fight against the odds for an ideal. So I fought. The romantic, self-sacrificial fight could not help being self-satisfying as well. I couldn't help thinking about myself and what people thought about me when I went into their homes or to dances or just walked down the street. I couldn't help admiring myself just a wee bit. It was like watching myself on the television of my brain. Much later, I was so busy caring for myself that I couldn't help caring less for others, and when I injured someone, I couldn't think too much about it because I had to think about myself, about the risks I was taking. I ignored the human rights of the people I injured but was very touchy about my own human rights. I was a hypocrite. In injuring human beings, I didn't cure injustice, I created new ones. I didn't realise then that my youthful, militaristic activities conflicted not only with Christian morality but also with the principles of democracy and democratic socialism. And I regarded myself as a democratic socialist, don't forget. Democracy means 'government by the people' or 'government by majority vote' and every adult citizen in a democracy has a say in who shall govern whom. For instance, when the people of Eire wanted to be rid of Cosgrave's government, they simply voted it out of office. It went out. Democratic parties and persons respect the will of the people as expressed through the democratic process, and in this way the people rule. But I didn't realise that by engaging in militarist activities, I was repudiating the democratic process and the will of the people, and was foisting my will

on them. I was, in effect, telling the people that they didn't know what was good for them and that I knew best. I was almost a little Left-Wing dictator.

But Shane's religious and political conversion cut little ice with the authorities because, even after he came off the blanket, he continued, in their eyes, to be a non-conforming prisoner. The reason for his continuing protest was to try and force the Home Office to transfer him to a prison in Northern Ireland, not least so that he could be near his family and in particular his mother, for whom the long and expensive journey to London was becoming increasingly arduous. No sooner had the gates of Wormwood Scrubs banged behind him in 1976 than Shane started to petition the Home Secretary for a transfer. His repeated requests were repeatedly refused. He became a prolific letter-writer and over the years, aided by the tireless efforts of his brother Eamonn who had become a teacher in Peterborough, enlisted the support of an army of public figures who championed his cause: they included Lord Longford, Cardinal Basil Hume, former Labour MP Phillip Whitehead, Cardinal Tomas O'Fiaich (Archbishop of Armagh and head of the Roman Catholic Church in Ireland), Bishop Daly of Derry and John Hume MP. They not only believed that his repentance was genuine, but argued, not unreasonably, that under any 'normal' circumstances Shane Paul O'Doherty would not be serving thirty life sentences in an English – or Irish – gaol. Had he been brought up anywhere else outside Northern Ireland, he would probably have been at university preparing for life and 2.1 children.

Sadie O'Doherty took the loss of her son very hard, the shock of the sentence he received only compounding the shock of discovering his involvement in the IRA. By now she was all alone. All her children had gone. In 1982 Fergal had emigrated to seek his fortune in America, following in the footsteps of his brother Bernard. He now teaches at university in New York where he is studying for a PhD. He tries to get over to Derry twice a year to visit his mother and family and see his brother in gaol.

With Fergal finally gone, Sadie lived for her monthly trip to England to visit Shane in Wormwood Scrubs, but that often made the loneliness worse. 'I used to visit Shane every month and then it got too expensive. I had to stay over two nights in bed and breakfast accommodation near Victoria station. I used to sit there at night thinking, "What the heck am I doing here, with all the family I've got, all alone in London tonight?" It used to make me feel so lonely.

In the morning I used to catch the tube from Victoria and change at Oxford Circus for East Acton. I knew every part of the journey to Wormwood Scrubs so well. You got a cup of tea there and the staff were so nice. Shane was so thrilled to see me. I used to go in and I was supposed to be cheering him up and Shane ended up cheering me up! Bishop Daly used to say the same. I used to come out in tears. I remember standing there crying, thinking, "My God, what's this come to? Me rearing all this family and here I am."' I suggested, gently, that she was there because her son had sent letter-bombs. 'Yes,' she agreed at once, 'he never resented that and he never complained about his sentence. The only thing he wanted was to get transferred to Ireland to save me travelling.'

But the more Shane continued his protest to be moved to a prison in Northern Ireland, the more unsuitable the Home Office considered him to be for repatriation, transferring him from Wormwood Scrubs to other prisons in England. Even as late as April 1984 the authorities continued to be dismissive about Shane's religious and political conversion because, to them, he continued to be a highly disruptive and subversive prisoner who repeatedly refused to conform to prison rules. Between March 1983 and March 1984, the Home Office listed seventeen offences in which he had been in breach of prison discipline, which included refusing to obey orders, damaging the contents of his cell, and smearing his cell with excreta. Shane accused the Home Office of resorting to 'utter lies and misrepresentations' in order to discredit his case, although he did admit that some of the alleged offences were committed to draw attention to his claim that warders had beaten up a black prisoner. Such behaviour prompted the Home Secretary, Leon Brittan, to note in a letter to one of Shane's most influential Roman Catholic champions, Cardinal Tomas O'Fiaich:

> I am aware that many people whose opinions I respect have claimed that Mr O'Doherty has broken his links with terrorist organisations and that he has renounced the use of violence to achieve political objectives. I have to say that I have reservations about this. Moreover, his behaviour while in custody has been such that there are bound to be very serious doubts as to whether he would co-operate with a normal prison regime on transfer.

Leon Brittan wrote that letter in April 1984. Later that year Shane was transferred back to Wormwood Scrubs where, according to the authorities, 'his behaviour became calm and his security classification was downgraded'. In September 1985 his mother's prayers were answered and, after the long campaign by Eamonn and those public figures who had fought for his cause, Shane was finally transferred to the Maze prison near Belfast, the first IRA prisoner to have been moved back to Northern Ireland in over a decade. Sadie could hardly believe it. 'It was the most marvellous day of my life when Bishop Daly phoned me and told me Shane would be back in Northern Ireland, and then the prison authorities rang and confirmed that Shane would be there and I could have a free visit. That was the most wonderful, wonderful day with Shane back on Irish soil again. It was the beginning of the end of my nightmare.'

In 1988 Shane was transferred to Northern Ireland's new high-security prison at Maghaberry. As you approach, it looks like any other high-security prison in the province with high fences, high concrete walls and even higher watchtowers. Getting in is almost more difficult than getting out. But Maghaberry is different: here there are no protests, no paramilitary structures as there are at the Maze prison, and no non-conforming prisoners. For many of its inmates Maghaberry is the gateway to the world outside after years of incarceration, and few are likely to do anything to jeopardise their chance of freedom by not co-operating fully with the prison authorities, who do a great deal to prepare them for their eventual release. To date 100 Republican prisoners serving life sentences have opted for transfer to Maghaberry, some, like Shane, putting the IRA behind them, others, although maintaining support for the organisation, deciding they had done their 'bit' for the movement. It was here, after months of negotiation, that I was finally allowed to interview Shane Paul O'Doherty. In fact the meeting came rather sooner than I had expected. I'd been to see the Governor, a man who could hardly be further from the Republican – or even non-Republican – stereotype of any prison Governor, let alone one in Northern Ireland. He first got to know Shane when he was Assistant Governor at the Maze prison and, although exasperated (and slightly amused) at times by his nit-picking challenges to prison rules, clearly felt that Shane had paid his dues to society and had more to offer it outside his prison walls than within. It was a view with which other senior prison officials whom I met concurred. None of them were men likely to have wool easily pulled over their eyes. I asked each one if they felt that Shane's recantation was sincere. They all tended to feel that it was. The Governor asked me if I'd like to meet the prisoner there and then. Shane wasn't expecting me and I wasn't expecting to see him so soon. I'd been warned I'd be lucky to get a word in. We shook hands and exchanged pleasantries for a few minutes. He didn't look at all like a man who'd spent nearly fifteen years in gaol. If the prison system grinds people down, it had clearly failed to do so with Shane. He was smaller than I'd expected, although I'd seen a recent polaroid photograph of him taken by the prison authorities with Fergal on a recent visit. His red beard, which matched his red hair, was still neatly trimmed. It was like meeting an alert and inquisitive student in his study. Maghaberry, I observed, seemed far more relaxed and very different from the Maze prison which I'd visited during the hunger strike. He smiled and said he agreed.

Around a quarter of the nearly 2000 prisoners in Northern Ireland's gaols are serving life sentences, the vast majority of them convicted for 'political' offences. Only 10 per cent of the total prison population are regarded as 'ordinary, decent, criminals', sentenced for traditional, non-terrorist offences. As a 'lifer' Shane's sentence was up for review and, as we spoke, his case was being examined by the Life Sentence Review Board. It was the fourth time his case had been considered. The Board is chaired by the Permanent Under Secretary at the Northern Ireland Office and consists of senior NIO officials, the Governors of the Maze and Maghaberry prisons (as of summer 1989), the Principal Medical Officer of the DHSS, a consultant psychiatrist and a Chief Probation Officer. Normally the Board reviews a prisoner's case after ten years, although it can do so earlier at its discretion. It also uses its discretion to decide the frequency of any prisoner's review. A life sentence is not in practice 'life': even a judge's recommended life sentence of twenty to twenty-five years can be reviewed by the Board, which is not constrained by such judgements. If the Board decides it is time for a life prisoner to be released on licence (which means he or she can always be called back), a recommendation is made to Ministers and then a date is set for release. Since January 1984, 132 lifers have been given release dates, and so far no licence of a paramilitary offender has been revoked. But before the decision to release a lifer is finally taken the original trial judge has to be consulted and the views of the Lord Chief Justices in Northern Ireland and Great Britain are taken into account. In Shane's case, the original sentencing judge has passed away so the decision is left in the hands of the two Lord Chief Justices. It is unusual for the judiciary to counter a decision made by the Life Sentence Review Board. Like all prisoners, Shane wasn't being too optimistic as he'd been disappointed on the three previous occasions when his case had been reviewed and rejected.

A few months later I returned to Maghaberry with my producer, Michael Dutfield, to film an interview for the television programme, *Families at War*. Shane had just heard that the Board had agreed to his release, although it still had to be ratified by the judiciary. No date for his release had been set. He was relaxed but not overexcited. Fifteen years in prison teach caution. Besides talking to him about his family and his days as an IRA volunteer, I questioned him about his change of heart, knowing that many would allege that it was but a cynical ploy to get out of gaol. Shane emphasised that his offences hadn't involved murder or attempted murder and few who knew anything about the penal system would say that he was getting out 'early' as he entered the fifteenth year of his sentence. He cited the case of a nineteen-year-old British soldier, Private Ian Thain, who was sentenced on 14 December 1984 for the murder of Thomas 'Kidso' Reilly, the first soldier to be convicted of murder while on duty in Northern Ireland. 'He served just over two years, was taken back into the British army and given a gun again. I'm going into year fifteen and I still haven't got a release date.' Private Thain served most of his sentence in England and was released by the Home Office. Shane also referred to the case of the IRA 'supergrass', Kevin McGrady, who was sentenced to life imprisonment in June 1982 for his part in three murders in the mid-seventies, and who was released by 1988, having turned Queen's evidence at his trial and identified ten of his former IRA accomplices.

I pressed Shane further on the sincerity of his rejection of violence. He stressed that, despite what people might think, he wasn't the only IRA volunteer who had left the organisation. 'Now the Northern Ireland prisons are littered with people who have left. Maghaberry is a monument to those who have quit paramilitary organisations – Loyalist ones as well. There are now wings set up in the Maze for men who have become opposed to the "armed struggle". Now it's quite commonplace. It doesn't matter to me if the British press or media, or individual MPs or others don't believe I've left the IRA. Everybody who knows anything about the Irish situation, be they politicians or clergymen, would accept that I have left the IRA – and that's it.' I asked him whether he would ever consider going back. He said categorically that he would not. 'I would never become associated with any form of violence again. I would never go back because there is no way that you can create a just society by heaping up a mountain of personal injustices and by wounding people, maiming people and killing people. There is very little support in Ireland for an organisation or party that has such an appalling record on human rights. I feel the continuing use of violence is not justified as a political way forward.' He wished to stress, however, that he still had his Republican ideals although they were now divorced from the 'armed struggle': he welcomed signs that the Republican Movement was now putting a greater emphasis on politics.

I finally asked Shane if he thought he had helped free Ireland, given the dreams of his youth. He was emphatic in his reply. 'No. I think I helped create a massive number of new borders within Northern Ireland, whereas previously there was only one. I think I have contributed to the polarisation of the community to the extent that Irish unity – that is unity between the Irish people, Catholic and Protestant – is a virtual impossibility in my lifetime. I think we have done an injustice to the ideals we sought to serve. We were possessed with the idea of the blood sacrifice and the armed struggle – but it possessed us. You have only to look at the state of Northern Ireland now to see that the fruits of twenty years of violence have put off the very ideals we sought to serve – and will do so for a long time to come. Yeats was right, "Too long a sacrifice can make a stone of the heart."'

As he walked away with the warders, I thought of all he'd been through and all that his family and victims had suffered. I thought of the hundreds of other prisoners too, whom years in prison had made bitter and ever more committed to the 'armed struggle'. However remarkable his experience, I felt it would be a mistake if people thought that all Northern Ireland's paramilitaries, both Republican and Loyalist, were likely to undergo a transformation similar to that of Shane Paul O'Doherty. The pull of history, I suspected, would be too strong.

Three weeks later I heard that Shane had been awarded a place at Trinity College, Dublin to read for an honours degree in English, starting in October 1989. I hoped the judiciary would be kind – but felt there was no guarantee that they would.

CHAPTER SIX

NEVER A DULL MOMENT

Mary Wallace – I shall call her that – lives in an area of Northern Ireland where the Troubles seem as remote as they do to most citizens in the rest of the United Kingdom. To the people in the village where she lives the images of violence on the TV screens are light years away from their experience. The green, rolling hills and the fish-filled lakes that surround her should be swarming with tourists but, to the relief of the locals, they are not. Were it not for the Troubles, weary estate agents say, Northern Ireland would be England's Dordogne. The fact is that more people die on the province's roads than die in the violence. For most of the time, 98 per cent of Northern Ireland is unaffected and people live normal lives facing the same problems that affect families everywhere – mortgage repayments, education and the cost of living. Unemployment is a problem; traffic jams are not. It may seem surprising, but more people than you would care to imagine say they would never live anywhere else.

Mary, her bank manager husband and two grown-up daughters, Jane and Anne, who have now moved away, could be a comfortably off family from the home counties – were the home counties as beautiful and uncrowded. Their lounge has a picture window with a stunning panorama of open countryside the like of which is photographed, enlarged and sold as wallpaper to those less fortunate in their view. Antique furniture and china line the room and the walls. Everything has its place in impeccable good taste. The gas-log fire in the hearth is so realistic I threw my cassette wrapping into its flames by mistake. Sitting there, it was difficult to imagine that Mary had just retired after serving ten years in the Ulster Defence Regiment (UDR) and her youngest daughter, Jane, was a policewoman in the RUC's anti-terrorist unit in one of the hardest and most dangerous Republican areas in Northern Ireland. No wonder father had stuck to the bank. Looking at Jane, it was even more difficult to imagine: a strikingly attractive 29-year-old, with long, dark curly hair and beautiful dark eyes – and twelve years' service in the police. When I met Jane for the second time, each time out of uniform, I hardly recognised her: on the previous occasion her hair had been cut short. I enquired about the change and was told, with a smile, that it was for reasons of security not style. Jane clearly gets her looks from her mother, whose elegant and well-tended appearance make it difficult to guess her age. She had laughed when she had told me she had had to pass the basic fitness test in the UDR to the standard of a 45-year-old man. She passed. She was fifty at the time. I suspected she could still get through.

Jane wasn't overenthusiastic when her mother told her, in 1976, she was going to join the UDR, the locally recruited regiment of the British army formed in 1970 after the abolition of the controversial 'B Specials'. She grumbled that if anything happened to her mother, she'd have to go and live with her granny. An exceptionally nasty shooting, even by Northern Ireland's grisly standards, had finally prompted Mary to join. On 5 January 1976, gunmen claiming to be from the Republican Action Force (a suspected cover name for a section of the Provisional IRA) stopped a minibus near Kingsmills, South Armagh. They ordered any Catholics to identify themselves. One Catholic did. They then mowed down the remaining ten Protestants. The gun used in the Provisional IRA's killing in March 1989 of two RUC superintendents, who were returning to the North after a meeting in Dundalk on cross-border security, is believed to have been one of the weapons used in the Kingsmills massacre. Mary Wallace, like the whole of the province, was sickened by the murders which were the climax to a horrifying round of tit-for-tat sectarian assassinations. 'I felt I should do something about it,' she remembers. 'It all seemed so useless and pointless. I'm not either a very keen Protestant or Catholic or Unionist or anything. I just want to see people living and getting on. I love this country. It's a lovely place to live in. The vast majority of the people get on together. I just wanted to be able to do something. I'd done nothing at that stage apart from looking after my children.'

Although the Troubles were distant, they occasionally touched the family. Both Jane and Anne had been weekly boarders, 'much against their will', at Princess Gardens, a fairly exclusive school on the fringes of Andersonstown in West Belfast, and every weekend had made the long journey home to be with their parents. Ironically, Mairead Farrell was a contemporary of Jane's at Rathmore Convent, the Catholic grammar school next door. The grounds of the two schools touched. Both girls had been at the school for six months when, one night, Anne pulled back the curtains in her dormitory and two masked faces appeared at the window. Both men were carrying guns. They asked the terrified girls if they were Catholics or Protestants. They were afraid to answer in case they gave the wrong reply and were shot. In the end they said they were Protestants. The gunmen appeared to lose interest and vanished into the night – perhaps, Mary thought later, making for the Catholic school next door which had all along been their intended target. But they left, having realised their mistake, with a warning to the dormitory not to breathe a word to anyone of what they had seen or they would be shot; and they reminded the girls they knew who they were. Anne was about fourteen years old at the time.

When she came home that weekend, her mother instinctively knew that something was wrong. 'When you have a family, you know the minute something is wrong with them. They're very quiet and they look unhappy. You just know. We took the whole weekend trying to find out. Jane, who was twelve at the time, was just dying to know. And we knew that if she found out, she'd tell her form and soon it would be round the whole school. Eventually Anne told me – on condition that I didn't tell anyone else. Once I knew, I realised I had to tell somebody so I spent the next two hours persuading Anne that if the headmistress wasn't informed, it was a great mistake and it could happen again. Anne finally agreed. I told the headmistress that night. Immediately she called a Board of Governors' meeting and the next morning there were bars on the windows, big lights outside, and guard dogs patrolling the grounds.' It was only several years later that Jane discovered her sister's secret.

Jane too had had her own experience of gunmen when her mother was driving her to school one day. They were waiting in traffic at Finaghy crossroads, the southern gateway to Andersonstown from the leafy avenues of the Malone Road, when a car pulled up alongside them. Suddenly a police car shot across the front. Jane, still looking at the other car, shouted, 'Look, mummy, they've got guns in the back!' They later assumed it was an IRA unit trying to get back to West Belfast and the police were trying to block their escape route. Jane noticed the panic in their faces as they scuttled around in the back of the car. 'I thought I'd find blood and gore on the way back from school,' Mary remembers, 'but there was no sign of anything. There was nothing in the paper and no word anywhere. I don't know what happened. It was just one of the many incidents, I suppose. It was my first memory of any terrorist incident. The girls were almost used to it: they knew more about low-velocity and high-velocity shots than I did, being at school on the fringes of Andersónstown which is like a huge, echoing saucer when the sound travels at night.'

When Mary joined the UDR, she soon learned the difference in the cracks of a bullet. At first she thought she hadn't been accepted. She had filled in the application form, sent if off and then heard nothing for two months. 'I thought, "That's it. Nobody wants me!" I was rather put out when I didn't hear by return of post. I didn't realise there was all this security vetting going on. In fact, I think they lost the application because somebody later came round and apologised.' Mary joined as a private and thought her local knowledge of the area would be invaluable, but again she was disappointed. 'I sat in the back of a Landrover and all I could see was behind – and then it was mostly night-time. I didn't recognise half the places I'd been until I later became an officer and sat up front!' She learned how to shoot, although "Greenfinches", the name for women members of the UDR, never carry a gun, and went on a training course with the Black Watch, to learn how to assemble a radio. Each of the five women on the course paired up with one of the Scottish soldiers. They were shown how to put the radio together; they assembled one side as their instructor did the other. 'I had great problems understanding the dialect but in the end I could take apart and put together the whole of the right half of the radio. But I could never do the left because the man always did that. I passed the course. It was perhaps the greatest thing I ever did!'

Besides getting used to the hardware, Mary also had to get used to the richness of barrack-room talk. 'I think that's what I noticed most when I joined the UDR. When I was a private, I used to sit in the back of the Landrover with the soldiers and they used to regard me as one of the boys. I remember counting the number of f—ings one of them used in one sentence. I counted twenty. Twenty in one sentence and one breath! And they don't think anything of it. The strange thing was that, when I became an officer, they never swore in front of me. As a result, we had hardly any conversation at all. They had to think twice before they brought out a new sentence. It was still all very friendly – but we didn't have long conversations.'

The hours were long, especially at night. Often Mary would come home at three o'clock in the morning but always made a point of getting up and having breakfast with the family. That, she felt, was the least she could do. The journey home ws sometimes as hazardous as the patrols she had just been on. Mary had been off duty for three months, nursing an Achilles tendon she'd broken on an assault course, 'which wasn't none too bright'. It was her first week back on duty and she had just finished two late shifts in a row. It was cold and dark and three o'clock in the morning again when she finished. The last mile home was the worst. She felt very tired and sleepy, winding down the window to let the shock of the cold night air keep her awake. She normally chewed gum to help, but that night she hadn't any with her. The lights of the house were clearly visible about a mile away. She wound up the window to get warm again, relieved that home was in sight. 'Just as I was coming down the long straight before the bend, I must have nodded off and gave what I thought was a telegraph pole a glancing blow. The moment I hit the grass verge, I woke up and regained control of the car. I thought I saw a kind of flash, but I thought it was me blinking. The following morning I found I'd put out half the lights in the village. It was most embarrassing. By lunchtime word had got round that the bank manager's wife had been coming home from a party drunk! You can't tell everybody you're in the UDR – it's too risky. So what else was a woman doing coming home at three o'clock in the morning if she hadn't been to a party and got drunk! I rang the electricity people and they were awfully decent. They said they were going to replace the pole anyway and I wouldn't have to pay for it. And the local policeman was absolutely sweet. He said, "Now are you *sure* a black dog didn't run across your path?" I assured him it had not – but I couldn't just tell him I'd fallen asleep. He was really doing his best. He was terribly nice.' But the superintendent was less understanding. 'He tried to take me to court. Luckily, at the last minute he was moved to another station and the case was dropped.'

The close encounter with the pole was more dramatic than her first trip to Crossmaglen, the IRA's notorious stronghold at the tip of South Armagh. She showed me a signed certificate to prove that she had been there. She had always wanted to see it for herself and was given the opportunity to do so when she overnighted in Bessbrook, the army's main base in South Armagh from which it supplies its border outposts. In what is known as 'bandit country', the police and army seldom travel by road. To do so may be suicidal as the long list of victims of IRA ambushes shows. Mary asked the commanding officer if there was any chance of a trip to Crossmaglen. As luck would have it, the CO said he was going there himself that day and she was very welcome to come. Mary boarded the helicopter and was airlifted into the military fortress in the centre of the town that overlooks the huge concrete square, constantly swept by the wind and softened by the addition of a few sad trees.

The troops stationed behind the mortar-proof walls showed Mary the scars of battle. 'The soldiers were awfully nice. They showed me the marks on the wall where they'd been shot at. They told me, when I went out on patrol, to turn sharp right and run flat out for forty yards – then I'd be under cover from the sangar. They warned me there was some loose ground and to watch I didn't fall flat on my face! I was damned if I was going to do that and have them pick me up. So I ran like mad, and then walked with dignity.' Crossmaglen was Mary's first encounter with a hard Republican area. She was shocked. 'It was the first time I'd had a really bad feeling from people. I always used to say "hello" as I passed, but here they just looked at you, and it was such a bitter look. Some of them pretended they couldn't see you. It was awfully sad that they were brought up like that. I remember vividly a wee girl who looked at us with great curiosity, but her mother dragged her on. About ten minutes later she came back to us on her own and stared at me. I was wearing army trousers and puttees [army gaiters]. She said, "Are you a lady?" There hadn't been any women on foot patrol in Crossmaglen before so you can understand why she wasn't quite sure. She must have been about ten years old. Then she said, "Are you a Catholic or a Protestant lady?" I asked her why it mattered. "Because my mother doesn't let me talk to Protestants," she said. And that was it. We had a long chat and we got on very well. She showed great enthusiasm for all the nice things we did. But I felt a bit sorry for her afterwards in case she'd gone home and got into trouble for talking to us. There she was, ten years old, and not allowed to talk to a Protestant!' 'There wouldn't have been too many of them floating about Crossmaglen, anyway,' Jane interjected.

Mary rose rapidly through the ranks and became Captain Wallace, the commanding officer in charge of all the Greenfinches in her area. 'I had the opportunity of meeting some of the most interesting people. I had lunch with Mrs Thatcher and Airey Neave after they'd paid us a morning visit. I sat next to him just before he was killed. [He was blown up by an Irish National Liberation Army (INLA) car bomb placed under his car at the House of Commons on 30 March 1979.] We had a long chat about Colditz, where Airey Neave had been a prisoner of war.' Mary also talked to the Prime Minister who was due to visit Mackie's engineering factory in Belfast that afternoon. Mary was clearly disappointed by the encounter. 'She's not a woman's woman. I think she's frightfully capable but I don't think she's time for a lot of women. She's living in a man's world – but then so was I. She was very different from what I expected. She seemed more preoccupied with her afternoon visit to Mackie's than she was with us. She didn't seem to ask us the questions you would expect anyone to ask us – to find out about us. I was disappointed. I didn't really think she had the interest.'

The UDR has paid a heavy price since its formation in 1970, with 180 of its soldiers killed by the IRA and INLA. The Republican paramilitaries have made the Regiment a special target in the hope of deterring men – and women – from joining to defend the part of the United Kingdom they seek to destroy. Many of the killings have caused particular revulsion as part-time members of the Regiment have been shot down or blown up at home or at their work. Greenfinches have not been spared in the IRA's campaign: they are not exempted because they are women and unarmed. On 8 October 1977 the Provisionals shot dead a 24-year-old Greenfinch, Margaret Hearst, in a caravan in front of her children. Because most of the members of the Regiment are Protestants, many Catholics see the UDR as a sectarian force, not least because over the years some of its soldiers have been found guilty of murdering Catholics.

Mary Wallace could not be further from any sectarian perception Catholics may hold of the Regiment. She gave ten years to the UDR – a period she regards as one of the happiest of her life. The event that perhaps gave her greatest pleasure was an auction she organised in 1983 for the UDR Benevolent Fund. Three hundred letters were sent out to every celebrity whose name and address Mary and her colleagues could get hold of. The letter said:

> There are some 800 girls serving in the Regiment and we are known as 'Greenfinches'. We are proud to be part of a Regiment whose task is to protect the people of Northern Ireland from the violence of the paramilitaries organisations.
>
> Inevitably the Regiment's casualties have been very high with 126 killed [that was by 1983] and over 500 injured. The Benevolent Fund helps those who are disabled and the widows and children of those who have been killed.
>
> This year an appeal has been launched to raise one and a quarter of a million pounds so this is why we really would appreciate any help you can give us by donating some personal souvenir however small.

Over 100 replied and sent Mary Wallace something to sell. 'Each day you looked, the office got fuller. It was like Christmas every morning! People were very, very generous. All these people were so absolutely super.'

Eric Morecambe sent one of his pipes; Chris Bonington the ice-axe with which he'd climbed Everest. Colonel Maurice Buckmaster, the head of the Special Operations Executive in France during World War Two (the forerunner of the SAS), sent his Légion d'honneur; Val Doonican a signed print of one of his original drawings; Barbara Cartland a signed copy of *Love and Kisses*, which she said had fetched £70 at a similar auction in Cheltenham. Tony Jacklin sent a golf glove; Paddington Bear a signed portrait; Enoch Powell a regimental tie; Rolf Harris a cartoon; Ken Dodd a tickling stick – complete with instructions: 'This tickling stick is hand-made and should be gently but firmly pushed out from the middle to make it fluffy.' David Bellamy sent a 'well used' sweat shirt (which didn't sell); Michael Crawford one of his 'Some Mothers Do 'Ave 'Em' ties; Major-General Menendez (involuntarily) a crested Argentinian dinner plate, courtesy of the army unit that had 'liberated' it from his flagship, crippled by HMS *Antrim* during the Falklands war. The cast of *Coronation Street* sent a signed photograph with an 'unstained' beermat from the 'Rovers Return'; James Galway a tin whistle; Michael Denison a signed copy of his book *Overture and Beginners*, signed too by his wife, Dulcie Gray, with a note that said: 'May the gallant contribution made by the UDR and its gallant volunteers help bring about a just and peaceful settlement – and, please God, soon.'

There were some very special donations. A well-known comedian commissioned a hand-crafted bowl from a Scottish potter. Its centre was to be a Scottish thistle with the words of a poem he wrote specially for the occasion running round the rim:

> In tears and in sorrow,
> In sadness in pain,
> The Greenfinch of Ulster
> Come sunshine come rain
> Stands guard in the night,
> Stands watch through the day,
> Protecting the weak
> In her own special way.
> So come fly, little Greenfinch,
> Fly high in the sky,
> For the joy of tomorrow will be yours

Bye and bye.
And the pain of today
Will in time only be
An old song from the past
But a proud memory.

There were disappointments too. Sir Robin Day said he had no
bow ties left, and Sir Rex Hunt, Governor of the Falklands during
the war, sent a signed photograph, when Mary really wanted a piece
of shrapnel from his back garden. Spike Milligan was approached
but declined, detailing his reasons in an unsigned letter, presumably, Mary reasoned, so it couldn't be auctioned. He wrote:

> Thank you for your letter. This may come as a shock to
> you, but I am a citizen of Eire, and I am actually for the
> reunification of Ireland. I don't support the IRA, but at the
> same time I am against Ulster not being part of what it was
> originally. I do hope you understand.

Mary understood. 'I admired him for it.'

The auction made £4500 and attracted wide publicity – and
inevitable controversy from a section of the Nationalist community.
A reader of the *Irish News*, the main paper read by Northern
Ireland's Catholic community, wrote that he had sent a letter of protest to many of those who had donated items to the auction:

> No doubt you have been painted a picture of some sort of a
> gallant band, defending democracy in the face of terrorism,
> and, in all sincerity, you believed this. Please allow me to
> show you some facts to the contrary which are a matter of
> public record . . .
>
> Over the past decade, the UDR has been involved in the
> murders of innocent Catholics, the most spectacular some
> years ago involving the Miami Showband* . . . Not a pretty
> picture you'll agree, but a factual one, and you, sir, have
> been conned into giving this body an aura of respectability,
> by use of your good name.

Mary Wallace saw tragedy too. Three of the soldiers she worked
with were driving along a country road when the IRA detonated a

---

* On 31 July 1975 three members of the Miami Showband were killed near Newry by a bomb
planted by Loyalist paramilitaries from the illegal Ulster Volunteer Force (UVF). They were
masquerading as UDR soldiers manning a bogus roadblock. It later transpired that one of them
was a sergeant in the UDR.

thousand-pound bomb from a derelict building a couple of hundred yards away. The bomb ripped the road apart from one side to the other, leaving the Landrover at the bottom of a crater thirty feet wide and thirteen feet deep. Three of Mary's friends were killed instantly – two young Protestants and one Catholic. Four others miraculously survived. It was the UDR's biggest loss to date and brought the Regiment's death toll to 100 and the province's to 2000. Mary was out on patrol at the time. 'I heard of the disaster and headed back to base. I spent all night in the ops room. You normally just say, "Oh dear, there's another explosion." But when it's three boys you work with . . .' Her voice tailed off, the sentence unfinished. 'I knew all three, but it was the Catholic family I knew particularly well. The father had been in the regular army and then joined the UDR. Two of his daughters were Greenfinches. People wrote from all over the world. Ian Paisley went to visit them too – and they were delighted. I thought, "More power to him". They got tremendous support. Another family just threw all the letters out. Years later they're still grieving and they haven't come to terms with it. It seemed so sad that all those letters, and they came in by the basketful, were just thrown out, unread.'

I asked Mary if she had thought of getting out of the UDR after a tragedy such as that. 'Oh no,' she said defiantly, 'you don't let people get the better of you. I won't be intimidated out. After something like that people join up, not resign.'

Jane had sat patiently listening to her mother, no doubt mentally checking her watch and listening to the chimes of the clock in the hall, thinking of the RUC hockey match she had to play in that afternoon, and all the things she had to get ready for her first-ever skiing trip the following day. She was tired, too, having been on a series of late duties, and would probably rather have been asleep than talking to me.

Jane joined the RUC in 1977, a year after her mother joined the UDR. She was eighteen at the time. She'd never had any burning desire to be a policewoman but had been very impressed on a tour of an RUC station whilst doing her Duke of Edinburgh's Award at school. 'I thought it was interesting and what a nice friendly bunch they were.' Did she ever think of the danger when she thought about joining? 'Not really. I didn't know that places like the Bogside and the Creggan, Ballymurphy and Andersonstown existed. No sooner was I out of the training depot than I found myself having to resolve big family rows and telling married couples how to sort their problems out, and here's me fresh from ten years at boarding school! If I'd been thrown out on to one of the big Republican estates, I'd never have coped.'

Marriage guidance apart, Jane was broken in gently. Her first posting was in the tiny fishing village of Kilkeel, one of Northern Ireland's beauty spots where, literally, 'the mountains of Mourne sweep down to the sea'. 'It was a lovely place to make a nice, gentle start. It was very, very quiet in those days. There was the odd little traffic accident here and there but that was about it. Obviously there was terrorism about but I wasn't switched on to it like I am now.' The next posting, to Bangor, a genteel seaside resort fourteen miles from Belfast, was hardly more arduous. 'I loved it there. It was a cushy wee station to work in. It was a nice drive around the sea front, helping little old ladies across the road, having a wee cup of tea here and there, and things like that. I didn't realise I was living.' Her mother wasn't sure the memory was all that rosy. 'But I remember you coming back and making my hair stand on end telling me about someone who'd had their ear cut off with a spade!' Jane shook her head. 'I don't remember. I suppose Saturday nights were a bit rough.'

But Jane's luck didn't hold. The next posting the computer threw up was one of the hardest Republican areas in the North. 'I was on night duty at the time and the sergeant rang me up and broke the news. That was it. I put the phone down and burst into tears. I didn't want to go. It was such a dangerous place to work in. Besides, I was very happy in Bangor. Another policewoman before me was supposed to be going but she raised a big hue and cry and managed to wangle out of it. I suppose I could have done the same. Then I started to think about it. I could have been going to places that might be even worse.' Such places would have been difficult to imagine, but Jane didn't make a fuss.

When she landed in the area, all her expectations were fulfilled. 'It was my every worst dream come true. It was absolutely terrible. You couldn't even park your car at the police station you were working from. You had to leave it elsewhere and then wait for the armoured vehicles to come along and take you to your work. When we got there, it was just like the Black Hole of Calcutta. That was my first impression. Everything was pitch-black. I just couldn't believe it. It was terrible – especially for a wee girl, there.' Initially she found her new colleagues a bit stand-offish; not surprisingly, it took her a few weeks to settle in. 'I was a bit miserable at the beginning,' she admits, not just because of the difficulty of getting used to new, and this time battle-hardened, colleagues, but because of the attitude of the locals. She'd never met anything like it before. Her mother's experience of the locals in Crossmaglen was nothing compared with her daughter's encounters. 'I just couldn't get over their attitude. You're walking along the pavement, and you don't even exist. They won't even look at you. It's horrible the first time you meet it. But now I'm hardened one hundred per cent. Now I'll say, "Hello. How are you? Nice day," and chat away – even though they'll totally ignore you. And I keep on chatting because I'd say it probably annoys them more.' During eight years of police service, Jane had never received a single complaint. That ended with her first night on duty in her new posting. 'I hadn't done anything. I can't remember what it was but the complaint was really pathetic. And I'd never had one before in my life. They've been coming in thick and fast ever since.' I asked if any of them were justified, hardly expecting the answer 'Yes'. She smiled. 'Certainly not in my case – not that I'm going to admit to you, anyway,' she laughed.

After two years at the station, Jane asked for a transfer, not back to the tranquillity of Bangor or Kilkeel, but to the RUC's specialist anti-terrorist unit, with its roving commission around the area in which she was stationed. Wherever there were bullets and bombs the unit would arrive within minutes. It was highly dangerous, adrenalin-pumping work. I wondered what happened to the person who broke down in tears when she first heard where she was going? 'I got fed up with patrolling derelict street after derelict street. Once you get over the initial shock of jumping every time you hear a bang or a bump, you find the comradeship down there is fantastic. You'd never get a better bunch of people to work with. In Bangor, you'd have to have your shoes beautifully cleaned; here it doesn't seem to matter as much.'

I remembered talking to Jane the first time I met her, just as she was about to go on duty the night of the seventeenth anniversary of internment, an occasion invariably busy. To my amazement, she relished the prospect ahead. 'I love every minute,' she said. 'There's never a dull moment!' Her mother, whilst delighted and proud her daughter is in the police, doesn't share her enthusiasm for danger. 'At first, I couldn't go to sleep until she was in. I used to wake up every half-hour to see if the lights were on and Jane was back. But you can't live with worry all the time. One night we'd been out and we heard that someone had been killed in Jane's area. For the first time ever, I rang up the station. You don't like making a nuisance of yourself.'

I was intrigued to know how the men she worked with – the

policemen and the soldiers – reacted to a woman like Jane. 'I felt a bit sorry for the soldiers because I was the only girl they'd seen in four months. One unit presented me with a lovely signed photograph of us all before they left. They were great.' What about her police colleagues? 'They hadn't had a woman serving in the unit for four or five years. We soon got used to each other. You'd never get a better band of people to work with.' Did she wear trousers? She laughed again. She'd ripped her skirt leaping over hedges in Bangor and it was trousers from then on. 'They're far more practical – especially with these new Landrovers with the high backs. You couldn't get in and out of them in a skirt!' Did the other members of the unit treat her like a lady? 'Well yes, silly things like opening the door and letting me through first. That's about the only special treatment I get. Sometimes it's the funny little things that remind me I'm a woman. We'll be driving along in a car and suddenly one of the lads will say "'Cor, look at that there!" It's even come to the state where I find myself looking round and looking too! I'm beginning to worry about myself!' Her mother laughs too. 'It's funny how very self-conscious everybody is becoming about the women's equality thing,' Jane reflects, almost as if she disapproved. Feminists might object but clearly the men in her unit do not. As her mother says, they just treat her like one of the boys.

Jane's unit, as you would expect from those that constantly share danger and depend on each other for survival, is about as close as any group of people can get. 'We would probably see more of each other than we would of our families.' The loss of one is like the loss of a father or brother. Jane knows the anguish. 'We were driving back to base in our Landrover when the last vehicle got hit by a bomb. The boys in the lead vehicle heard the bang but saw the other Landrover carrying on, and assumed the missile had missed. It just carried on under its own steam, driven by its own momentum. Then they realised it had hit its target. There were three men in the vehicle. We found Mike had nearly had his scalp taken off, Jim had perforated eardrums – and Dave was dead. He was like a brother. We were very close. I still see his wife. You're stunned at first. You just can't believe it. It hit us all really hard.' Jane was living away at the time and asked to come home for the night. 'She just wanted to be with somebody,' says her mother. 'She didn't get back till four in the morning.' Jane had worked with Dave for a long time. 'It was so shattering. You get to know them so well. You can't believe it until it does happen to someone you know.'

I asked if there was any desire for revenge. 'I don't know if I ever felt that. It's very hard to have feelings of "revenge" when you don't know the person who did it – although, to be honest, we've a good idea who was responsible. It's very frustrating.' Did Dave's death make her think of leaving the RUC? 'That's initially the way I reacted. I felt I'm going to have to get out of here, I can't stick it any more. It was like that for about a week. Then I thought, what's the point? What good am I going to be able to do? At least down there, I'm doing a bit of good – I might be able to be of some benefit.'

I wondered whether Jane looked forward to the day when she could hang up her uniform and lead a quiet, more normal life. 'Some days at the station I think I'd like to pack it in. And then other days I think, "My God, what would I do?" I've twelve years done now and it's become a way of life for me. I think it would be very hard to settle down into ordinary life again. Some days, when I feel like packing it in, I think of settling down and having a family. And then other days I think, "No way, I couldn't." How would you put your day in at home? At the end of the day it's the comradeship I would miss.'

I finally asked Jane and her mother if they thought the IRA could be defeated. Jane paused and thought. 'Not overnight,' she said. 'It's like a game of one-upmanship. Maybe the IRA get a shoot here and then maybe we get one back on them. It's like points. We get one and then they get one. And yet at the end of the day nobody's any further on.' Her mother sighed. 'I just didn't believe it could last that long.'

CHAPTER SEVEN

ARMY BARMY

There are similarities between British army 'squaddies' and IRA volunteers. Most potential recruits are in their late teens and early twenties and many come from similar backgrounds, although separated by the Irish Sea and centuries of history. Listening and talking to young soldiers as well as families from whom the IRA draws much of its raw material, you can almost imagine one side wearing the other's combat gear, had their birthplaces been reversed. Many come from working-class areas in urban conurbations where, in many parts, poverty and unemployment are the norm, whether they be in Liverpool, Glasgow and Newcastle or Belfast, Derry and Strabane. In many cases, home to both sides is a council-house estate. Both use the same rough language and similar high-velocity weapons. The IRA has no qualms about squeezing the trigger, nor have the soldiers if the circumstances demand, and as in war both sides known who their enemy is: the difference in Northern Ireland is that, for the most part, British soldiers fight in uniform and the IRA does not, its berets and gloves being reserved for largely ceremonial occasions. As in war, too, both sides know what they're fighting for. The IRA is fighting a guerrilla war to remove the British presence from the North in order to reunify Ireland, and the British army is fighting a counter-insurgency campaign, such as it has fought in Kenya, Cyprus, Borneo and Aden, in order to defeat terrorism and maintain Northern Ireland as part of the United Kingdom as long as that remains the wish of the majority of its inhabitants.

No doubt there are a good number of British soldiers who feel that they're wasting their time being shot at and killed in Northern Ireland, but it must be said I found them thin on the ground amongst the many soldiers I talked to in the Royal Green Jackets. A surprising number said they actually enjoyed serving in Northern Ireland because it was 'real' soldiering – although the majority seldom see action at all. One colour sergeant, a veteran of half a dozen tours spanning most of the twenty years, said he'd fired a total of six rounds, all during the same incident when the IRA opened fire on his unit from across the border. Most soldiers probably never fire even one. When I asked them if they thought it was all 'worth it', there was a remarkable degree of unanimity. Even those who didn't like it – and there were, as you would expect, many – said that if they weren't there, the blood would flow even more freely as Protestants took on the IRA and the Republican areas that are its stronghold. Although not all 'squaddies' would be Conservative voters, most clearly supported Mrs Thatcher in her determination not to let the IRA win. All this could, of course, have been brainwashing but I suspect it was a genuine gut feeling.

Corporal Jim Miller, no doubt like many of those on the opposing side, was brought up the hard way. His parents separated when he was eight years old. 'My father was a Lancashire lad and he stayed up there. He was a drunk and a rowdy and my mother says he used to beat her up.' Jim and his mother moved south to live with his grandmother, but not for long. Mother and daughter rowed all the time and when Jim's mother fell for a local man and got pregnant, his grandmother kicked them both out. They then went to live with his mother's new boyfriend. Jim ended up in a local authority home and from there the council sent him to a boarding school which he hated – apart from the art lessons. 'When everybody else was doing PT and cross country, I was doing art for a teacher who had great plans for me. The problem was, apart from the set work he made me do, I was always drawing aeroplanes, tanks and soldiers. I was "army barmy".'

Jim couldn't wait to get out of school and join up. His uncle had been a Regimental Sergeant Major in the Royal Green Jackets, and the Green Jackets, or the 'Black Mafia' as they're often called because of their dark-green uniforms, seemed his natural home. The Regiment's philosophy, which he probably learned from his uncle, also appealed to him, as did its reputation. He explained it to me, clicking his 'Zippo' to light another Marlboro cigarette. 'People tend to get on at us because we're Green Jackets. "Oh," they say, "f—ing Green Jackets!" It's hatred, but it isn't hatred in the true sense of the word. It's envy of what we are, what we've done and how we act. Other Regiments have different reputations. We call one "Starchers", for example, because all they do is starch everything. They tell me it makes them look smart. "Great," I say, "but is it bullet-proof? Will it win a war?" There's an old Green Jacket saying that sums us up: Why stand if you can sit? If you can lie down, why stay awake? That's our attitude. If it doesn't need to be done, don't do it for the sake of doing it.'

But Jim's mother had other ideas: if her son was bent on being a soldier, at least he could be a useful one and learn a trade. He tried for the REME (the Royal Electrical and Mechanical Engineers) because he liked fiddling around with cars but failed the test. 'I wasn't bright enough to become an apprentice. They asked me what else I'd like to do. I mentioned the Green Jackets and that was it!' Although Jim wasn't considered suitable to take tanks apart, the army soon discovered he had more conventional and equally necessary military skills: Jim was a crack shot. Although he's modest about his ability behind the sights of a rifle, there's no doubt he would clear out the stalls on any fairground, even if the barrels were bent. I watched him on the rifle range put half a dozen rounds through the nose of the pop-up 'enemy' target. During his Rifleman's training he won the Green Jackets 'Crossed Rifles', an award only won by two or three men in a battalion of over 500. 'It's a competition between you, the recruit, and them, the staff. The staff always win. They always will do. That's the way the game is set out.' But Jim's life at that time was never simple. He injured his cartilage in training, got fed up and obtained a medical discharge. But he got even more fed up out of the army and at the beginning of 1969 re-enlisted and started his training all over again. This time Jim was in the Green Jackets for good.

Apart from being accomplished behind a rifle, Jim is also pretty useful with a fishing rod in his hand. Beside his cigarettes, his Zippo and his scrapbook on the table lay a copy of *Angling Times*, which he flicked through before me, shaking his head and saying, 'I love fishing. Every time I buy it, I say never again!' I assumed he meant it only fuelled his addiction. He remembers fishing in a competition at the end of a pier in Swanage during his leave in the early part of August 1969. He didn't win but it didn't matter: it was a beautiful summer afternoon and he'd caught a couple of mackerel. As he was walking down the pier, the competition over, his wife came running up to meet him. 'She said, "You're going to Northern Ireland!" I said, "Get lost, you're winding me up!" – or words to that effect! She assured me she wasn't.' A message had miraculously found its way to his father-in-law's caravan in which they were staying: he was to return to Battalion Headquarters at Tidworth as soon as possible and prepare to embark for Northern Ireland. 'That cut my holiday slap down the middle. It was the first of my many jaunts over there.' Ironically, Jim and his mates on holiday with him had been talking about the situation in the province only the night before as they were walking back after an evening out. It was late on a warm, dark August night and the rain had just stopped. As they passed a house, they noticed images of Northern Ireland flickering on the television news through the window. 'We could see all this rioting going on, and my father-in-law said, "Will you get involved in that?" "No," I said, "there's no chance. They won't send us there!"'

Jim, like just about every soldier in the British army, Irishmen apart, had never given Northern Ireland a moment's thought before August 1969, and preparation for the emergency was, given the speed at which things happened, inevitably of the most cursory kind. 'We'd no idea what would meet us. I can't even remember having briefings, which was most unusual given that normally you can't pick your nose unless you're told *when* to do it, *how* to do it and *what time* to do it! It was a simple case of rushing over.' Jim had no idea how long he was going over for and doesn't ever remember looking forward to going home. He initially ended up in a Territorial Army drill hall in Dungannon, County Tyrone. He doesn't recollect ever feeling any sense of danger or risk. 'There was none at all. The only danger I faced was behind the wheel of a car – because that's where I learned to drive. It was nice out there. Enjoyable. We were eighteen, free and happy. The hardest thing about being there for the first time was having to put up with the company commander and the restrictions on not being able to go out. The time you had to get back depended on your rank. The more rank you had, the later you could stay out. We had to be in by eleven o'clock. Blokes used to go out on the piss, get drunk and get carried home. I got carried home a couple of times myself. But it was just like being back in England. There was no real trouble as such.'

The soldiers used to mix freely with the locals, and when off duty always went around in uniform, not least because they had no civilian clothes. For an off-duty soldier to wander around Dungannon today in uniform would be considered at best unwise. They used to sit around in coffee bars, playing cards and listening to the locals reminisce about the 'old' Troubles, having their ears bent to endless stories about the shootings and explosions, the popular legends of a time long past. In the telling of such tales, the opposition was invariably the police and 'B Specials'. 'They were the enemy then, as we are now. But then we were on a swan. There was no fear of being shot at or blown up. I can't remember any aggravation or being scared about what might happen to us. As for the IRA, they were marginal as far as the army was concerned. They were just an entity that had been there before and were considered no risk.' Jim got to know some 'B Specials' and began to understand what Catholics went on about. 'The father of one of the girls a mate was trying to knock off was a "B Special" and he had lots of stories about "B Specials" beating the shit out of Catholics. He asked me if I'd like to come shooting at the weekend. I had visions of shotguns. "No," he said, "SMGs – Sub Machine Guns!" I was amazed. "Yeah," he said, "we've got stacks of bullets and I can put my hands on lots. We'll just fill the boot up with guns and ammunition and go shooting rabbits." With SMGs! That's the way it was in those days.'

Meeting the local girls was no problem, even if coming to terms with the etiquette in a country market town did cause bewilderment and confusion amongst groups of eighteen-year-old 'squaddies' let loose on the ladies. 'In England, if you asked a girl for a second dance, you thought you were in there. But where we were posted, if you asked a girl for a dance you had to dance with her for three dances. And then she'd walk away. We all thought it strange but when we discussed it amongst ourselves, we found it was happening to everyone else too. Then the "civvy" blokes filled us in. After three dances, you had to go back and ask again. If the answer was "No" that was it. If it was "Yes" you were in with a chance.' But when the unit transferred to Catholic West Belfast for the last six weeks before Christmas, they found no such inhibitions at the dances. 'The girls loved us. It was brilliant. Unbelievable. There were blokes fighting over one woman and she didn't care who got her. They just wanted to get out of Northern Ireland and we were the ticket. There was nothing there for them to do. They couldn't get out without a skill or a husband. I know Northern Ireland's only about 150 miles from England but it could be 2000 miles away. It's a separate country, really.'

For most of those last six weeks in Belfast at the end of 1969, Jim found himself patrolling up and down Forfar Street, a line of Victorian terraced houses parallel to the Springfield Road. It was known as the 'Bun Run'. A couple of Riflemen would start patrolling from the top of the street and a woman would come out and ask them if they'd like a cuppa and some breakfast. A pot of tea and a big plate of toast or sandwiches would then be produced and the grateful Riflemen would stand there and eat it and then walk on. Four or five doors down, someone else would pop out and also ask if they'd like a cup of tea. They never said no because experience, and mothers, had taught them that to say no meant never being asked again. This performance would be repeated all the way down the street. 'We'd end up cramming "baps" and buns down our flak jackets and into our pockets and we'd walk on with thirty or forty bits of toast stuffed everywhere. You could drink endless cups of tea and go and have a pee down an alley. But there was a limit to the number of buns you could put away.' Jim was unlucky – or perhaps lucky – because he missed most of the 'Bun Runs'. He invariably drew the 'dead man's stag', the patrol between the hours of two and six in the morning: at that hour the buns were mercifully limited, but one old lady did relieve the monotony and the cold every night by leaving a couple of flasks of tea and some sandwiches behind the hedge by her front gate. 'That was 1969. That was the goodness of Northern Ireland. Then it was simply Catholic versus Protestant and vice versa. There was no one there to say, "Right, let's get the 'Brits' out!" It was great. Then we were the Catholics' saviours. We were there to help them and not the Protestants. Then slowly but surely we went full circle. Now we're pig in the middle and everybody hates us. In 1969 it was fun: it was nice.'

When Jim returned eighteen months later, in the early summer of 1971, it was neither fun nor nice. Soldiers no longer stood in the middle of the rioters, trying to keep the two sides apart: they themselves had now become the target. 'To a "squaddie", a riot is like a sheepdog and a gang of sheep. The "squaddie" is the sheepdog and the rioters are the sheep. The dog runs miles and miles to get the sheep where he wants them, and it's the same with us with the rioters: trying to push them back, trying to cut them off, whizzing here, whizzing there. It's hard work with a flak jacket, a big gun and a big pair of boots – on a nice sunny afternoon when you'd rather be on the beach. You used to get really pissed off.'

On his second tour Jim had to look out for bullets and bombs as well as petrol bombs and bricks, and was now trained to watch everything that moved. 'There was always the fear that someone would pull the trigger on you in the Lower Falls, but it never used to go through your mind all the time – and you were trained to avoid it. You used to walk round the street – and I still do now – looking at windows. "Squaddies" look at windows. When a car goes past, *you* look at the *car*, perhaps because you like the car. But *I* look at the driver, never the car: I've been conditioned to do that.' During the height of the violence that followed internment, Jim went home on R and R (Rest and Recuperation), not realising how much those frenetic and dangerous weeks had taken their toll. Half a mile from his married quarters in England was a chip shop and a Chinese takeaway. He was walking back from the Chinese one evening when a car came round the corner and backfired. 'I've got my arms full of Chinese, and I've hit the floor before the Chinese had left my hand. This guy who was walking his dog asked me if I was all right. I kicked the paving stones, pretending I'd tripped, trying to cover up, and he said, "Are you a 'squaddie'? Made you jump, did it? It made me jump and all – but I never thought anybody would react like that!" That's how keyed up I was, we all were, without realising it.'

The shooting, as Jim and his mates personally discovered on that and subsequent tours, was for real, and they learned never to underestimate their enemy. On one tour they walked straight into an IRA ambush. Jim and another Rifleman, 'Staz', were in a house keeping watch on a well-known Republican bar. Two men with large overcoats walked into it and there was the sound of what Jim thought were shots. The two men came running out, first running one way and then the other, 'just like a Laurel and Hardy film', and then made off. Jim and Staz radioed base and said there'd been a possible shooting at the bar. Another Green Jacket patrol in the area was alerted and dispatched to the scene within minutes. But instead of stopping round the corner out of any possible line of fire, their two Landrovers screeched to a halt in the middle of the road right outside the bar. As the soldiers leapt out, the IRA sprang the ambush. Jim could see where the shooting was coming from but couldn't shoot back because soldiers were still tumbling out of the vehicles and were directly in his line of fire. One Rifleman was hit by a ricochet and another by splinters from the back of the Landrover as it was ripped apart by a bullet. As soon as Jim thought all the men were safely on the ground he opened fire, taking the beret clean off the head of one of his mates who thought the coast was clear and chose to get down from the Landrover at just the wrong moment. Bullet were flying and men were running for cover as Jim and Staz took turns to fire from the one small window that offered a view. 'I was changing magazines, with Staz in the window banging off down the street. Then it was my turn to go to the window. As I took up position, a bread van pulled out about 300 yards away. I aimed at the driver – and then, not being sure whether he was involved, thought better of it. So I put my sights all the way up to 600 and aimed a shot above his head. I pulled the trigger and he ducked. Then it all went quiet. Then the major arrived and asked me if I'd fired at the bread van. By this time the bread van had gone. I said, "No, sir. What bread van?"' The major informed Jim that he'd asked everybody the same question and all had denied any knowledge, which he said was a little surprising as there were thirty-nine holes in the van and the driver was dead, shot through the head. Jim's heart sank, his reaction unprintable. 'But', continued the major, 'you obviously saw something as we found him with an Armalite tied to his wrist.' Jim's relief must have been audible. 'I'm not saying it was me that blasted him on the head, but he was a gunman, he had an Armalite on him, and therefore he was fair game. It all happened in minutes.' Whilst the bullets were still flying, the driver of an army Saracen armoured car had put his foot down flat on the floor and rushed his two wounded colleagues to hospital, letting nothing stand in his way.

Jim and his fellow Riflemen weren't great ones for 'hearts and minds', and displayed no obvious enthusiasm for suggested football matches against players who, once the final whistle went, would try to kill them. But they would still get the odd cup of tea, a rare event that merited a mention back at base and a visit from the intelligence officer, who would suggest they pop in again in a week to see if they could pick up any scraps of information. But Jim and most soldiers believe that the number of 'tea stops' is not directly related to the support the IRA enjoys in such areas. 'Of all the people in Northern Ireland, probably only about five per cent are the lunatics that go around blowing up and shooting people. Another fifteen to twenty-five per cent support them – and the rest can't wait until it's all over. But they've got to conform. If they don't, there's a knock on the door and "bang!" The IRA rules by fear. They don't just pick their victims out of a hat: they know who they are. Maybe some lunatics just walk down the street and don't care who they kill – that's what a lot of "squaddies" think, having talked to a lot of people in Northern Ireland. A lot of them will just act up for show, especially when they're with their mates out on the street. When they're in a gang, even the "wimpiest" will have a go because he's got to prove he's "macho" and save face. Get him on his own, and he's very different.'

Some of Jim's mates weren't so ready to turn the other cheek. Discreet treatment was occasionally meted out to those a patrol would know were involved or active in the IRA. 'Sometimes one of our patrols would stumble across them at night – and some of them were the guys that ran the protection rackets. They'd always be in a gang, never on their own, to make sure they always had witnesses. They'd get given a hard time. It was a simple case of the patrol letting them know a couple of things: that it knew who they were and they'd better not forget it!' Jim admits a few stupid things were done sometimes, but points out that many of those who did them were only eighteen. 'It was the sort of thing that people did because others were doing it. No one wanted to be a "wimp". If they got caught, they got suitably punished: if they didn't, well that was that. But it only used to happen now and again. We were not a gang of hooligans going around armed with rifles.' The fact that incidents did undoubtedly happen from time to time is a measure of the frustration and anger young soldiers often felt, fighting an enemy they seldom saw and against whom, when they did meet them walking in the streets, they were powerless to act. The fact that there were not more serious incidents more frequently is perhaps an indication of considerable self-restraint.

I asked Jim if he thought the army was fighting a war against the IRA. He said he thought it was and most soldiers, he imagined, would agree with him. 'It's a war I don't think we can win. There's no way to win a war like that. You know who the enemy is but you never see them. It's a war, but it's a pain in the arse as well.' Why did he think it was a war? 'Because the IRA are trying to kill us. We are the target. Every now and again a "civvy" gets hit or a police station or an army barracks: but they're always aiming at us, the "squaddy" on the ground, because we're always there; and they know we'll always be there, wandering around the streets and around the countryside. They don't put claymore mines or culvert bombs out there to blow up "civvies": they're put there to blow up "squaddies". It's as simple as that. You can't call it a war in the true sense of the meaning of the word "war", but it gives us the opportunity to go out and do what we're paid to do. If you get shot at you're looking for someone to shoot back at. It's just getting your own back, I suppose. It's the same in all wars: you get shot at and you want to shoot back at something or somebody.'

Jim can speak from experience. For an ordinary 'squaddy' to get an IRA 'kill' is a rare event. The SAS, with specialist operations like Loughgall, succeed more frequently because that's what they're trained to do. This doesn't necessarily mean that 'squaddy' kills are few and far between, more that finding evidence of the 'kill', a body with a gun, smoking or otherwise, is exceedingly rare. Jim saw both the body and the guns. He was manning a covert observation post (OP) in the roof of a derelict house, with another Rifleman known as 'Knuckle'. They had drawn the short straw and lost. 'OP' duty was seldom popular as it invariably meant sitting in a tiny space with no room to move for twenty-four hours and defecating in a plastic bag. Because it was such an unpopular and, for the most part, intensely boring duty, soldiers sometimes reported that they had been spotted, which meant they had to be got out fast. Jim and Knuckle, however, were warned by their Company Commander that they compromised this OP on forfeit of their lives. The reason was that this particular OP was located in the heart of a fierce Republican town where there had been a lot of IRA activity and where the 'boys' were known to parade around and operate openly with their guns, and not always with their masks. Jim and Knuckle sat there all day in the tiny roof space, most of it taken up by a giant water tank. Knuckle, living the Green Jackets' philosophy, 'if you can lie down, why stay awake', took his boots and clothes off and settled down in his sleeping bag between the rafters whilst Jim sat on his flak jacket (to protect his privates in case bullets came up through the ceiling) and kept watch.

As there was no skylight or hole in the roof, which would only have increased the risk of the OP being compromised, the previous occupant, a young platoon commander, had created a small slit by propping up two slates with matchsticks which he'd snapped in half. Unaided, Jim could see nothing, but when he pressed a huge pair of naval binoculars against the gap in the tiles he had a panoramic view of the streets of the town and much of the surrounding countryside. Every hour, on the hour, he would give a signal over the radio that all was well. He sat there for hours with the binoculars pressed to the slit, seeing nothing but local people going about their business. During one of his contacts with base he was told to watch out for a stolen van which had been hijacked from a garage nearby. Jim made a mental note, thinking at least it might add some point to his long, uncomfortable vigil. As dusk was falling, a van came into view which fitted the description he'd been given. To his amazement, it stopped some distance away. He focused the binoculars and saw something sticking out of the window which he'd initially taken for a wing mirror with a long stem. The 'something' was clearly an AK 47 assault rifle – and there were other guns too. Jim woke Knuckle, told him to get his act together and then called up base and relayed the sighting. The voice on the other end asked him if he was sure. He said he was positive. Jim waited whilst checks were made to ensure that there weren't any army patrols in the area – not that they were likely to be carrying an AK 47 and waving it out of the window.

By the time base came back with a 'negative', Jim had no doubt he was looking at IRA gunmen on an operation and about to open fire. He tried to smash an opening through the tiles with the end of his rifle to create space for a decent shot but didn't have a great deal of success. 'I got behind my gun, but couldn't see properly through the sight because the hole wasn't big enough, so I just aimed as best I could out of the hole and fired three times, not certain if I would hit one of them. Then my weapon jammed. I cleared it in four or five seconds but when I looked out again the gunmen had gone. Knuckle was cursing and swearing because the hole wasn't big enough. By this time, he's got his boots on. He tells me to get out of the f—ing way, lies on his back and with an almighty kick rips a bloody great hole in the roof. Suddenly I'm sat in the middle of nowhere, trying to hide behind what's left. And suddenly there's a gunman again. I aimed at the bloke and missed him. I was really pissed off. I'd always thought of myself as a good shot. He hadn't a clue where the fire was coming from. How he missed seeing me, I'll never know. It all happened in a matter of seconds. I was looking for something else to shoot at to test my sights and I thought I'd have a go at a chimney-pot.' The gunman was still in view and perceived as a threat, so Jim made a rapid adjustment and 'banged off' at him and at another man from the van he saw with a gun. He hit both and shot them dead. The man with the AK 47 was a Provisional high on the army's wanted list. 'When he was identified, I could hear everyone going loopy in the "Ops" room.' The other gunman, who was fatally wounded, also featured on the intelligence files. Both received IRA funerals with full 'military honours'. Jim summed up the experience: 'I gave them a taste of what they gave a lot of "squaddies" – they didn't have a clue where it was coming from.'

Jim did several more tours in Northern Ireland, and on one occasion actually asked to be sent back because he couldn't stand the boredom of being back at the barracks. I wondered if he'd ever thought about what he was doing there and if he'd ever considered getting out. 'Many times,' he said. 'It's a waste of time and a waste of money: your money, my money, the taxpayers' money and the government's money. But it's a job that's got to be done. The simple fact is that, if we went, we'd have to go back anyway because they'd shoot each other up and the place would be like Beirut, all blown up and shot up.' I suggested that if soldiers weren't there they wouldn't be targets, but Jim wasn't going to be led up that particular path. 'Even if you built a wall all the way around Northern Ireland and searched every single house and found all the stuff, in a short time it would come back and then it would start all over again. It's like banging your head against a brick wall.' Jim shook his head and lit another cigarette.

CHAPTER EIGHT

ACROSS THE DIVIDE

Paul Sayers has not been shot, wounded or injured, nor has any member of his family. His wife Julie, and her family too, remain physically untouched by the Troubles. That does not mean to say that they have not been affected by the suffering of others. To have remained unmoved by the human tragedies of the past twenty years would have been insensitive and totally untypical of them. Paul and Julie can feel and share other families' grief. People often say to me, 'Why don't you tell the good news about Northern Ireland? Why do you and your colleagues always concentrate on the bad?' The Sayers are a good news story.

Paul and Julie have spent most of their lives in Derry. Although Paul is a Protestant, he calls the city by the name most Catholics use. To an outsider spending time in the city, the problems start with its name. The official British name for the city is Londonderry and the Irish name is Derry. The city was given its 'London' prefix in 1613 in recognition of the contribution merchants from the City of London had made in financing James I's 'plantation' of Ulster. If you call it 'Derry' in Protestant company you're likely to be mentally noted as a Catholic sympathiser and, very occasionally, corrected. If you call it 'Londonderry' in Catholic company, you're likely to be seen as a supporter of the other side. To make this semantic minefield even more hazardous, the City Council, which now has a Nationalist majority, has officially changed its name to 'Derry City Council', and many Protestants who live in the city still call it Derry. But as a rule of thumb, Protestants who call it Derry, like Paul Sayers, would be liberal or 'sunny day' Protestants, rather than flag-waving Loyalists. Having said that, there will still be Protestants who would resent being placed in the latter category and who would still call the city Londonderry.

To an Englishman all this may seem absurd and confirm all his prejudices about the Irish when they can't even agree on the name of a city; but in Ireland it matters because the name touches the nerve of the Irish conflict, whether Northern Ireland is Irish or British. Above all, the name of the city matters to Protestants because 300 years ago the Protestant Apprentice Boys bolted the gates against the army of the Catholic King James II, who was seeking to regain the throne he had just lost to King William of Orange in the 'Glorious Revolution' of 1688–9. The siege lasted 105 days. Around 15 000 men, women and children died, most of them from starvation. According to chronicles of the time, many ended up living off dogs, cats, rats and mice. The lifting of the siege marked the beginning of the end of the attempted comeback of the Catholic King James. The symbolism of that Protestant victory remains deeply rooted today as Protestants see themselves under threat from a British government prepared to do business with the Irish Republic under the aegis of the Anglo–Irish Agreement. There's a huge slogan painted on the walls of the Protestant Fountain estate, within Derry's ancient city walls, that says '1989 – Londonderry Still Under Siege'.

As a young Protestant, born and bred in the city, Paul Sayers would know the history but today would no more think of marching to commemorate the anniversary of the siege than he would of flying to the moon. Nor would he feel that Protestant fears of a 'sellout' to Dublin were justified, and even if they were, you feel that Paul wouldn't lose any sleep over it. He regards history as being the curse of the country and wants his two-year-old son to grow up free from the prejudice, hatred and political extremism that have cast their dark shadow over the past twenty years.

The house that Paul was born in and where he lived until 1969 is now no more, knocked down to make way for new terraces of shiny red brick, witness to a housing revolution that has swept Northern Ireland since the days when housing was an issue that fuelled the civil rights movement. Paul's childhood home was part of the Bogside, the vast tract of formerly marshy land beneath the city walls where Catholics settled when they came to seek work in the city from the hinterland of Donegal. But in the fifties and sixties the Bogside was not an exclusively Catholic area. Paul lived on a mixed estate, next door to the Christian Brothers Brow-of-the-Hill school that stands at the top of the hill overlooking the Bogside. Paul's playmates were both Catholic and Protestant. Sometimes he'd go a few hundred yards up the road to the Protestant Fountain estate, not consciously to play with Protestants but because it was just another part of the town. There were no sectarian tensions then, and even today they are far less noticeable in Derry than they are in

Belfast, perhaps because the two cities are the reverse of each other: Belfast is two-thirds Protestant and Derry is two-thirds Catholic.

In the sixties most of the areas of the city were mixed and, as in any mainland British city, people would move freely and unconsciously from one part to the other. It was only after the Troubles began that the two communities began to divide, mainly, each thought, for reasons of self-preservation. Protestants tended to move across the bridges of the River Foyle to the Waterside district on the east bank, whilst Catholics spread across further on the west. Yet it would be a mistake to imagine that the city is rigidly divided into two opposing camps, like the Shankill and the Falls in Belfast. Beneath the surface of Derry, the two communities mix to a degree that would surprise those who prefer to stereotype Northern Ireland and its people. Paul, who exemplifies this attitude, would like to think that nothing has really changed since those days when he was a boy in the Bogside. 'Everybody mixed in together. It was a good wee community. There was a real community atmosphere. That was the best thing about it. My happiest memories are of living round there.' I asked him if, growing up in the Bogside, he was conscious that he was a Protestant. 'Not a bit, not a bit. The first time I became aware was when we moved across the river to the Waterside in 1969. We had to move because the tear gas kept drifting up to us from the Bogside, and when barricades started appearing at the end of our street, my mother said we had to go. Most of the street was moving at that time. It was getting rough.'

Paul was eight years old in 1969. Did he know what the rioting was about? 'No, I'd no idea because it came so quick. I don't think we had a TV in those days, so I don't really think we would have known what was going on. Anyway, you can't take it in at that age. I knew something was happening because I saw the army on the streets, but I didn't know what. I remember everyone was very friendly to them at that stage. There was none of the aggravation there is now.'

The moment the young Paul joined the Protestant exodus to the Waterside, he knew he was different. For the first time he saw the paving stones of the new streets in which he was to play painted red, white and blue, and Union Jacks flying everywhere. But it was only when he got to his new school that he really felt the change. 'That's when it began to click that I was a Protestant. That's when it starts to hit home. That's when you start to be indoctrinated. At school. It was confusing at the start, a weird experience coming from a real community to one of those horrible estates where things get so bigoted. It was culture shock, a completely different way of life, moving from one side of the river to the other.' Like most children of that age would have done, Paul fell in with the norms and attitudes of his new school pals. To have done otherwise would have been to risk cultural ostracism and several bruises into the bargain. To a community under siege, and that was how the Waterside saw itself in 1969, those who were not with it were against it. Paul, being a sensible lad, had no wish to swim against the tide. 'At school, they'd always ask you who you were playing with and where. Politics were always talked about – but they were always one-sided politics. Suddenly, there were places in the city you couldn't go. Suddenly, all these divides came up and all these massive barriers started appearing.'

But Paul did go back across the river on a regular basis, to St Columb's Church of Ireland cathedral where he sang in the choir – and where he'd done so since 1966, before his enforced migration. The beautiful cathedral, despite repeatedly being damaged by IRA bombs planted to devastate adjacent buildings and shops, still rises magnificently above the city walls from within the Protestant heart of the city. Inside the cathedral entrance stands one of the cannon-balls fired into the city during the Great Siege, and in the vestry there is a photograph of the choir from nearly twenty years ago on which we based one of our three television programmes. In the photograph the young Paul Sayers is one of the choirboys. 'I only went to church because of the choir – not that I had anything against the church, it's just that I'd got better things to do on Sundays. But I really enjoyed the choir. We met a lot of people and it was good 'crack' – plus the extra money we got from singing at weddings and the like.'

Going home from choir practice one night with his cousin, Paul had his first direct experience of the horror of the Troubles. He was thirteen at the time. They were walking down Shipquay Street, the steep hill that leads from the cathedral down to the Guildhall square, when a bomb exploded somewhere at the bottom. Paul remembers no blinding flash, just 'a big rattle and a bang'. The IRA had planted a booby-trap bomb for the security forces. 'Something came flying past us. We went on down because we were curious and we were young. I remember it was dark but around the Guildhall it was always well lit. We had a look around and there were torsos everywhere. The thing that came flying past us, although we didn't realise it at the time, was a bit of body. My cousin kicked it, thinking it was a seagull. It was somebody's foot out of the boot. It was very horrific. I used to always think, "When the bombs go off, will the coats still be on them?" It was very graphic. There were bare torsos: the clothes and everything had been burned off but they were still recognisable as people. It wasn't covered in blood or anything. It was just a chest with no head. It was gruesome. I couldn't sleep for weeks after it. There must be hundreds of children in Northern Ireland who've seen things like that. I think the main effect was making me think, "Why do people do this to each other?" It made me change my mind on a lot of things at the time. It was a big fright for a thirteen-year-old.'

Besides singing in choir, Paul's other Sunday pursuit was going to observe the Sunday afternoon riot. The start was usually two o'clock and the venue was a football pitch between the Protestant Waterside and the adjoining Catholic area, Gobnascale. The preliminaries consisted of the two sides coming down from their two estates, waving their two flags, the Union Jack and the Tricolour. A few stones would be thrown and then it would escalate into a full-blown riot. The police and army would then arrive on the scene and they, in turn, would become the targets. 'It was an arranged thing every Sunday afternoon. There wasn't much else to do. It was, like, fun, but occasionally it would spill over into the night and then there'd be petrol bombs. At first it was just sport. Then it would get out of hand with blast bombs. After a while it wasn't sport any more. It became pure hatred.'

By the time he was fifteen Paul had had enough. He wanted to get away and he wanted to find work. In Derry the two were often synonymous. On his sixteenth birthday he joined the navy, following in his father's footsteps who had been a sailor during the war and who, like so many English sailors, had met his wife in Derry. Paul wasn't the only Irishman in his unit or the only one from Derry. He soon teamed up with a Catholic from the Creggan area of the city, the huge Catholic estate built above the Bogside. 'We remained friends for a long time although we both came from opposite camps, him from the Creggan and me from the Waterside. But we were too intelligent to let it bother us.' I wondered if the others expressed any interest in the fact that he came from Northern Ireland. 'You'd get some abuse,' he said, and then, assuring me he didn't wish to appear offensive, added, 'You know, typical English, they'd call you a "Boggie" or a "Paddie" and things like that. The fact that you were a Catholic or a Protestant didn't make any difference. We were all Irish. I suppose it was resentment of the Troubles. I suppose blacks had it the same. You had to work that much harder to prove yourself. I suppose it did surprise me at first. Obviously you start to wonder why you're getting more abuse than anyone else, but after a while you get used to it. We all used to go around in groups. The Scots stuck together. The English stuck together. And the Irish used to go around with the blacks. I suppose there was a sort of bond. We got on together. I suppose it was strange, looking back.' But the racist jibes didn't stop once Paul had ceased to be a raw recruit. The petty officers were some of the worst offenders. 'It really used to annoy me. You couldn't argue back. You had to take the abuse.'

The worst day for being an Irishman in the Royal Navy was 27 August 1979 when the IRA assassinated Lord Mountbatten whilst he was fishing off Mullaghmore in County Sligo. That same afternoon, they lured eighteen soldiers to their death in a double bomb attack near Warrenpoint, just inside Northern Ireland. 'You'd feel blamed for what was happening. You'd get snide remarks in the bar and barmaids wouldn't serve you. You'd find yourself apologising and trying to assure people that not all Irishmen were like that: that I had nothing to do with people getting killed. At that time, I felt very, very angry. It wasn't my fault these people were getting killed and soldiers were getting shot and blown up.' Paul understood the hostility in the wake of Mullaghmore and Warrenpoint, but felt that the general attitude displayed towards the Irish and the abuse they constantly faced was largely based on ignorance. 'They didn't understand the situation in Northern Ireland and they'd probably never been there. I remember we once had to take a minesweeper over to Belfast, and their attitude changed. We had to catch the bus from the harbour out to the airport to fly back to England. We got abuse all the way over on the boat for being Irish, but once we got on the bus no one said a word. They kept dead quiet all along the motorway. They were very, very frightened. But once we got on board the plane the abuse started again.'

In 1981 Paul left the navy. The constant racist abuse was, he says, a contributory factor. But he had no regrets at having had the experience. 'It was a totally different way of life. You met different people who weren't interested in the Troubles and a lot of Irish people from over there on neutral ground. Those years in the navy knocked all the stupidity out of me and made me realise that people could live together.' Paul returned to Derry and the Waterside, but soon found himself attracted to the brighter Catholic lights in the bars and clubs on the other side of the river. 'That was where the fun was, that's where the "crack" was. There was only one disco in the

Waterside and that was in a crummy hotel. The bars were stagnant. The life was across the bridge. I sometimes feel sorry for the people in the Waterside – but if they did come across there'd be no room in the bars!'

It was in one of these bars that Paul met Julie. Julie was a Catholic but such things didn't worry Paul any more. Her family too had lived in the Bogside, in Cable Street. She says, with a smile, that she thinks it's now become the Sinn Fein office. I asked Paul his reaction when he first met Julie in the bar. She has all the classic features of the Irish colleen, with beautiful auburn hair, clear skin, free from make-up, and gentle eyes. But it wasn't her looks that impressed Paul but the fact that she was drinking Guinness – and buying her round. 'That impressed me even more, a woman who buys drinks back!' Julie was four years younger than Paul and doing her A-levels at the time. It was six months before they met again, in January the following year. In June, as Julie was preparing to go to university, Paul proposed sitting on a bench with a can of Harp on Castlerock station, 'the crummiest wee station in the world'. Julie says she thought he was joking at first when he kept putting hypothetical questions, like, 'If you got married, who would be your bridesmaid?' But Paul wasn't joking and Julie said yes.

The fact that Paul was a Protestant and Julie was a Catholic was of no concern to either. It was only when they started to make the wedding arrangements that family differences in religion surfaced. There was never any question where the wedding would take place: in Julie's Catholic church. This didn't bother Paul, who was prepared to get married in a synagogue if necessary. 'I really wasn't interested. We decided if there couldn't be agreement, we'd end up in a registry office. We had this romantic idea of getting married in Gibraltar!' But Julie, being an independent woman and not a fervent Catholic, had reservations about having to give a verbal undertaking that her children would be brought up in the Catholic faith. 'I didn't like doing that. I didn't like talking about something that wasn't going to happen for a long time. I'm not sure if it was a *condition* of the church agreeing to marry us but I felt I was being put on the spot – and that I don't like. Then I was asked to *sign* the agreement. I didn't want to. I thought the verbal agreement was enough. It galls me now when I think of it. I didn't pass comment, I just signed. We never think about being Catholic and Protestant. The only time I think it occurred to us after the wedding was when a relative gave us a religious picture for the house – of Christ and a child praying. We keep it upstairs – behind the bedroom door.' The two families accepted the mixed marriage, although one or two of Paul's relatives weren't exactly over the moon at the prospect. One had even stopped going to St Columb's when the cathedral acquired a Celtic Cross, which he equated with Republicanism in its highest form. One of Paul's aunts refused to go to the service, saying she had no wish to be sprinkled with holy water lest it bewitch her and convert her to Rome. Another relative came to the church, delivered a present and left. The gesture was appreciated. Paul's family, who were as unfamiliar with Catholic ritual as their son, were guided through the service by the Church of Ireland Dean of St Columb's cathedral, the Very Rev. George Good, the man who was the driving force behind the choir. Dean Good helped fortify them before the service by taking them on a slight detour. 'They all arrived with a hint of "the water of life" on their breath,' remembers Paul. 'I'm very glad he was there.'

After they were married, Paul moved back across the river to what had become the predominantly Catholic west bank where he had been brought up, and where he now felt completely at home. It would have been unthinkable that the young couple would have settled in the Protestant Waterside which Paul didn't like and where Julie never felt at home. 'It's only across the bridge a quarter of a mile away, but there's a massive difference. I'd say the Derry side is still a community. Even when people moved out from the Bogside to Shantallow [the huge new Catholic estate on the outskirts of the town, barely a mile from the border], they took that community feeling with them. You do round those areas and the doors are still all left open, some with the keys in the lock.' It's something I had noticed myself, not just in Shantallow but in other Catholic parts of the town. I remember my surprise at seeing so many doors left wide open and so many keys left jangling in the locks. I wondered if it was to let the 'boys' (the IRA) in. 'No, no,' Paul laughed dismissively. 'When you think of an estate of between two and three thousand people, there's maybe only two or three who'd let the "boys" in.' I suspected that might be a underestimate. The keys were left in the door, it was pointed out, because families were large and there simply weren't enough keys to go round.

Paul knew Shantallow quite well and had once seen the 'boys' operating there. Julie's experience was limited to once seeing a masked gunman in a garden and remembers being terrified lest he should see her peeping through the bedroom window. Paul was working in Shantallow at the time, painting numbers on lampposts for an electrical contractor. It was summer, he was out of work, and it was the only job he could get. 'I was up a ladder painting a lamp-post when an open-top wagon came round the corner with three or four gunmen sitting on the back. One of them jumped down, came over to me and told me to pack up my stuff and get out. They were wearing masks and carrying AK 47s and 9mm pistols – the lot. I was amazed at how calm he was. I said, "Fair enough," and shot out of the estate. It was frightening at the time and it was even more frightening when I got home and thought about it. I was still shaking. It was just like the western movies: they came flying round the corner and jumped out of the wagon, just like a commando raid. Then, as calm as you like, they just jumped back on the wagon. There was no threat to me.' Julie interrupted. 'There would have been if you'd said no!' I asked if there'd been any reported incident after the encounter. 'They brought in a bread lorry and a couple of buses and then set fire to them.' It was the kind of incident that, in Northern Ireland, would barely make the news.

Paul and Julie bought a house in one of the dozens of new estates springing up all over the city where land is not at a premium. I noticed that where they live very few of the houses are for sale, and those that are appear to have kept their value. In Derry, a new three-bedroomed, semi-detached house can be had for just over £20 000. In contrast, in a similar new housing estate on the outskirts of the Waterside, where the occupants would be largely Protestant, I saw row upon row of houses for sale, with vendors unable to sell them except at a considerable loss. It was almost as if the Protestant exodus from the west bank to the east was now moving even further afield, away from the city altogether. One young Protestant couple I spoke to from the particular estate, Michael and Wendy Jordan, were leaving for England where Michael had found a job. But they were leaving without having sold their house. They told me, with great sadness, that they could not face the prospect of having a family and raising their children in the bigotry and hate of Northern Ireland. Michael also featured in our programme about St Columb's choir. Michael's and Paul's view of their city could not be more different. Michael has left Derry, and Paul is only too happy to stay.

On one of my several visits to Paul and Julie's house, I noticed a framed, type-written poem hanging, of all places, behind the bathroom door. I read it and noticed at the end that it had been writ-ten by Paul and dedicated as a present to Julie. It was called 'The Southern Irish Horse':

Dublin 1916
The wives and mothers stood,
Whilst in the fields of Flanders,
Their loved ones' blood had flowed,
The drummers rolled, the cannons fire,
How deafening the sound,
The sickness in the morning air,
The dampness of the ground,
It took just thirty minutes,
'Til history ran its course
Then died one thousand men from
The Southern Irish Horse.
Cannon fodder lying round,
So many young lives gone,
Dying for a country
Where none of them belong.

The loss of limbs how will they cope,
The loss of soul, where is the hope,
The loss of faith, the gain of hate,
The young lives that the generals take,
Remembering mother Ireland,
My lush and pleasant place,
The heather and the bracken,
The sun upon my face.
The days I spent with Molly,
I'll be with her no more,
Ireland is so far away,
From Flanders distant shore,
Dublin 1916
The teenage widows stood,
As in the fields of Flanders,
The trenches flowed with blood.

Paul told me that writing poetry was one of his hobbies and that he had written the Southern Irish Horse after watching a Remembrance Day service from the Royal Albert Hall in which a regiment was mentioned that had been wiped out during the First World War. Paul was moved and wrote the poem. I suspected that 'Molly' was Julie. 'I thought of young Irishmen going out from Dublin to fight for a country that at the same time was fighting against them. In 1916 England was executing Irishmen who'd seized the GPO. I was trying to imagine how their families in Tipperary or Donegal would have felt waiting for their sons and husbands to come back from fighting in these strange, foreign fields. It all seemed very stupid to me. I didn't understand why any Irishman should have gone.' I had to remind myself I was listening to a Protestant talking. In a sense, the unexpected attitudes of Paul the Protestant mirrored those, on the other side, of Marie Kelly the Catholic who features in the next chapter. Marie became a Catholic Unionist and Paul seemed to have become a Protestant Nationalist. But when I questioned him it was clear that he hadn't. His views on a United Ireland were purely governed by economics. 'At the moment, the economy would be the pits. But if the Republic progressed quicker than it is now and if it were put on a financially sound footing, there'd be nobody left in Northern Ireland.' Paul admitted he'd love to bring his young son, Connor, up in the South where he could go to school without fear, without the risk of booby-traps going off. 'I'd love him to grow up not knowing the difference between Catholic and Protestant – the same as I am now, although being like that all through his life.' Julie agreed. I asked them whether they considered themselves, living in Northern Ireland, to be British or Irish. Both said they considered themselves 'Northern Irish' – neither 'full Irish' nor 'British'.

Although Paul would like to live in the South, were it economically more attractive, he would never consider following Michael Jordan, and many other young couples from both communities, who have emigrated from Derry to England. When he was out of work in 1988, he went to London to look for a labouring job. The experience cured him of any desire to work across the water. 'It was the first time harm has ever come to me since I left the navy. I was coming back on the bus from my first day on the building site. I was sitting upstairs and two men came and sat down behind me. The next thing I knew, there was a knife at my throat, a hand in my pocket and all my money had gone. They ran downstairs and made off. And it was a bus full of people! I thought, "What the hell is happening here?" It would have been different if it had been half-past eleven at night on a darkened bus, and me the only passenger. But it was six o'clock in the evening, in broad daylight, coming home from work in a crowded bus. And nobody lifted a finger to help me! I felt frightened on the underground too. I never feel frightened in Derry – never. I was so glad to get home again. I'd had enough of London. The first night was horrible; the second night I got mugged; and the third day I never got paid because I decided it was time to go home. London sickened me.' Julie was glad to see her husband back and, after much discussion, it was decided that he should apply for university. Paul was successful and he's now studying philosophy and literature. She too feels the same way about Derry, despite the dangers of the Troubles. 'Derry is a safe enough place to be. I can walk home at night without fear. Our children aren't going to grow up being drug addicts because we don't have that kind of problem in Derry. That's why we're so very, very lucky. It's safe to walk the streets. There's very little petty crime or sexual abuse. It's amazing, you can actually remember the last rape in town – about three years ago, near the Guildhall. In London, it happens every day.'

But, when challenged, they do admit that this somewhat idyllic picture of the quality of life in Derry is overshadowed by the Troubles. The fact that the violence so seldom impinges directly on people's lives means that for most of the time most are able to ignore it. 'People here have become desensitised to the violence. The Troubles don't affect your everyday life.' But when they do the effect is traumatic. In between my visits to Paul and Julie, two young soldiers were killed when their vehicle was blown up by an IRA bomb close by where they lived. 'You can actually see the spot where it happened from upstairs. The explosion nearly blew our windows in. The windows in the house round the corner came in like a big balloon. Julie thought it was someone banging at the door.' Julie felt very emotional. 'It means more when an incident happens close by. If I'd heard that two soldiers were killed in Belfast, it wouldn't have meant as much. But when you can look out and see the ambulances, that's when it affects you. It was only about half a mile away. I can remember Paul was watching a football match on TV and he went out to get some cigarettes – and just at that precise time two people were killed. You always think it's somebody's son, somebody's brother, somebody's been made a widow, no matter who's killed. It does have an effect, although it's happening every day. The next morning it was old news. It didn't even feature on the bulletins.'

Paul now lives for one other thing besides his wife and young son: Derry City football club. The club, which has had a remarkable renaissance in recent years, plays in the Brandywell district of the Bogside. The team was thrown out of the Irish League (the name of the Northern Ireland League) some years ago after supporters burned a bus, but those days are now long behind it. In the 1989 season Derry City won the Southern 'treble': the League, the League Cup and the Irish FA Cup. Its fans, and Paul Sayers is one of its biggest, are as fanatical as any English fans, but in Derry soccer hooliganism is unknown. There are few barriers to stop spectators rushing on to the pitch, no fences to segregate the fans, and there's not a policeman in sight – although security, with the ground in the heart of Republican territory, is an additional reason for their absence. But for Paul what makes Derry City football club unique is the fact that its supporters, like the players, are drawn from both communities. 'To me it represents a great community, of both religions, and a great afternoon out. The atmosphere you get in the Brandywell every Sunday is the atmosphere you used to get in the "Bog". There are no tricolours. No Republican songs. There's no fighting, no aggro. Their supporters stand in front of us and beside us and we chat away. There's never any problem. And when we play away in wee small towns in Ireland, people don't lock up their shops as if Millwall and Chelsea were playing. Our supporters are welcomed with open arms.' I went to a match with Paul and found that most of what he said was true, although I did see a few tricolours flying in the sea of red and white, Derry City's colours. But of course they could have belonged to the visiting team's supporters, Shamrock Rovers from Dublin. Sadly Derry City lost a dull game.

The morning before the match, I had been to see the Lewers, the Protestant family across the river in the Waterside who feature in Chapter 12. I told them where I was going that afternoon. 'Don't be taken in by all this stuff about the fans being Catholic and Protestant,' cautioned Mr Lewers. 'Not many Protestants are going to take the risk of going down there in the first place. You can count the Protestants on the fingers of one hand.' Paul was clearly one of them. Looking round at the match, I suspected the caution I'd received that morning was right. I suspected too, on reflection, that the tricolours were being waved by the home side's supporters.

I remembered Paul saying that if Catholics and Protestants could get together to watch football, why couldn't they get together in other ways too. No doubt they do, and in Derry perhaps far more than elsewhere. But you've only to look at the football crowd in the Brandywell, and then at Northern Ireland as a whole, to realise how far integration has still got to go. It's something that Paul, being realistic, recognises. 'It's unlikely to happen that the two communities would come together as I would wish them. It could happen, but it's very improbable when there are individuals on both sides who are intent on keeping the pot stirring.' If all Protestants and Catholics were like Paul and Julie Sayers, the problem would scarcely exist. But the fact remains they are not.

CHAPTER NINE

TRUE BRITS

Marie Kelly was born into a Catholic family that cared nothing for religion or politics. They went to church like all good Catholics in the border area where she lived (bad Catholics being a rarity), but showed no interest in the issues that were moulding Ireland. There was no Republican blood on either side of the family, no stories of heroic blows against the British to be handed down at mother's knee, no awareness of partition and no ill feelings against Protestants. The Kellys' main concern, like that of thousands of rural Catholic families, in the years between partition and the birth of the civil rights movement nearly fifty years later, was living from day to day and worrying about where the next meal would come from, not dreaming of the day when Ireland would be united. Certainly the Kellys did not blame partition for their poverty. Marie looked across the border and saw families far worse off than her own. To her, in the wake of the welfare state, Britain was the friend to be thanked, not the enemy to be cursed. 'When families from the "Free State" came to visit us,' she remembers, 'I couldn't understand the poverty of these couples with large families. They had no income and no family allowance until they'd had three babies – and even then it wasn't much. They got two and sixpence a child. We got five shillings. It was terrific. And they didn't have free milk and free vitamins.' Marie's gratitude to Britain was to grow ever stronger with the passing of time.

Marie has always lived in a border area where removing the line drawn on a map in the wake of the 1921 Treaty between Great Britain and Ireland remains an article of faith for many of her neighbours. Here the IRA's writ runs over the fields, farmhouses and villages beyond the sandbagged outposts of the army and RUC, where a solitary Union Jack reminds those both inside and out that Northern Ireland is part of the United Kingdom. This is where the family settled in the 1920s after Marie's mother had emigrated to America, returned on holiday, met her husband and stayed to put down her roots.

Home was a tiny cottage and a few fields in the shadow of the border hills – which sounds romantic and looks it on the postcards – but the land was not kind and life was hard, even harder after Marie's father died when she was twelve years old. Her mother kept a few chickens, a few cows, and 'a pig or two'. The main capital investment was 'a brooder' – a Tilley lamp running on paraffin oil that encouraged the hens to lay in winter when eggs were in short supply and fetched the best price. Money was scarce and barter was the currency of the day. 'We'd help each other out in that area in those days. Money would never change hands. I'd go round to the neighbour's and swop. We'd let him have some potatoes and then he'd come round and help my mother out on a Sunday.'

When Marie married her husband, Kevin, another native of the border country, life didn't get any easier. They bought a small farmhouse, again with a few fields, and here raised nine children. There was no bathroom, no toilet and no running water. 'I had to carry the drinking water maybe a mile and a half from a well in the middle of a field. It was even worse in summertime because cattle used the well. I also had to carry the water for washing all the nappies and towels.' On one occasion the well almost claimed Marie on a freezing, cold morning with frost on the ground. 'The memory's still vivid. I'd got all the children off to school and took the toddler to get the water to do the washing. I had to go down three stone steps. They were covered in ice. I slipped and fell into the well, right up to my waist in freezing water. If I'd gone in on my head, I'd have drowned and the child would have come in after me. I managed to drag myself out, picked up the toddler and went back to the house. That was an awful situation to be living in.'

The house had no creature comforts as there was no money to afford them. Kevin worked away in a nearby market town from Monday to Friday and his small wage fed the family and little more. The house revolved round the kitchen, which served as dining-room, living-room, washing-room and bathroom. Its centrepiece was an ancient black cooker that ate coal at a speed determined by the direction and force of the wind. 'Whether you got a cup of tea in half an hour or two hours was entirely at the mercy of the elements.' Permanently squatting on top of the stove was a huge galvanised pot that provided the family with constant hot water – wind speed per-mitting. This boiled the nappies and filled the tin bath. I asked if all the family used it. 'Not at the same time!' she laughed.

Leading off the kitchen were two other rooms, or to be more pre-cise one other room and a partitioned-off area. These were the bedrooms. Marie and Kevin slept behind the partition, sharing the tiny space with two cots, whilst the rest of the children slept in the other room, three in a double bed, two in a single and one in a cot. (I never quite managed to fathom out how nine children fitted into eight spaces.) From time to time even Marie had to remind herself just how many children she had and who was who, a process that entailed starting with number one and listing them off on the fingers of one hand and then the other.

I asked Marie if she'd ever had a holiday. 'No. We scarcely had a night out between being married and him [Kevin] dying. We didn't drink and we didn't smoke.' There's no 'holier than thou' boast in the answer, or sense of the martyred mother. Marie isn't like that. Everything is matter-of-fact. There's no embellishment, no preaching and surprisingly little emotion. The answers are clipped and direct. The clear eyes don't wander. They fix you and reply. I wondered how a woman who had been through so much, and now in her sixties, could look so untouched. No doubt a hard life had hardened her too. Was Kevin a good husband? 'Yes.' Did he work hard? 'Yes.' Did he drink? 'No. Not after we were married.' Whether Kevin had given it up of his own accord or had been persuaded or ordered to do so by Marie was something I never established. Her answer suggested the latter. Marie's account of the family's situation is borne out by her eldest daughter, Patricia. She remembers her parents going out once – to see *The Sound of Music* in a cinema across the border. 'Looking back for us as children, we didn't mind the life. I suppose it was quite enjoyable in many ways. She was an excellent mum, very dedicated to her family. If she put her mind to something, she would do it. If she objected to something, she would say it – and not think of the consequences.' That single-minded determination to do the best for her children and the stubborn refusal to bow to those who stood in her way are the driving force behind the story of Marie Kelly.

However appealing the rural idyll in hindsight, Marie was set on beating down the doors that stood between her family and something better. The first step was to get her hands on a council house, and council houses were few and far between in the early sixties – for any religion, despite the popular myth that only Catholics couldn't get houses. Protestants too found it difficult to obtain a scarce resource but tended to do so more successfully than their Catholic neighbours because, as historically they regarded Northern Ireland as 'their' state, they saw themselves as first in the queue for such benefits as the state had to offer. They were, as a rule, always served first. It was this sense of grievance, in particular over the allocation of council houses, that fuelled the civil rights movement in 1968. But, according to Marie, in her part of the border country, where Protestants were few and far between, the pecking order was different.

When she saw the foundations of half a dozen council houses being laid down in the village, she set about finding out how to get one. She went round to see the local councillor. He didn't appear to be in but his wife was in the kitchen. Marie told her she'd come about the new houses, to see if she could get one. 'Oh no,' the councillor's wife replied, 'those houses is all let.' It was never quite clear to whom the houses had been let but Marie remains convinced that they had been allocated by the local Nationalist council to Catholic families from across the border, to increase the numbers of the Catholic minority in the North. She then discovered that sixteen more houses were going up. She tried again, to be told she wasn't eligible because she already had a house. Undaunted, she tried another avenue. She spoke to the welfare nurse, who used to visit the family to look after the children, to see if she could help. The nurse was treating Marie at the time for rheumatoid arthritis which had been diagnosed, by the nurse, not Marie, as having been brought on by hard work. She warned that Marie would end up in a wheelchair, surrounded by eight children and not able to do anything for them. The nurse spoke to the doctor and the doctor spoke to the councillor and in December 1964 Marie finally got her council house. 'It was terrific news. I was elated. I was going to have water on tap and light at the flick of a switch. And then the Troubles started.'

I asked Marie if she'd been aware of the Troubles. 'We'd had a TV since 1965,' she said, 'but I didn't have much time for watching it. I was aware of civil rights but I couldn't understand it. I couldn't figure out what civil rights Catholics in the North wanted when Catholics in the South had such poor living conditions. Catholics were complaining about not getting council houses. They *were* getting them in my area – and from across the border!' The bitterness is still there when she says it. To Marie, Catholics from 'the Free State' were the queue-jumpers, not the Protestants.

Few had any doubt that Marie Kelly and her children were different. Just before the Troubles began, Marie's youngest daughter, Anne, was asked to write an essay in primary school on 'Our Flag'. Anne arrived home full of excitement at the idea and Marie got hold of an encyclopedia to help her with the project. 'The flag she was going to write about was the Union Jack because I don't think she'd ever seen any other flag – even in our part of the world.' I asked if Marie was sure, assuming that in those days that area was alive with tricolours, defiantly aflutter in the breeze. No, I was emphatically assured, tricolours there were not – at least not that the children would come across. The only flag they saw was the Union Jack, flying atop the RUC station on their way to mass. Could she remember what Anne had written? Marie screws up her eyes as she searches for the memory. 'There's a flag on our police station,' she recalls, 'and it's the nicest flag I've ever seen. And they call it the Union Jack and its colours is red, white and blue.' Had she written orange, white and green it would not only have rhymed but gone down better with the teacher. 'Now, the teacher didn't say anything to anybody. But she knew from the flag she wrote about what the politics were at home. All the other children wrote about "another" flag which Anne didn't understand much about. After that they seemed to have spite about the child.' The difference between the world outside and the Kelly household continued to cause confusion through the children's early lives. The worse the Troubles became, the worse the confusion. Marie's last child, Angela, born in 1968, had problems at the age of four sorting out the goodies and the baddies. At home, the soldiers were the 'goodies' and the IRA the 'baddies'. At school, it was the other way round. One day she came home from school and asked her mother whether the soldiers or the IRA were in Long Kesh, the internment camp thrown up to house mainly Republican detainees in 1971.

It was not surprising confusion arose in the young minds when they saw one brother, David, join the RUC and another, Michael, the British Army. For one member of a Catholic family to join the police in such a Republican stronghold was a rarity; for another to enlist as a soldier was almost suicidal if the family had any intention of continuing to live in the area. Marie Kelly was not the sort of woman who would pack her bags and go just because her sons had decided to serve their country – not least because it would have meant leaving her much fought-for council house. She knew the risks and was prepared to take them. After all, it had been she who was instrumental in getting David, her first-born son, into the police force in the first place. David, according to his mother, had always wanted to be a policeman: it was just a question of his making the effort to do it. And the climate in 1969, the year David joined up, was very different. Few ever imagined that the situation would escalate in the way that it did and that over 250 RUC officers and reservists would die at the hands of the IRA. Unable to find work near his home, David migrated to Belfast at the age of eighteen and found a job in a scrapyard. If little else it was work, a scarce commodity for Catholic youths his age. David was happy there but his mother thought he could do better: he'd been to technical college and the scrapyard seemed a poor reward for a young man of his intelligence. 'Mum made an effort to get Dave organised,' remembers Patricia. 'She pushed and he eventually succumbed. He joined the RUC.'

David lasted thirteen months as a policeman. As he was completing his basic training at the RUC school at Enniskillen, one of his great friends and a fellow officer was blown up by an IRA bomb. A car had been reported stolen and turned up a few days later in David's village where his friend was the local policeman. The car was spotted parked in a side road and his friend and another officer went to investigate. The car, booby-trapped with twenty pounds of gelignite, exploded and the two officers died in hospital of their injuries. Both were in their mid-twenties. The statistic attached to their deaths gives some idea of how comparatively little violence there had been by that stage: the two officers were only the ninth and tenth members of the RUC to die since 1956, the year that marked the beginning of the IRA's last, and relatively ineffective, campaign along the border. The Prime Minister of Northern Ireland at the time said:

> The outrage committed last night was a crime against the whole community in whose service Policemen do their duty. All decent people will want to express the profoundest sympathy with the relatives of those young men who have been the victims of as cowardly an act as any of those which for too long have stained the pages of our history.

The deaths of the two young officers hit the Kellys hard. They knew them well and were accustomed to see David call in on his friend for a chat on his way home from work. That evening David had changed duty and hadn't come home. Had he done so, he would have called in on his friends as usual and gone off to help investigate the stolen vehicle. That was the incident that really brought the Troubles home to Marie. 'The fact that David could have been killed with them really hit me. It was horrible. Some of the locals were upset. Others thought that somebody, somewhere had struck a blow for Ireland.'

Several weeks later, one of the local priests decided to say a special mass for the two policemen. Marie stumbled upon it by accident when she called into the church to say a prayer, which at the time was part of her daily routine. She found it full of policemen in plain clothes and then realised what it was. She decided to stay and take part in the mass. Sometime later, Marie discovered that a note had been taken of the names of all the locals who had attended the service. Her name was on the list. I asked who took the note. 'The IRA.' How did she know? 'Because I was told – and I was told I shouldn't have went.' By whom? 'A neighbour – and she said what an awful tragedy it was that the priest had said a mass for the two Protestant policemen because Protestants don't get to heaven. I disagreed and told her that Protestants must go to heaven, but I didn't take it any further because she was from a staunch Republican family, and older than me anyway.'

Shortly after losing his friend to the car bomb, David had a second narrow escape. Another of his friends in the village, with no security force connections, was abducted by the IRA one night in the belief that he was David. They threatened to shoot him despite his insistence that he wasn't the man they were after, nor was he a policeman or a soldier. His captors were only convinced when he produced his Northern Ireland driving licence, which unlike the English equivalent contains a photograph of the owner. The photograph saved his life. David, his life spared twice, wasn't inclined to take any more chances. He left the RUC. Few will have blamed him. He now lives in England and never comes home – even for a family wedding.

Remarkably, David's experience did not inhibit his younger brother, Michael, from joining the British army, or deter his mother from seeing her second son join the security forces. He'd first been attracted by the prospect while at technical college, where an itinerant recruiting officer had regaled the boys with wonderful stories of what the army was like. Michael joined up as a boy soldier at sixteen. There were others too from the area who took the Queen's shilling, his mother insists, although she admits there weren't many. Ironically, the day he enlisted was the day of internment – 9 August 1971 – the day Catholic enclaves throughout Northern Ireland exploded in anger as their fathers and sons were carried off and detained without trial as IRA suspects. Over the next three days, twenty-two people had been killed in the worst violence the province had seen since 1969. Many areas were literally ablaze. In the Ardoyne area of Belfast over 240 houses lit up the sky. That was the moment Marie Kelly took Michael to Belfast to enlist. She hitched a lift to the nearest market town that ran a bus service to

Belfast but found no buses and the town alight. To her amazement, there was no traffic and no fire engines in sight. 'I saw women breaking windows, lighting rolls of paper and pushing them in to burn the shops. It was horrible.' They hitched another lift to the next town – of more Unionist persuasion – and found the buses still running to Belfast. On that inauspicious day Michael Kelly enlisted in the Royal Irish Rangers, the army regiment recruited in Northern Ireland but which, until 1988, never saw service there. The only time Michael spent as a soldier in his native province was whilst undergoing initial training in Ballymena for the first few months.

At the end of 1971, he had three weeks Christmas leave and came home to spend it with the family in the village. After a few days it was clear to Marie that her son was unhappy. 'He was ashen and so nervous.' She asked him what was wrong. He said he wanted to return to Ballymena and asked her to ring the depot to see how he could get back. 'I said, but your three weeks is not up yet. He said he knew, but wanted away out of here. I knew to look at him he was frightened. I wanted to know what had happened. He wouldn't tell me but I knew he'd been threatened. Somebody had said something to him.' Michael was asking his mother to go out and make the phone call because clearly he didn't want to leave the house. When it got dark, Marie left the house and found that none of the phones in the village was working. She went on to the next village and rang the police station from a shop. At 8.30 that night three plain-clothes policemen arrived at the door and said they were taking Michael out because it was dangerous. 'It was the last time Michael was in the house. Like David, he never came back.'

It was only the firm hand of his mother that prevented Michael from becoming involved in the IRA. His sister Patricia remembers that Michael's best friend did become involved. 'There was a great pull there but mother decided that the British army uniform was better than the local one. We used to go around as children shouting "Up the IRA". We hadn't a clue what it meant but we thought it was good fun. Mother told us that under no circumstances were we to shout or say such things.' From a very early age, Marie instilled in her children what her attitude was towards the IRA and what she expected theirs to be too. 'I made it clear there were going to be no IRA men – or women – in my house. I told them what could happen if they did any of these awful things that these IRA bosses made them do – that they could be found at the side of the road with a bullet through the back of the head. And they could,' she added emphatically.

I asked Marie how easily young people could be drawn into the IRA in an area with such a strong Republican tradition. It was clear the odds were stacked heavily against families such as hers. She told me of how she believed Michael had almost been sucked into the organisation when he was just sixteen and just before he opted for the British army uniform. Apparently, one of the teachers at his school was well known for his Republican symphathies and had a natural hold over many of the boys because of his strong personality and the fact that he ran the Gaelic football team. Football wasn't Michael's strong point, but he used to go along to matches as a first-aider, with a bottle of water and a couple of plasters. One evening he told his mother he was off to a match and departed with a warning to watch himself. Michael wasn't away long. It transpired that the football match had been a recruiting meeting for the IRA. 'Everybody was there,' says Marie, 'and they all joined the IRA. They handed out forms and kids as young as eight years of age signed them. As far as I remember, they were green forms. And there was boys from very good families signed on the dotted line that evening.' I expressed some surprise at Marie's recollection, not only at the notion of eight-year-olds being invited to join but at the likelihood of membership forms being handed round. Joining the IRA – even the Fianna, the junior wing – isn't like joining the Rail Riders Club. But, as usual, Marie was adamant. She asked Michael why he hadn't signed. He said he couldn't come home and tell her that he'd joined the IRA. And what about his friend? He had signed and taken his form home to his mother. And what did she say? She didn't say anything. The friend joined the IRA and Michael joined the British army.

In bringing up her nine children Marie's other main concern – the first being to keep them out of the IRA – was to give them the best education possible. Like the battle for the council house, that too was a fight. Marie's expectations for the education of her children were apparently different from most of her peers. It was generally accepted by working people that only the children of shopkeepers and teachers went to grammar school: the ordinary 'five-eighths' did not. Most accepted their lot; Marie Kelly refused to do so. She went to see the headmaster of Patricia's school and asked if she could sit the eleven plus. Eventually she pushed him into letting her do it. It was the first intelligence paper Patricia had ever seen. She failed. Convinced the fault was not her daughter's, Marie went to see the headmaster again and asked for a transfer to another school. She says the headmaster told her that because the children weren't going to get jobs, there was no point in educating them. Marie was affronted. 'His own children were in grammar school. He wouldn't accept that excuse for his own children, so why should I accept if for mine?' As ever, not taking no for an answer Marie kept on pushing, and finally got the transfer she wanted, to a school outside the area. Patricia came third in the class and this time passed the eleven plus. She went on to read medicine at Queen's University and is now a doctor in Belfast.

Marie remains convinced that her daughter's success was a source of considerable bitterness and envy in the community. 'When Patricia got her A-level results, a well-wisher told her to "watch herself" – to be very careful. It was meant as a piece of friendly advice. Some no doubt found it a difficult pill to swallow that somebody from a family that had been so very, very poor had passed their A-levels and was going on to study medicine. They resented it because in that area they believed that Catholics would get nowhere under the British system – and here was a girl able to get into Queen's to study medicine. They didn't like that. It disproved the theory.' But Patricia wasn't the only family success. Through sheer persistence, and the children's own ability, Marie has since put three more of her children through university. There are now three graduates in the family and a fourth is at university. The achievement is all the more remarkable given what happened to the family.

By 1972 Marie Kelly was a marked woman. She was not only seen as a trouble-maker in the local schools, with ideas above her station, but had sent two sons into the security forces, the cardinal sin in the eyes of many of the locals. She had also singled herself out by refusing to participate in the rent and rates strike, the protest against internment which was supported by broad sections of the Nationalist community, not just by supporters of the IRA. She remembers the rent collector coming round and being terrified by the crowd that gathered outside her door, hurling abuse. The collector, a friend of the family, came in and stood on the floor, terrified. 'He took a cup of tea but wouldn't sit down. He was afraid they'd beat him up because he'd been sent out to collect the rents – or at least to do the rounds. I didn't pay him because I thought they'd steal the money off him. Normally, I would have done so. But I went up to the office afterwards and paid it directly.'

The intimidation grew worse. Windows were smashed and shots fired across the house. Paint was thrown at the gable end. Harassment became a way of life. 'I remember one evening. There were two cars parked on the corner outside the house. A crowd gathered and started jeering and cheering and hammering on the cars as hard as they could. We could see them all by the street lights. I knew them all. There was thirty-three local chaps that night, aged from nine up to thirty. I counted them all but I couldn't name them all. I've tried many time since. It was half three before they dispersed.' But they all knew Marie Kelly. I could imagine Marie lying awake at night many years later, still trying to remember the names.

In the early seventies Marie returned home from a funeral to find a letter from a Catholic policeman who had been stationed in the village but had moved on to another station on promotion to sergeant. 'He was a great man, a terrific person, and he knew about the problems I had.' The note was scribbled on a bomb-damage claim. He asked Marie to get in touch: not to telephone but to call in and see him at the station. Marie did. He told her to be very, very careful and to 'watch' herself: it was just a bit of information he'd picked up; 'they' were going to do something. Marie heeded the warning – not that it could have come as any great surprise under the circumstances. She had already tried to get a transfer from the housing authorities but met with no success. The family was obliged to stay put, an ever more prominent target.

A few months later she went to a special ten o'clock mass conducted by a group of Franciscans and Capuchins on a mission to the village from across the border, 'to make us better Catholics and Christians'. She came out of the mass about 10.30 and went into the draper's shop. As she was coming out, a girl who worked in the supermarket scross the road came running out and said, 'Mrs Kelly, there's a bomb in your house! It hasn't gone off. It was due to go off at ten o'clock and now it's twenty to eleven.' Marie suddenly felt horribly alone. 'I didn't have many friends and the fact that I had a bomb in the house meant that I had even less.' She tried to ring the police station but there were the usual problems in finding a phone. She was trying to get through from a telephone box when the man who owned the chemist's shop came over and offered to help. Mrs Kelly's predicament must have been well known by 10.45. The chemist phoned the police and Marie went up to the station. She found it manned entirely by soldiers. They seemed very hostile. They didn't know Marie Kelly from any of the other Catholics in the village, which they regarded as enemy territory. They perhaps suspected the bomb story might be a hoax to lure them into a trap. Six days earlier in a town not too far away four soldiers had been killed by a booby-trap bomb when they got into their car after coming out of a hotel. The following week soldiers were taking no risks. A young officer walked up and down the small room and started to ask her questions. Where was her husband? What was his name? Where did he work? He then proceeded to go through the rest of the family. Marie answered all of the questions. Then he came to Michael. What was his age? Where is he? 'In England.' Whereabouts? 'Warminster.' What's he doing there? 'He's with the Royal Irish Rangers [a regiment of the British Army].' A surprised silence and a pause. 'Can you give us his number?' Marie rattled it off. At a nod, a soldier left the room. Seconds later he returned. 'The atmosphere changed. The questioning stopped. There was a cup of coffee. 'They'd been hostile at first because they didn't know where they were or who they had. Now they wanted to keep me in the station lest anything happen to me. When they heard about Michael being in the army, they had a brave idea why the bomb was in the house. Then a very nice officer seemed to appear from nowhere. He was very reassuring. He wanted to know if there was anything he could do to help and offered to run me back to the village. I thanked him but said I didn't want to get anyone killed and preferred to leave on my own.'

A neighbour gave Marie a lift back home. Surprisingly at this stage the street wasn't cordoned off. For most the bomb was still a rumour. The rumour was confirmed by some gypsies who had been camped a short way from the back of the house and who told Marie that they had seen about half a dozen men go into the house with guns and a package the size of a shoe box. By the afternoon, there was still no cordon around the house but the street was closed to traffic. It was a beautiful day. Then soldiers started appearing and helicopters out of the sky. Groups of people stood round waiting with dangerous curiosity for something to happen. Soldiers were getting ready to go into the house. Marie told them she'd rather they didn't as someone was likely to get killed. Couldn't they just blow it up or burn it or something from a distance? They said they just wanted to get the house cleared so they could get her back into her home. No doubt by this time word of her son's occupation had got round. Four soldiers, one a bomb disposal expert, approached the house. 'Seconds later, there was an almighty explosion and the whole house went up. The soldier underneath the front window was blown across the wall and into the road. He must have died almost instantly. The other was dead in the ruins alongside the house. A third one was lying under a mattress blown out of the bedroom, his face streaming with blood. The mattress saved his life. There's total confusion. I'm in shock at this stage. Somebody says there are loads of stretchers being heaped into a helicopter and lots of soldiers are dead. They say it in jubilation and I'm very, very angry. Although I'm sedated by now, I'm still taking everything in.' Marie then recognised the nice officer whom she had met at the police station that morning. He told her her home was destroyed and asked what she was going to do. She said she didn't know. He put her in his car and drove her to his own home to rest for the night. Marie never returned to her village.

Patricia, who was away at the time, saw news of the explosion and the deaths of the two soldiers on the television. 'It was unreal, yet it was there.' Why did she think the IRA had done it? 'The house was blown up because mother dared speak her mind. To her, soldiers were "someone else's hard rearing". She would say that openly. We were in the way. A lot of things that local Republicans would like to have done, they didn't get doing because mum was sitting there. Once they'd bombed our house, the grip on the community was much stronger. After we'd moved, mum met neighbours who said that they'd been warned that if they stepped out of line, they'd get what we got.'

Today, Marie Kelly lives in a neat council house on a mixed estate in a different part of Northern Ireland. It's as well ordered and immaculate as was, no doubt, the cold, stone farmhouse in which she reared her family. Despite a life of adversity, compounded by the death of her husband in a car crash, she's fit and well and as active as ever, now doing an adult education course in criminal law. And she still votes the way she's always voted – Unionist. 'I'm very grateful to Britain,' she says. 'I'd still be poor in the heart of the country were it not for the help I'd received with the family allowances and the children's education. I'm not poor now. I may not have much money, but I have what I need. I'm proud of my children – and I'm very proud that there's none of them in the IRA, out there killing somebody else's son or husband or father. It was a horrible fight,' she reflects with a sigh, 'but I think I won it.'

CHAPTER TEN

A PROBLEM OF IDENTITY

I arranged to meet Steven O'Neill and his wife in an Indian restaurant in Belfast. For once I was early. I sat in the reception area with a hovering, solicitous waiter, a drink and a bowl of those curried peanuts which are there to be nibbled but, without the exercise of considerable self-control, can easily end up as the main course. I watched an endless succession of people come in, well-dressed, prosperous and relaxed. By eight o'clock the well beneath me was packed with diners enjoying a Friday night out. The Troubles could not have seemed further away. This was normality just outside the centre of Belfast.

I looked at my watch. A middle-aged couple came in through the swing door. I thought they must be the O'Neills. I went to greet them and introduced myself. They looked suitably pleased before they realised I wasn't the restaurant manager and they had been mistaken for somebody else. I tried again and this time I got it right. Mr and Mrs O'Neill apologised and said they'd had problems with the baby-sitter. I hadn't met Steven before, as was apparent from my mistake, so I wasn't quite sure what to expect. He seemed a quiet, rather mild-mannered man, with the air of a civil servant, the sort of person you might meet in an office at the DHSS. I guessed he was in his forties, although at which end I couldn't tell. He had sideburns beneath a thinning head of wispy hair and spectacles with very thick lenses. I knew little about him except that he was a Protestant.

The solicitous waiter showed us to our table, where there was scarcely room to unfold a napkin without banging your elbows against the person at the table next door. It was one of those restaurants where any conversation risked being drowned by the neighbours. However 'lively' the restaurant, it wasn't best suited to any discussion of sensitive matters, not that I had any idea what Steven was going to tell me. I asked if it was possible to have a quieter table and the waiter grudgingly obliged. I put my tape-recorder down between the popadums and the chicken korma.

Steven had been brought up in one of the larger market towns in Northern Ireland, one of the few Protestants living on an estate that was 85 per cent Catholic. He was only dimly aware that he belonged to a different religion. In the late fifties, when he played for the local football team, he was the only Protestant in the side. The difference only occurred to him when the priest came out to congratulate the boys on a win and shook all their hands bar his own; and his mother's tolerance for the Roman Catholic church was severely strained when a priest came round to the wrong house (No. 17 instead of No. 15) and berated the wrong Mrs O'Neill for her son's absence from school. As Steven grew older through the sixties, his awareness of the difference grew. He still played for the football team, but when there was a match on 12 July, the most sacred day in the Protestant marching calendar (the anniversary of the Battle of the Boyne in 1690 when the Protestant King William III defeated the Catholic King James II), his mates in the team would ask him why he wasn't marching instead of playing football. 'I told them I'd no interest in marching, although I used to go off with my father to watch the Orangemen leaving for the parade. I was totally, politically naive.'

When Steven passed his eleven plus and went to the local Protestant grammar school, he realised for the first time that there was a pull between his Catholic friends at home and his Protestant friends at school. The older he got, the greater the pull became. 'It was very difficult when I got to sixteen and seventeen. Which way was I to go? My Catholic and Protestant friends just didn't meet. Should I go to the Protestant youth club or stay playing around with my Catholic mates? I was "piggy in the middle".' Steven kept on playing for the local Catholic football team, but by 1968–9 even the football matches had become sensitive. 'I can remember the word going round before matches, "There's a prod, there's a prod!", and my mates saying, "Don't worry, leave him alone, he's one of us." It was awful.' But in the early days of the Troubles, things were not as clear-cut as they later became. Steven remembers some of his friends from the football team joining the newly-formed UDR. 'They used to be as proud as punch in their uniforms, marching through the streets of the town to the UDR depot. Then they got warned [by the IRA] to get out – and they did. Some other members of the team joined the RUC. They got warned too and they got out.' Steven stuck with his Catholic friends, but as the political temperature rose his presence became more and more embarrassing and potentially dangerous. He remembers someone shouting, 'The "B Specials" are coming!' and being told to go home because he was 'a prod'.

Steven had to decide which side he was on. He chose his own. As he moved up the school he began to associate with junior Orangemen, for whom permanent Protestant supremacy is written in tablets of stone. Their views pervaded the classroom. 'When our history master told us that King "Billy" was blessed by the Pope, there was uproar. The boys just wouldn't believe it. I got more and more involved and indoctrinated by the Loyalist side.' Soon Steven outstripped his classmates in their fanaticism. He was invited to join the Orange Order. 'I turned it down because it wasn't extreme enough.' He was invited to join the UDR but says he turned them down too. As there were no Loyalist paramilitary organisations to speak of, like the Ulster Volunteer Force and the Ulster Defence Association, organised in the area where he lived, he fell back on associating with a gang of youths whose views were as extreme as his own. 'There was nothing organised. People just knew each other and had a few shotguns.' By this time Steven had gone on to university, but failed his exams. I spoke to one of his lecturers who remembers him as a 'strange' character who used to wear his white laboratory coat over a mackintosh. (I couldn't help thinking that there might be a touch of the 'Walter Mitty' about Steven.) Whilst waiting to resit his exams he found work with a road-haulage firm and became involved with an even harder crowd of Protestant bigots. 'We used to zoom backwards and forwards across the border. I thought we were chasing Provos but it transpired we were smuggling floor tiles. The army used to stop us at the border, but they didn't care what we had as long as it wasn't guns.'

In the climate of the time, and given the views of the O'Neills' extremist son, it wasn't long before the family had to move out of the Catholic estate. The police advised Mr and Mrs O'Neill to get Steven out of town. The estate became 100 per cent Catholic. If Steven is to be believed, his departure deprived the security forces of a valuable source of intelligence. 'Living in the middle of the estate, I knew people who were in the Provos and I used to pass on bits and pieces to the army. We became the eyes and ears for one unit. In return, they used to leave us alone. Most of the soldiers were good but there were exceptions. I remember one army commander newly arrived in the estate who went around with a baton saying he and his men had just "taken" Ballymurphy [one of the IRA's strongholds in West Belfast] and they were going to do the same with our area. He went around the town saying this. The next night, a soldier was shot. They asked for it.'

It wasn't long before Steven and his mates got the reputation they deserved – and presumably relished. How much of that reputation relayed to me over curry and rice is fact and how much is bravado is impossible to say. 'I associated with fellas who drove down footpaths to look at the shop windows. There was no problem in driving across the border to the nearest town on the other side, sticking replica guns through the windows and watching the residents run.' Steven alleges there was an even nastier side to some of the activities in which his friends were involved. 'They were suspected of carving the letters "UVF" on somebody's chest with a milk bottle and of hanging people over bridges by their feet. I never did it but I was seen with those who did. I was a very angry, aggressive, bitter, violent person. I took intense pleasure in "destroying" my enemy.'

In 1973 a dramatic change came over him. 'I remember receiving a letter from a friend who said that the only answer was the gun. "If you have problems, terminate them," he wrote. At the time we were as thick as thieves.' Then, suddenly, his friend became a Christian. He invited Steven to a retreat in Greystones, County Wicklow, south of Dublin. Steven went, although why he's not quite sure, perhaps just welcoming the opportunity to get out of Belfast. 'It was great to get out of the city. I was amazed at the quietness. I just sat and looked at the sea, looked at the sea, looked at the sea and looked at the sea.' I counted the times that he said it as he relived the experience. 'I was noisy inside and outside there was not a sound. There were people there who befriended me after years of "watching out" for myself. They could accept me at face value. It was fairly obvious to me they had something I didn't have and I wanted what they had. But I didn't know how to get it. For a country that's so religious, that's awful.'

But there was no immediate conversion. Steven says he went back to Belfast and returned to his studies but was thrown out of college for being disruptive. He then spent a year unemployed, on the brew (a phonetic Ulsterisation of the 'bureau' where the unemployed register). 'I couldn't rest. I was smoking sixty to eighty cigarettes a day. I went for three solid nights without sleep. I opened the bible. I wanted to know how to be saved. I got down on my knees and kept reading and reading and reading. In the end I reached the bit where it says, "If you confess with your lips that Jesus is Lord and believe in your heart that he was raised from the dead, you shall be saved." I just said out loud, "Jesus is Lord!" and got back into bed. I fell fast asleep and slept for the first night in three days.' Something happened. Steven became a different man. 'I had a conscience and my conscience returned. I knew what it was to do right and wrong.'

He rejected all the established Protestant churches in East Belfast and at the end of his search joined a 'house' church whose members gather together to worship under each other's roofs. All its congregation regard themselves as Christians: Catholic and Protestant denominational differences are irrelevant. It was here that Steven met a Catholic woman called Patricia Kelly, who worked as a doctor in Belfast. Patricia is the daughter of Marie Kelly, the subject of the preceding chapter. Steven and Patricia married ten years ago. The original purpose of our meeting in the Indian restaurant that evening was for me to talk with Patricia about herself, her mother and the other members of the family. I'd simply suggested she brought her husband along.

CHAPTER ELEVEN

SONS AND GUNS

There is an interesting collection of books on Mrs Maura McKearney's shelves. Alongside the line of encyclopedias stands Delia Smith's *Complete Cookery Course*, General Sir Frank Kitson's classic work on counter-insurgency, *Low Intensity Operations*, and *The Last Post*, the chronicle of IRA dead. As in most family parlours, the walls and mantelpiece display photographs of children and grandchildren with well-scrubbed faces and neatly combed hair, framed with proud parents. The first impression of the room, with its glowing coal fire and neat lace on the table, is not that given by many Republican homes in Northern Ireland with crucifix on the wall and lines of crafted artefacts from Long Kesh set wherever space will allow. Mrs McKearney serves tea in Royal Albert bone china and brings in sandwiches and cake neatly wrapped in cling film, lest her visitors be late on their long journey from Belfast.

Mrs McKearney could not be further removed from the British stereotype of the Irish Republican mother. When she opens the door of her three-bedroomed bungalow and greets you on the step, it is difficult to imagine the distinguished-looking, white-haired lady screaming abuse at British soldiers or banging a dustbin lid. Anyway, it's the kind of middle-class area where the residents probably have bins on wheels with non-detachable lids. It is immediately apparent too that she's not from the North, with her soft, gentle accent from County Roscommon. Her husband, Kevin, who's been in business in the town for over forty years, clearly *is* a man from Northern Ireland whose family goes back many, many years. And there's Protestant blood in it too. His grandmother's name was Powell ('I hope no relation to Enoch!') and is said to have been married to the local tax inspector. The ancestral home remains in the family, now lived in by Mr McKearney's youngest son, Kevin, and still retains the memorabilia of the days when the Powells were the servants of the Crown. Kevin now works in the family business.

Maura and Kevin McKearney had six children: four sons,

Tommy, Padraig, Sean and Kevin; and two daughters, Margaret and Angela. Margaret and Angela now live in Dublin, Margaret working part-time in an accountant's office and Angela reading European Business Studies at university. I met Margaret in Dublin. She's a bright, attractive, articulate woman who recognises the debt the children owe to their mother. 'When we were growing up, all she wanted for us was a good education. She did her best to see that we all went to good schools. We didn't have everything, but we had sufficient. We all aspired to third-level education. That's what their dreams were for us – ordinary, everyday parental dreams.' All the McKearneys did well, going on to grammar school and collecting a basketful of O-levels. Their parents are proud of them all.

At my request, Maura went to a cupboard in the corner of the dining-room and from the top shelf took down a huge pile of scrapbooks devoted to the lives of her children. Somewhat incongruously 'Postman Pat' adorned the covers of several of them. All were stuffed full of newspaper cuttings, photographs, letters and an assortment of bits and pieces. Among them is a photograph of four of her children. It is one of those photographs that mothers keep that convey a moment in time in a way that words never can. It was taken in the playground of the local primary school in 1964 and shows Tommy (aged 11), Margaret (10), Padraig (10) and Sean (8). They have their hands on each other's shoulders as if they are playing trains. All the boys have short back and sides, with fringes of hair, meant to be combed back but falling across their foreheads at forty-five degrees. Margaret, far plumper then than now, has her hair tied back in a bow. All are dressed in the pullovers and cardigans of the time. The four McKearneys look like any group of brothers and sister in any playground anywhere in the United Kingdom in the early 1960s. Five years later, when the army intervened in Northern Ireland, all of them were teenagers at one of the local grammar schools. The Troubles took over their lives. Tommy is serving a life sentence for murder, Padraig was shot dead at Loughgall by the SAS, Sean was blown up by his own bomb, and Margaret is in Dublin, afraid to return to the North lest she be arrested. Mrs McKearney's three elder sons all joined the Provisional IRA. 'My mother's probably lost everything a mother would hold dear,' says Margaret, 'or at least a large portion of it.' There's no doubt too that collectively her sons have caused at least equal grief to other mothers during their time in the IRA.

The three boys followed in their grandfather's footsteps. Maura McKearney's father, Tom Murray, was another veteran Republican from the 1920s who was adjutant of the North Roscommon brigade of the IRA. He had no sons and neither of his two daughters, Maura and her sister, became involved. 'Girls didn't join organisations in my time. I married and my sons got involved. Tom Murray was committed for the same reason as my children – to end British rule. He was prepared to go out and fight and die if he had to.'

Like a good number of his colleagues from the 1920s, Tom Murray survived into the early 1970s to see the regeneration of the organisation he had lived and fought for. He came North to live with his daughter in 1969. Although not all veterans of that early period gave the Provisionals their seal of approval, a good many did, seeing them as their natural heirs in the long and bloody campaign to drive the British out of the remaining six counties of Ireland. When his grandchildren used to visit him at his home in Roscommon, 'Granda' would take them on tours of sites where he'd skirmished with British soldiers half a century before. 'He was very fond of one particular place, Scramogue,' remembers Margaret, 'where a British army officer, Captain McPeake, was killed. The officer was running away from an ambush when one of the volunteers stood up very, very calmly in the middle of the ambush, trained his rifle and shot him – an excellent shot in those days.'

Maura McKearney was very close to her father although he spent a lot of time away from home in those early days, on the run in the hills. While he was away she helped run the small County Roscommon farm of ten acres. 'The farm wasn't enough to keep us so he did weekly work for the Land Commission [the government body which broke up the huge estates of the English aristocracy and sold the bits to small farmers]. We passed the primary school exam, but because my father couldn't afford the £14 a year we couldn't go to grammar school.' Mrs McKearney stills feels the lack of that secondary education and in particular what she feels is the limitation of language it has imposed upon her – a limitation which is not at all apparent in conversation. She speaks with a quiet passion and natural rhythm which are the product of hard experience and self-education not the classroom. 'People with degrees don't realise what it's like to be just a primary school person trying to talk their way through the world. It's one of the biggest drawbacks one could have.'

The horizons for girls with no more than a basic education were strictly limited in County Roscommon. Being maidservants was about the best they could hope for. Maura's aunts, her father's four sisters, emigrated to the United States like so many families in a similar position (which also helps explain how the IRA has long been able to look to America for much of its financial support). 'One of their daughters now sells computers to banks, so they've come up in the world a long way since ten acres in the bogland of County Roscommon.' At the age of twenty Maura came North to look for work, becoming housekeeper to a Protestant doctor and his family who treated her well and for whom she still retains affection. It was the first time she became aware of 'Protestants' as such. 'In the parish I'd lived in, there wasn't even one Protestant. In Roscommon town itself there were seven. It was something you didn't think about in the Irish Republic. Living with the doctor's family gave me a different view. I realised Protestants were just like ordinary everyday people – that is, no different from Catholics.' Settling down and marrying in a mixed country area confirmed her in her belief that all Catholics and Protestants were equal. 'I'd never experienced the ghetto mentality that I would have done had I been brought up in Belfast, as either a Catholic in the Falls or a Protestant in Sandy Row or the Shankill. All the Protestants I've come across in this part of the world are normal, decent, responsible, hard-working people, no different to the honest to goodness working-class Catholic. We do business with Protestants and Protestants do business with us. And it's something I've always instilled in the children all through life, that all people are equal and that no one person is intrinsically better than another.'

Such a declaration may seem offensive coming from the mother of three IRA men most of whose victims would have been Protestants, but there was no doubt the views were sincerely held. Her sons, had they lived, would have claimed that their targets were the uniforms not the religion of those who wore them. The fact that, British soldiers apart, many of the IRA's victims are members of the RUC and UDR, the vast majority of whom are Protestants, means that such distinctions cut no ice with the Protestant majority in Northern Ireland, many of whom see the IRA waging a war of genocide against them, in particular in the border areas. Maura McKearney is genuinely offended at the thought. 'My mother is what an awful lot of people aren't,' says her daughter Margaret, 'a Republican born and bred. It's like being a Catholic: she has the same devout faith. She's not just a blind follower, or a blind mother who says "my children right or wrong".'

I wondered how much Mrs McKearney had directly influenced her children. Whether she had fed them on Republican propaganda? Whether she had filled them with dreams of fighting and dying for Ireland? Whether she had hoped that they would succeed in arms where their 'Granda' had failed? Margaret says her mother wasn't like that. 'She encouraged a sense of "Irishness", but not rabble-rousing Republicanism. I suppose through bedtime stories and things like that we were always understanding Irish history.' I wondered about the bedtime stories, with visions of Mrs McKearney sitting on the edge of the bed, recounting the epic deeds of IRA heroes from long ago. I was assured she didn't – at least the heroes weren't members of the IRA. 'We'd sit down in the house and ask what had happened at such and such a time to such and such a person – like Brian Boru.'* Clearly the theme was much the same: noble Ireland standing alone against those who came to oppress her, be they Norsemen in longships or British soldiers in armoured cars. But Mrs McKearney was also concerned to give her children a wider knowledge of the world. Margaret remembers her mother making them sit down and watch the funeral of U Thant, the former Secretary General of the United Nations, on television. This didn't surprise me given Ireland's deep commitment to the organisation he led. But she also made them sit down and watch the wedding of Princess Margaret – a typically English fairy tale of May 1960 that would seem to have little appeal to an Irish Republican family. 'We were only kids at the time. Mother told us she was the sister of the Queen of England. She was very keen that we understood the topics of the day.'

By 1970 Tommy McKearney had passed seven O-levels and three A-levels. He knew, according to his mother, that even with these qualifications he could not apply for a job on merit and stand a chance of getting it, as he would in England, because he was a Catholic. 'He was torn. Did he go to university? Or did he fight for his country? He never put it that way, but he made his decision.' In 1970 Tommy McKearney joined the IRA, but not without consulting his mother first. 'He came in one day and said he was anxious to join the [Republican] Movement. He said that if I was dead against it or it would upset me too much, he wouldn't. I said he was eighteen and old enough to make his own mind up. I warned him it would be a very hard life – I'd seen what my father had gone through: that he'd never have a day's comfort and face nothing but hardship; but if that was to be his decision, so be it.' I was rather taken aback at all

---

* The first 'Irish' national hero – the High King who defeated the invading Norsemen at Clontarf in 1014.

this, not expecting many IRA recruits to have talked it over with their mother first. I asked Mrs McKearney why she hadn't said he was out of his mind, that he'd probably end up dead and that would only bring more suffering, hardship and misery? She smiled sadly and shook her head. 'If you make a bad lot, that's it. The choice is yours. If he got into a motor car, he could end up dead.' I suggested the risk wasn't quite the same and that drivers didn't go around deliberately trying to kill people. We let the analogy rest. Had she expected her son to raise the matter with her? 'It was a surprise without being a surprise. So many young men were joining, any son of mine could have joined because of the tradition and the background.'

I asked if she had had the same conversation when Padraig had joined in 1971 at the age of seventeen. 'Yes. To a certain extent he was following in the footsteps of his bigger brother.' And when Sean joined in 1971, when he was eighteen? 'Yes.' What about Margaret? Had there been a similar conversation? 'No. And I'm not just saying that to protect her.'

'Granda' Murray lived to see some of his grandchildren become active in the IRA, but not long enough to see them die. Margaret remembers the Troubles giving him a new lease of life. 'He used to be dying in the armchair sitting by the fire, dying a little more every day. Then through the window he'd see a "Brit" checkpoint at the bottom of the road. All of a sudden he'd put his hat on, grab his walking stick, and fly down the road giving abuse to the British army.' The fact that the boys were involved was never a household secret, nor would one have expected it to have been, given those conversations with their mother. 'No matter what time of night Tommy and Padraig would come in "Granda" was still awake,' remembers Margaret, 'praying for them with his prayer book and rosary beads. (Old people are like that, particularly in Ireland.) They used to discuss their campaign with him and compare it with his own all those years ago. He used to say he couldn't see any difference, except the IRA today had better guns. One of the things he did teach them, with his walking sticks, was how to drill. They were proud to be taught.'

In 1972 the local post office was blown up. By this time both Tommy and Padraig were in the IRA. I asked Mrs McKearney if they had been involved. She said she didn't know as her sons never discussed particular operations with her – although they appear to have done so with their grandfather. 'They must have known Tommy was a member. They raided our house and searched through all the cupboards and sheds.' It was the first of many such searches. 'The army always did the searching and were always civilised in our house. Not at any time did we suffer any physical or mental abuse. They would take away every book we had.' Including Delia Smith? 'Including Delia Smith.' Would tea ever be offered? 'The only one I ever made tea for was a UDR Greenfinch because she'd sat here for about four hours.' In fact, Padraig was arrested for the bombing of the post office and held for six months on remand in Crumlin Road gaol before being released when the charges were dropped against him for lack of evidence.

By this time Tommy had left home, not wishing to suffer the same fate, and fled across the border to Monaghan. Many a Sunday his parents would drive across to see him 'and take him out for something to eat'. At that time Monaghan was a safer haven for IRA men and women on the run. 'In those days, they wouldn't have sent a fellow back,' says Mrs McKearney bitterly, reflecting on the way the authorities in the South now readily extradite those wanted in the North for IRA offences. For years IRA fugitives could claim immunity from extradition by claiming that their offences were political. To the anger and dismay of their supporters, recent Supreme Court rulings in Dublin have now closed the loophole, and in the climate of co-operation created by the Anglo–Irish Agreement, extradition has become less politically contentious for the Irish government.

By the end of 1972 the McKearneys were a marked family, not just by the police and army but by Protestant paramilitaries too. They received a typed warning purporting to be from the commanding officer of the local unit of the Ulster Volunteer Force. I came across the original in one of the family scrapbooks, badly typed and badly punctuated. Tidied up, it reads:

WARNING

You have two sons associated with the IRA. This command has decided that if there are any more explosions in the area or shootings at the security forces, you and your family have to get out within two days. This is final.

The necessary arrangements have been made regarding this matter. So watch your sons' behaviour, they are being watched.

By 1974 Tommy and Padraig were both out of the way. Tommy was arrested in the Irish Republic and sentenced to a year in Dublin's Mountjoy gaol for IRA membership (at the time, the word of a senior police officer was sufficient evidence for the court); and Padraig was sentenced to seven years in the North for blowing up a local factory. By this time, their younger brother Sean had also become active.

Just before midnight on 13 May 1974, Sean and another eighteen-year-old IRA recruit and lifelong friend, Eugene Martin, drove an Austin Maxi belonging to Eugene Martin's father (the local under-taker and auctioneer) into the forecourt of a filling station just out-side the town – and less than a mile from the Martin home. It contained a twenty-pound bomb which exploded prematurely. One badly mutilated body was found immediately, and several hours later parts of the other body were still being located. Two thousand people attended the funeral and a volley of shots was fired over the coffins. 'He joined at Easter and was killed in May,' Mrs McKearney reflects. 'It was possibly the first thing they sent him out to do. It's hard to explain the shock. You don't expect your son to die: you expect him to live on when you're gone. I live with the fact knowing that my sons may die and I hope and pray that they won't. But I live knowing that there is that possibility. I think it fortifies you for it. The grief and heartbreak is no less but you're hardened. If your son is killed in a car crash, you wonder if it would have happened if you hadn't let him take the car to the party. I live with the fact that when my sons joined the IRA, although I hoped they would live to be old men, they could die at any time. It's like the mother who has a son in the British army. She knows that the moment he puts on that uni-form he can come home in a coffin, although she too hopes he will live to be an old man.' In Sean's case, she never thought death would come so quickly.

By the time Sean died, his sister Margaret was already across the border on the run from the authorities in the North. She was wanted for questioning by the RUC in connection with shots that were fired at an off-duty UDR man whilst he was shopping in a nearby town. In the ensuing confusion, Margaret is said to have been stopped by a British soldier. She allegedly broke down in hysterics and the soldier, thinking the outburst was occasioned by the trauma of the shooting, is said to have consoled her and let her go. In 1975 Mar-garet McKearney hit the national headlines. 'Britain's deadliest woman named by bomb squad' proclaimed the *Daily Mirror* (echoed by its competitors in more or less lurid language) on the front page of its edition on 5 September 1975. 'Terror Girl' declared the dramatic block headline above a photograph of a smiling, attractive young woman who was alleged to be Margaret McKearney. The media went to town on the basis of the photograph and a statement put out by Scotland Yard. Commander Roy Habershon, head of the bomb squad, described her as 'probably the most dangerous and active woman terrorist operating over here'. The statement said:

> Margaret McKearney is known to have been closely involved with terrorist incidents in this country since last Autumn and has been identified in connection with activities at Southampton which culminated last September with two policemen being shot and wounded; with the bombings and shootings in London last winter, which led to the murder of PC Stephen Tibble in Hammersmith in February and, as recently as July this year, with events in Manchester and Liverpool which involved the shootings of three more policemen, the capture of five terrorists, and the finding of a huge quantity of explosives, arms and ammunition.
>
> . . . She has a trim figure, blue eyes, well-shaped legs and favours blue coloured tights when not wearing trousers. She acts mainly in the role of terrorist courier, bringing supplies of explosives and money, and is known to travel extensively between here and Ireland . . . Her arrest is sought as a matter of urgency.

For days the story ran, with newshounds the length and breadth of Ireland in hot pursuit of Margaret McKearney, already tried and sentenced by the media, fired by the Scotland Yard statement that was not notable for its profusion of words like 'alleged' or any other such qualification. The case – and it was neither the first nor last of its kind – ended in recrimination between the authorities on both sides of the Irish Sea. Two months later Margaret McKearney was arrested by the Garda, the Irish police, questioned and then released because they said there had not been enough evidence against her. Another row ensued. Her last sighting by the press was her wedding to a former Republican internee from the Ardoyne in Belfast, Jim O'Neill, in Monaghan cathedral, 'almost within binocular distance of British soldiers patrolling the Ulster side of the border'. Margaret McKearney was then allowed to pursue more domestic concerns.

When I met her in Dublin with her husband and two little girls ('one called "Tommy" [Thomasina] after her uncle serving life') I asked her about the time when she was 'Britain's most wanted woman'. She asked me what I meant. She chain-smoked and hugged herself, shivering from time to time as if permanently cold. It was something I'd noticed the first time I'd met her. How did she react to being hunted by the media? 'Let's face it, you don't expect anything more of that sort of press,' she said with contempt. 'But let's be honest, it wasn't something I was ever ashamed of. It didn't psychologically damage me for the rest of my life. It just gives you a higher profile.' She sent the girls off to fetch her some more cigarettes and to buy themselves some sweets. I pulled out the *Daily Mirror* headline and showed her the photograph on the front. She asked me if I thought it looked like her. I said I thought it did – a bit. Then I asked her if she *had* been on active service in England – clearly not a question that expected the answer 'yes'. The question seemed to take her aback. She denied the allegations. She confirmed too that, unlike her brothers, she had never had a conversation with her mother about joining the IRA. The volunteers who operated in Britain, she said, were 'soldiers behind enemy lines'. The McKearneys – in the shape of her three brothers – operated solely within 'the occupied area', within Northern Ireland itself. The 'most wanted woman' chapter, as far as Margaret and her family are concerned, is closed.

Having served his year in Dublin for IRA membership, Tommy McKearney returned to the North and became active again. But he didn't enjoy his freedom for long. On 28 October 1976 the IRA shot dead a 29-year-old part-time lance-corporal in the UDR called Stanley Adams; he also worked as a postman. It was one of those particularly nasty killings that stick in the mind. The IRA is thought to have set Mr Adams up by sending a letter to a remote farmhouse about two miles south of Pomeroy in County Tyrone and then lying in wait to ambush him as he delivered it. Stanley Adams was shot down after he'd delivered the letter and was getting back into his van. The gunmen then picked up the letter he'd just left in order to destroy the evidence. Thomas McKearney was one of those charged with his murder. He was found guilty and sentenced to life imprisonment. That is where he is today, having served twelve years of his sentence in the Maze prison.

I remembered Stanley Adams and the way he'd met his death, and I was also familiar with the name Thomas McKearney before I met his mother. But with so many tragedies and horrific events involving so many names, I failed to associate the two until I met the

McKearney family and started to study their history. Then I remembered. I'd devoted several paragraphs to Thomas McKearney in a book I'd written a decade ago called *Beating the Terrorists*, which investigated allegations that (mainly) IRA suspects had been beaten up by some RUC officers during interrogation in the 1977–8 period. I concluded that some of them had been ill-treated, a finding confirmed by Amnesty International and, indirectly, by the then Labour government's own subsequent inquiry, the Bennett Report. The object of these tactics, that appear to have been limited to a relatively small number of officers, was to extract confessions from suspects during periods of interrogation that, under the Prevention of Terrorism Act, can last up to seven days. On the basis of these statements suspects could be tried and found guilty by a single judge sitting in the non-jury Diplock courts that since 1973 have tried terrorist offences in Northern Ireland. Found guilty, that is, unless the judge was satisfied beyond reasonable doubt that the statement had been obtained using torture, inhuman or degrading treatment. Most trials of the period began with 'statement fights', in which defence counsel would try to convince the judge that the statement should be ruled inadmissible because of the manner in which it had been obtained. Occasionally the defence won.

Thomas McKearney, like scores of others at the time, challenged the statement he had made during his seven-day detention at the RUC's interrogation centre at Castlereagh following his arrest on 18 October 1977. Concern about the ill-treatment of suspects at Castlereagh was first raised by a courageous police surgeon, Dr Robert Irwin. He examined McKearney following his interrogation. This is what I wrote in the book:

> At the beginning of his examination, McKearney was reluctant to complain or say anything about his interviews. It was only after Dr Irwin had questioned him about his injuries that he was prepared to admit he'd been assaulted . . . When he examined McKearney, Dr Irwin was angry. The prisoner had come from Castlereagh, pale and trembling, with a black eye, bruising and abrasions and no note from the medical officer at Castlereagh to explain how the injuries had been received. Dr Irwin believed that the injuries were consistent with the allegations he had had to drag out of McKearney, and did not think, from the position of some of the bruises, that they were likely to have been self-inflicted.

The judge rejected McKearney's counsel's plea that the statement had been obtained improperly and sentenced him to life imprisonment.

Mrs McKearney believes that her son was wrongly convicted. 'He wasn't there,' she insists, 'although I'm not saying that he wasn't at other things. Two thousand people didn't die in Northern Ireland without someone pulling the trigger.' Nevertheless, I pressed her on the way Stanley Adams had been brutally ambushed. 'My reaction to any shooting is sympathy, regardless of who they are. My sympathy for the Adams family is complete. The mother has lost what I've lost, but we are all in a war situation. I lost two sons because of the war in Northern Ireland. Mrs Adams lost a son because of the war in Northern Ireland.' Having questioned the notion of what constituted 'a legitimate target' in the eyes of the IRA, I asked her whether she agreed that Stanley Adams had been gunned down in a particularly cowardly way. 'IRA units do operate in a way that horrifies people. But I'm not a spokesperson for the IRA. I am not, and never have been, a member of the IRA. A man who wears the uniform of the British army must take the consequences. A young man who takes the oath to the IRA has to take the consequences too.' But what had shooting a postman got to do with fighting a war? 'Is a UDR man – or an IRA person – ever off duty?' It was pointless trying to extract any condemnation where clearly none existed, so I gave up.

The way in which Thomas McKearney and hundreds of his colleagues in the IRA were arrested, interrogated, tried and convicted sowed the seeds of the hunger strike of 1981 in which ten men starved themselves to death. The issue at stake for the prisoners and the government of Mrs Thatcher that confronted them was the perception of the conflict in which both were involved. The IRA maintained that its incarcerated volunteers were prisoners of war, and eligible for treatment as such by being allowed to wear their own clothes and being excused prison work. The government would have none of it. It insisted they were common criminals and thereby entitled to no special treatment. In the famous words of Mrs Thatcher, 'Murder is Murder'.

The 1981 hunger strike was the result of a gradual escalation of the protest in the prisons which had started after Labour's Northern Ireland Secretary, Merlyn Rees, had announced on 4 November 1975 the abolition of 'special category' status, which both Republican and Loyalist paramilitary prisoners had long enjoyed, living in POW-type compounds which they ran in a way reminiscent of

World War Two, with each compound having its own command structure. IRA prisoners protested by first refusing to wear prison clothes and going 'on the blanket' and then by smearing their cells with excreta, 'the dirty protest' (the Provisionals called it 'no wash') – in which 342 prisoners were ultimately involved. Although both protests brought the world's press flocking back to Belfast, they succeeded in moving the British government, both Labour and Conservative, not one inch.

The hunger strike is the ultimate weapon in the IRA's traditional armoury of protest and can only be undertaken as a last resort when sanctioned by the organisation's ruling Army Council. In the autumn of 1980 it gave authorisation for selected prisoners in the Maze to embark on a hunger strike. On 27 October seven Republican prisoners refused food and began their 'fast to the death'. One of them was Thomas McKearney. He told his mother and father, 'I'll put all my cards on the table. I'm going on hunger strike. If and when I die, I want to be brought back to Roscommon and be buried alongside my "Granda" . . . Don't let people try to influence you, your only friends will be the Republican Movement. If I die, never let the family be ashamed. If I die, I'll die in the knowledge that my life was for the cause and for the other boys here. If at my funeral the press say, "See how the IRA let your son die", just say, "My son died as an Irish soldier, not a British criminal".'

Tommy McKearney went without food for 53 days. Great pressure was applied on Mrs McKearney – and the other families – to persuade their sons to come off. As Margaret McKearney remembers, her mother would not hear of it. 'I remember her saying, "He's twenty-eight. At twenty-eight a man can make his own decisions." That's always been her attitude. She understands why they do what they do. She would never interfere.' Tommy came within hours of death. Mrs McKearney had begun to alert all the cousins and nieces and to get the house ready for the funeral. 'In the last few days, the authorities let us in nearly every day. Tommy was like someone dying of cancer. He was just a bag full of bones. How they ever come back to normality after such an experience, I'll never know.' The hunger strike was called off on 18 December 1980 after the prisoners were led to believe they had won significant concessions from the government. But the concessions proved illusory, and two months later the IRA prisoner, Bobby Sands, began the final showdown. This time it was to the death. Nine others followed him.

By the time Tommy McKearney had begun his hunger strike, his brother Padraig had joined him in gaol, sentenced in 1980 to four-teen years for possession of a loaded sten gun. But unlike his brother, Padraig McKearney got out early, unofficially – on 25 September 1983 along with thirty-seven other IRA prisoners in the biggest gaol break in British prison history. Padraig was one of the handful who was never recaptured. He appears not to have made straight for the border where every blade of grass would be watched but to have sought refuge, literally, under the floorboards of a 'safe' house within the North.* And he wasn't alone. Remarkably, seven other escapees are said to have shared the space with him, which was directly under the living-room of the house. At one stage the smell was so powerful that they were ordered to pass out their socks for washing lest it attract the sniffer dogs that roamed the area still in pursuit of the escapees. They stayed there for two weeks. There were said to have been heated discussions about the direction the Republican Movement was taking – not least over the political path down which Sinn Fein President (and Westminster MP) Gerry Adams and the Belfast leadership seemed intent on taking it. Padraig McKearney, it seems, was advocating the 'third phase' of the struggle, what he termed 'the strategic defensive' in which the RUC, UDR and army would be denied all support in selected areas following repeated attacks on their bases. During the long hours and even longer days in the cramped conditions under the boards, some of the men started to pray, a gesture most had abandoned long ago. Padraig adamantly refused to do so, declaring that it was a well-known fact that there was no such thing as God. He was an atheist and a communist too – like his brother Tommy who was subsequently to split with the Provisionals and form his own revolutionary socialist movement, Congress '86, which, nevertheless, did not forswear 'the armed struggle'. What Padraig and Tommy McKearney both questioned was the military strategy and direction of the leadership of the Republican Movement.

I asked Mrs McKearney how she reacted when she heard that Padraig was 'out'. She said she just wondered how long it would be before he was recaptured. Occasionally, once he was safe in the South, she would see him, having got a message that he needed a pair of boots. For Christmas he said he wanted a jumper and a couple of shirts: they'd be more useful to him than a video or a cassette. 'A strange existence, a strange existence,' she mused staring

---

* This account is based on the book, *Out of the Maze*, by Dublin journalist Derek Dunne. The book is based on interviews conducted with some of the men who evaded capture.

down at the tablecloth, almost oblivious of my presence. I wondered whether she'd tried to persuade him to leave the IRA once he'd escaped, to minimise the risk of recapture or death whilst on an operation. 'I suppose I'm a bad mother, but I don't think I ever asked him to leave,' she said, looking up. 'I can't answer for that side of my make-up. He didn't fight for personal gain. When he died, he had 10p in his pocket. In his bag were two shirts, a paperback, *The Year of the French*, and a pair of trunks. They were all his belongings. That was his wealth in this world.' She keeps the zip bag upstairs in the loft.

Margaret was very close to Padraig, as brother and sister both born in the same year. She was obviously deeply upset when I raised the subject and needed some time to compose herself before she could bring herself to discuss it. She asked me if I had any brothers and sisters. She said she didn't know how to explain her feelings without sounding dreadful. 'In every family you love everybody, but there's always one to whom you feel terribly, terribly close – a natural affinity. It doesn't affect your love for the rest, it's just one person you can go to with your troubles. Padraig was that person for me in my family. I was extremely upset when he was arrested for the third time [in 1980] and I thought I'd never see him again. [Margaret was unable to cross the border and visit him in gaol lest she be arrested herself.] I always saw him as my "big" brother because I was so small and he was nearly six foot.' It was over two and a half months after his escape before Padraig got to Dublin and saw his sister. He arrived at the beginning of December 1983, almost like a ghost from her past. 'I always remember him coming through the door. He just looked so small, thin and tiny. He'd been living in ditches and under floorboards, literally, and it had really taken its toll. I was shocked when I saw him. I thought, My God, he's not my "big" brother. He seemed so shrivelled and shrunk. He was literally physically wrecked, and mentally wrecked too. He just wanted a little bit of time to get his body and self together.'

By the beginning of 1984 Padraig had recovered, managing to remain at liberty whilst, in ones and twos, his fellow escapees were gradually being picked up. At the time of writing, nine of the thirty-seven escapees are still at large. Surprisingly, to an outside observer, Padraig didn't stay in the South but returned to the North on active service, a process known as 'going across'. He remained active for the next three years until his death in the ambush set by the police and SAS at Loughgall RUC station on 9 May 1987. I naively asked Margaret whether Loughgall was his first major operation after his escape, having failed at the time to have worked out the chronology clearly in my mind. She laughed. 'It was more like his hundred and first! He was extremely active. He would 'go inside' and stay in for six and seven months at a time. The danger in the North is crossing the border. Once you're in you stay in. After I'd seen him that Christmas, he went back inside and never really left the North after that.'

If there had been a price on her brother's head it would have been high. For three years Padraig McKearney's unit bombed and killed around the border and central areas of the province – apparently, judging from the operational pattern of those years, trying to put into practice the 'third phase of the struggle' that McKearney had discussed during his fortnight under the floorboards. RUC stations were attacked and mortared, and contractors who tried to repair them were killed in order to try and deny the security forces control of more and more areas. Between January 1984 and the end of 1986, there had been over seventy attacks on RUC establishments and more than thirty-five policemen killed, nine of them in an IRA mortar attack on Newry RUC station on 28 February 1985, after which the IRA warned it would shoot any builder who worked on repairs. Padraig McKearney was, in the words of the Republican Movement, 'a key figure on some of the most daring and innovative missions in the last few years . . .'

In the eyes of the police and army Padraig McKearney, at thirty-three, was one of the most experienced and dangerous terrorists in the North. The history of the eight weapons analysed by the security forces in the wake of the ambush at Loughgall gives some idea of the extent of his activities and those of the seven other IRA men killed. RUC forensic experts traced them to over thirty incidents. One of the weapons was a .357 Ruger revolver which had been used in six incidents. It had been seized from a dead police officer in one of the attacks in which Padraig McKearney was said to have been involved. At 6.55 p.m. on 7 December 1985 an IRA unit which apparently included Padraig McKearney launched a gun and bomb attack on Ballygawley police barracks. One member is said to have shot dead two police officers, Constable George Gilliland and Reserve Constable William Clements. The Ruger revolver was then taken from Reserve Constable Clements; it was said to have become Padraig McKearney's personal weapon. The revolver was subsequently traced to three killings, one of them of John Kyle, a man from the Omagh area who, the IRA alleged, had been supplying concrete to a number of RUC establishments, presumably to repair the damage the IRA had done.

During this three-year period of frenzied and bloody activity, Margaret occasionally saw her brother in Dublin. The last occasion was around Christmas and New Year 1986–7, when he spent two or three weeks in the Dublin area. 'He came down to me out of the blue one Sunday evening. We had a few drinks, well perhaps more than a few, and we sat and we talked about death. He told me he knew he was going to die at some stage. I found it very hard, because I knew it was probably true. It wasn't inevitable but it was a risk.' Her observation was an understatement given the charmed life her brother had led since his escape from the Maze three years earlier. The last time Margaret and her mother saw Padraig was on 24 March 1987 when Margaret had arranged a family get-together for a Mother's day meal in Monaghan. She had managed to get Padraig to come. 'He was on the best of form that day,' recalls his mother. 'It was the last time I saw him.'

On 8 May 1987 two of the IRA's most experienced units, one from each side of the border, combined for an attack on the small RUC station in the County Armagh village of Loughgall. It was to be a carbon copy of an attack the previous summer on another RUC station at Birches, again in County Armagh (in which the police are said to believe Padraig McKearney was also involved). Around 6 p.m. the IRA took a mechanical digger from a farm near Dungannon and placed a 200-pound bomb in the front bucket. They also hijacked a blue Toyota van. Dressed in boiler suits and trainers and armed with six high-powered rifles, a Spaz shotgun and the Ruger revolver, the eight IRA men – three on the digger and five in the van – made for Loughgall RUC station. They didn't know that the station, which was only manned on a part-time basis, had been cleared in preparation for the SAS ambush. The digger rammed the station, the bomb went off and the police and SAS opened up, killing all eight IRA men. The precise order of events is unclear. The result was not. Eight of the IRA's most experienced men, including Padraig McKearney, were dramatically removed from the scene. Anthony Hughes, an innocent civilian, was also killed, and his brother Oliver seriously wounded. Tragically both were in the wrong place at the wrong time. There were few complaints about 'shooting to kill'. The security forces – and the government and most of the British people – were jubilant at the success at what was obviously a brilliantly planned and executed operation, tempered only by the tragedy the Hughes family suffered. It was the IRA's biggest single loss since 1920.

The ambush caused bitter recrimination in the Republican Movement. There was the inevitable search for an informer but none was found. It remains almost inconceivable that the operation could have been carried out without some kind of detailed inside intelligence – such as there was in the killings that the former Deputy Chief Constable of Greater Manchester, John Stalker, investigated when an MI5 agent within the IRA had pinpointed targets for the police. The McKearney family was exceedingly bitter, convinced that Padraig had been betrayed taking part in an operation of no military value. Had the IRA's mission succeeded, it would have been a classic example of 'armed propaganda' – the kind of 'theatre' on which experts believe that terrorism thrives. But this time the ending was changed.

Padraig McKearney was buried in the same plot as his brother Sean. The family did not allow Gerry Adams or any of the leaders of the Republican Movement to give the oration at the funeral. Sinn Fein leaders Danny Morrison and Martin McGuiness paid their respects at the wake. Mrs McKearney knew it was an unpopular decision. She's not bitter against the soldiers and police who pulled the triggers. 'I'm not blaming the British soldiers who shot my son dead. It was one soldier fighting another. You wouldn't have to be very bright to work out that Loughgall knew they were coming.'

Margaret is as bitter and unforgiving as her mother. 'I haven't a lot of trust in the IRA of the moment – because somebody betrayed my brother. Someone, somewhere, for whatever reason, wanted my brother dead – whether for pure money or political advantage. I can't make my mind up whether someone just went and took British gold to put my brother and his friends in the grave,* or whether it was part of a preconceived plan for internal reasons – with their little plots and schemes to become part of the constitutional process – when there were men like Padraig who would stand there and say "No". He would have been very concerned about the political developments – but he was prepared to give them a chance. But Padraig would have stood firm against any "sell out" after twenty years. He was taken out for pure greed or because he stood in the way.' Given the obsessional – and understandable – secrecy that surrounds such operations, we shall probably never know the answer. But the odds are heavily on British intelligence, not on some Machiavellian plot within the Republican Movement.

* Like the IRA 'mole' working for MI5 in the Stalker case who was paid £30 000 over a period of time for his information.

In conclusion, I asked Mrs McKearney the inevitable question: what had the deaths of her two sons achieved? She paused and gave a long sigh. 'I suppose the straightforward answer is to say it hasn't achieved anything.' There was another long pause while she thought. 'You couldn't pinpoint something they'd really achieved. Their life would have achieved more than their death. Sean was only a short time involved but I would say that Padraig with sixteen years involved has left his mark, his pressure, on the history of this country. All my sons fought for equality on the island of Ireland.' To Mrs McKearney her sons were revolutionaries, more socialist than nationalist. And yet the prerequisite of their socialist or Marxist revolution was first getting the British to withdraw from Northern Ireland. I suggested that after twenty years of strife the British showed not the slightest inclination to go. 'I don't know, I've no idea,' she said sadly. Did she mind? Did she still want the British to go? She sighed for the last time. 'I think if the British left the Irish alone, the two traditions on the island would be forced to come to terms with each other. People would die, but there wouldn't be this bloody civil war.' She put down her teacup and stared out of the window with sadness in her eyes. There was nothing more to be said. I thanked Mrs McKearney and left, with nine heavy scrapbooks under my arm.

CHAPTER TWELVE

GOD HELP IRELAND

Flo Lewers is a remarkable woman. There aren't many Olympic medallists in the Waterside area of Derry, or in any other part of the city for that matter. Flo suffers from viral encephalitis, a disabling disease that left her paralysed in the legs and in part of her right arm. During her rehabilitation she took up archery and table tennis to build up her stricken muscles, and then, having discovered a natural talent, developed it through the Northern Ireland Para-plegic Association's Sport for the Disabled. Soon, to add to her skills in archery and table tennis, Flo could put a shot and throw a javelin from her wheelchair. Having won a gold medal at the National Paraplegic Games at Stoke Mandeville, she was selected for the Olympics in Jerusalem in 1968 and won a silver medal for table tennis and a bronze for archery. In 1977 she was awarded the OBE and presented with it in person by the Queen at Hillsborough Castle during Her Majesty's visit to the province in Jubilee year. 'The thing that impressed me most,' Flo remembers, 'is that she seemed to know what I had done. "How on earth do you play table tennis from a wheelchair?" she asked.' Flo probably let down the arm and demonstrated.

Flo doesn't readily talk about her achievements. She's far too modest for that. When I asked if I could have a look at her medals, she said they were up in the loft somewhere, tucked away in a box. As we were discussing just how table tennis *could* be played from a wheelchair, her husband Arthur got up from his place by the fire, put down his pipe and left the room. Five minutes later he came back with a box of medals, ribbons and pins in which he obviously took great pride. It was refreshing to talk about something other than the Troubles.

Flo suffers from another disability too. On 19 August 1979 she was attending an interdenominational carol service in aid of Cancer Research in the city's Guildhall when a massive car bomb exploded in the street outside. 'There was a tremendous bang, a colossal

167

bang. I'll never forget it. The windows opposite where I was sitting burst rather than broke. Thank God nobody was killed.' Remarkably, the service continued although it was cut short on the advice of the police. Afterwards the cupboard in the Mayor's Parlour was opened and everyone was offered a stiff drink. Flo remembers talking to Bishop (now Archbishop) Eames. 'I couldn't hear a word he said, although I assumed he was asking me if I was all right.' The bomb blast has permanently affected her hearing, so she is now afflicted with constant noises in the ear, like the high-pitched squeak you hear when you turn the television off at closedown at the end of the day.

You soon become totally unaware of Flo's disability which, I'm sure, is exactly as she would wish. Like so many disabled people she has an outlook on life that often surprises the physically fit. Whenever I met her, and I'd often call in when I was passing, she would always be cheerful, always be welcoming, and always most concerned that I'd eaten properly. Any assurance that I had was invariably disregarded as tea and sandwiches and Blue Riband chocolate biscuits (which I hadn't set eyes on since I was a child) were produced from the kitchen. Flo and Arthur are God-fearing folk and you can feel the Christian goodness in the house, not in any obvious way but in its warmth, courtesy and kindness. I wouldn't have been surprised to see a 'God Bless This House' tapestry on the wall, but clearly it wasn't necessary as God appeared to have blessed it already.

Flo, Arthur and their two sons are Church of Ireland Protestants but to them their religion is a personal matter, not a sectarian banner behind which much of the community on the Waterside stands. The kerbstones on the approach roads to the council estate on which the Lewers live are painted red, white and blue, although the paint is fading now – which shouldn't be taken as a sign that the 'loyalty' of Flo's neighbours is fading. In the Lewers' household attitudes are no doubt conditioned by the fact that Flo and Arthur were both brought up as Protestants in the Irish Republic. Flo was born in Dublin in 1932 and is eternally grateful that her liberal parents sent her to a mixed school. 'I always say, thank God for that. I put that down to the reason I can still mix. I was always taught to mix, it was just natural. I think that's where the problem in Northern Ireland arises: the children, or most schools, are divided from the word go.' At school Flo was never conscious of being part of a minority, a Protestant in a Catholic country. Growing up, she was never aware of any difference between the two religions, not least because once a month her parents would invite the local parish priest and the rector to dinner when Flo had to be on her best behaviour. Arthur was born in the North, in County Tyrone, and went to a Church of Ireland school, but like Flo came from a home where religious differences were never emphasised. His father worked for the Great Northern Railway, one of the few cross-border institutions, that wound its way from Dublin to Dundalk, Portadown and Belfast, touching other parts of the province as far away as Enniskillen. I thought it was a pity the line still wasn't open as it would have provided a magnificent scenic tour of some of the most beautiful areas of the province: but I wondered how long it would last with the Provisionals bent on destroying the only link that still remains, between the border towns of Newry and Dundalk, as the train runs from Dublin to Belfast. Arthur's father rose to become a stationmaster, which meant that one moment he could be in the North and the next in Dublin or at a small station in the middle of nowhere in County Monaghan. They ended up living in Ballyshannon, County Donegal, where Arthur finished his education in another Church of Ireland school. In 1947 he went to work in Dublin as a psychiatric nurse, and it was there that he met Flo whose father was head gardener in the grounds of the hospital where he worked. They married and in 1953 moved to Northern Ireland when Arthur got a post at a psychiatric hospital in Derry, and where he stayed until his retirement in 1986. (The Lewers tend to call the city 'Derry' because it's shorter.) He loved every minute of his work.

Despite the IRA's desultory border campaign between 1956 and 1962, which came to a prompt end when the governments north and south of the border interned IRA suspects simultaneously, the Troubles were nothing but folklore in the post-war years to most people in Northern Ireland. Derry, which was included in the North under Lloyd George's scheme for partition because Unionists would not tolerate the inclusion of their historically sacred city in the South, was the scene of some of the most bitter sectarian violence in July 1920. Sinn Fein had won resounding victories in the local elections which only confirmed Unionist fears of being subordinated to Nationalist control in the city. In her massive work on the creation of the Irish state, *The Irish Republic*, published in 1937, Dorothy Macardle vividly describes the scene in the city on the night of 19 July 1920:

> On that night, armed mobs rushed upon the Catholic
> quarter of the city, setting fire to houses, shooting, looting

and wrecking shops; they carried the Union Jack and the military did not intervene. During four nights and days, the street fighting went on; over fifty persons were wounded and nineteen were killed. At last, the military intervened, but only to fire upon members of the IRA who had undertaken to protect property and were standing on guard.

The old couple living next door to the Lewers remembered those days and of an evening would come over and reminisce with Flo and Arthur. 'They'd talk about the old times, about the riots in the twenties and we'd sit there laughing. Could you ever imagine that you couldn't go out and walk up the street because people were shooting at one another? It was unbelievable. We thought it was all exagerrated.'

When history was replayed nearly fifty years later and sectarian violence erupted again in Derry, as Protestants saw the civil rights movement as another IRA plot, it all seemed unreal to those who were not directly involved or who, like the Lewers, didn't feel threatened. 'You saw it on the telly so you knew it was going on. Most of us wondered what all these marches were for. We thought, "What have we got that they haven't got?"' The evening after a Protestant mob attacked civil rights marchers at Burntollet Bridge – a few miles down the road from the Lewers' home – Arthur was bemused to face a hostile reception from the Catholics he worked with at the psychiatric hospital. He was puzzled and couldn't understand it. A few nights later, when the heat had subsided, he took the matter up. 'One of the girls said she'd been on the march at Burntollet and had ended up being chased across fields. She said, "And I suppose you were out there." I said, "In the name of God, girl, what would I be doing out there?" She said, "Surely you'd have been out there because you're a Protestant and you must be an Orangeman." I couldn't believe it. I just dissolved into laughter.' I asked Arthur if he ever had been an Orangeman. 'Not at all,' he said as he laughed and waved his pipe. 'They assumed that all Protestants were alike. I then asked them what their grievances were and they went on about "one man, one vote", and Protestants getting all the jobs and Protestants getting all the houses. I said, "Well, all right, I'm a Protestant, you name me one thing that I've got out of life that you haven't got out of life." They said you had to be a Protestant to get a job. So I looked round at them and said it was funny I was the only Protestant there!'

Flo and Arthur were appalled at the Burntollet 'ambush' and saw the results at first hand as Catholic marchers, some with bleeding heads, streamed through their estate, shouting and screaming and still trying to escape their pursuers. Arthur, who was peacefully digging his garden on a quiet Saturday afternoon, was shocked. 'That's what brought home the viciousness of it all. It made you feel ashamed. It made you inclined to think, "To hell with Catholics and Protestants, to hell with the lot of them. If this is religion, if this is Christianity, then it's not for me!"' The Lewers were glad to see the army arrive, 'with their funny tin hats and rolls of barbed wire being welcomed by those who now want to murder them'. Arthur, like most people on both sides, assumed that order would be quickly restored and things would return to normal. 'Everyone thought it marked the end of a short, sharp, brief encounter. We thought, "The war's over. Those fellas will be off the streets in the morning. Thank God, that's the end of it." I thought people would say, "Now let's have a bit of wit and a bit of sense."'

Flo and Arthur's main concern, as their boys were growing up in the early seventies, was to keep them out of any involvement with the Loyalist paramilitary organisations (most notably the UDA) which were born in response to the IRA and out of frustration that the conventionally constituted forces of law and order, the police and army, were not being tough enough. Like the IRA, these Loyalist organisations claimed their legitimacy from history, when Protestants had armed to confront what they perceived as the Nationalist threat. Looking at the Lewers family and knowing the moral values of the household, it is difficult for an outsider to imagine how involvement in paramilitary activity could ever have been considered a threat. Arthur assured me I was wrong. 'Our boys could have become involved very, very easily. Young people are young people and they're attracted by the glamour of these organisations. The mood of the time was that the country was under attack, the Protestants were all going to be murdered and sombody had to stand up and do something. I can understand how young Protestants got involved and how young Catholics got involved too. Of course, we warned our children. Sometimes they'd come home from school with emblems and secret bits and pieces from the UDA or some such organisation. We just threw them in the fire and told them that those sort of things weren't wanted here. The boys protested – but they did as they were told. Gradually we hoped we'd get them out of it.' But as another family told me, if boys were of a mind to join, the only way parents could stop them was to lock them in their bedroom and throw away the key. Flo and Arthur didn't have to resort to such drastic measures.

It wasn't as if their boys were at a loose end and were at risk because they were bored and had nothing else to do. One of their sons, Mervyn, was particularly active in the St Columb's cathedral choir and most of his spare time, and most of his friends, were based around it. 'There wasn't much going on at night for young people,' he remembers, 'especially for that age group. We used to go to choir practice three nights a week and then to church three times on Sunday. We were all very close, like cousins and brothers. All of them were my friends. Although we would have our "off" days, we were great mates and we'd share everything. We were just like a unit. The choir was fantastic, brilliant – the best days of your life, to be honest.' One of Mervyn's friends in the choir was a young Protestant called Lindsay Mooney, who had been head choirboy before his voice broke: he then went on to join the adult choir and also became a Boy Scout leader. Lindsay was a model son and the kind of boy with whom any parent would be delighted to see their own sons associate. One weekend, at the end of March 1972, Lindsay came to call at the Lewers' house to see if Mervyn and his brother were ready to go out. By chance, Flo and Arthur were at home. They normally used to go away for the weekends, across the border into Donegal, but that weekend was an exception. Arthur answered the door and asked where the football match was. Lindsay said they weren't going to a match but to a rally in Belfast.

Four days earlier, on 24 March 1972, Edward Heath's Conservative government had 'prorogued' the parliament at Stormont through which Northern Ireland's Unionist majority had governed the province since partition. The government announced that henceforth the province would be administered directly from Westminster, with a Secretary of State of Cabinet rank and a team of junior ministers. The apparent abolition of what the majority of the majority had always regarded as 'a Protestant parliament for a Protestant people' was, for the Protestant community, one of the most traumatic events of the past twenty years. They saw it as a betrayal by the British government and a victory for the 'men of violence'. In the climate of the time feelings were running incredibly high. The Loyalist leader, William Craig, who had been the hard-line Minister of Home Affairs in the Stormont government, declared he would make the province ungovernable and force the British government to negotiate with the Protestant majority. The instrument through which he planned to force the government's hand was an organisation he formed called 'Vanguard'. At one of the first rallies held in Belfast's Ormeau Park over 50 000 men heard William Craig threaten:

We must build up a dossier of the men and women who are
a menace to this country, because if and when the
politicians fail us, it may be up to us to take action.

On 27 March nearly 200 000 Protestant workers answered Craig's
call for a stoppage, and the following day Craig presided over an
even greater mass rally of a 100 000 Vanguard supporters outside
the Parliament Buildings at Stormont. That was the rally to which
Lindsay Mooney was planning to take Mervyn and his brother
Alan. Arthur would have none of it and told Lindsay to 'rally ahead'
on his own as he wasn't having any of his boys going to such a thing.
Lindsay went on ahead. Alan was furious and rushed out, banging
the door, saying he wouldn't be back as he was off to Belfast to 'join
up'. Twenty minutes later he was back when he found that his lift
had gone. He rushed up to his bedroom, banged the door, and then
banged the door again. Arthur could understand his son's frustration and anger. 'All his friends had gone and he probably felt he
was letting the side down. He knew too that he'd probably get it
taken out of him at school and be called "worse nor a Fenian" – the
biggest insult a Protestant can hurl. Had our sons gone to that rally,
that would have been it!'

On 17 March 1973, almost a year to the day after that first
Vanguard rally at Ormeau Park, nineteen-year-old Lindsay
Mooney was dead, blown up on St Patrick's day by a car bomb he
was trying to plant outside Kirk's Bar, a pub in Cloghfin, County
Donegal, a few hundred yards across the border. Inside, over 300
people were celebrating St Patrick's Day. Thirty were injured when
the car exploded just after it had been parked by the gable wall. It is
thought that the bomb went off when it did because Mooney had
difficulty in finding a parking space outside the crowded pub. Parts
of his body were found in a field fifty yards away. The UDA in Derry
announced that Lindsay Mooney was a 'sergeant' in their organisation. At first they announced that he had been kidnapped by the
Provisionals and taken across the border, but they then changed the
story and alleged that the Provisional IRA's Army Council was
holding a meeting in the pub that night. That, the UDA now maintains, was the reason for Lindsay Mooney's mission.

He was given a full 'military' funeral with a volley of shots fired
over the coffin. The service was conducted by the Very Rev. George
Good, the Dean of St Columb's cathedral. Some members of the
choir went to the family home to sing a psalm in remembrance, and
one of them recalls being deeply upset by the sight of masked men

standing guard over the coffin. Dean Good was also upset and disturbed by the paramilitary trappings. Newspaper death notices announced that Sergeant Lindsay Mooney gave his life for Ulster and died in a foreign land. His mother is still shattered by the loss and has never recovered. His father, whom I met, is a kind, gentle man, not at all like most would expect the father of a 'terrorist' to be. He told me that, were it not for the circumstances of the time, his son would never have become involved. 'I would say we all felt a loyalty to our country. If you look at history, whenever Britain was in bother, our fathers and our grandfathers went to her aid. We just saw it as our duty. The same sort of loyalty existed at the time – except we were under threat and that's how all the lads got involved.' Grieving families on the Republican side would also say the same thing, although the cause for which their sons died was on the other side of the historical mirror.

Shortly after Lindsay Mooney's death, the boys in his scout troop came to his father and asked if they could start a band in memory of their leader's name. He agreed. From its noisy origins in a neighbour's back garage, the Lindsay Mooney Flute Band, with Mr Mooney on cymbals, has now become famous throughout the west of the province and has trophies to prove it.

The tragedy the Mooney family suffered shocked the close-knit choir, and in particular the Lewers who had known Lindsay so well and who could so easily have ended up with a similar bereavement had their sons gone with him to Belfast that day. Lindsay's death meant that Mervyn and his brother needed no further persuasion about the folly of any paramilitary flirtation. Mervyn was devastated by his friend's death. 'None of us ever dreamed that Lindsay was involved. He just didn't seem that sort of person. He was as quiet a fellow as you could find and he would do anything for you. I was really desperate at the time. But in a way, I suppose there was good that came out of it because I decided I was going to stay clear. I remember being shocked at the funeral when I saw two men with black masks and paramilitary uniform standing by the coffin. I was scared. I was glad to get out through the door. It was frightening – a big eye-opener for me.'

Flo realised it was a turning point for her sons and told them that if they wanted to defend Ulster, they should do it the proper way. 'I said if you want to do anything for your country, put on the Queen's uniform and serve with pride.' When Mervyn left the choir, he found he missed the camaraderie and, as the social life of the Waterside didn't seem to have much to offer, he finally took his mother's advice and joined the police. In 1977 he became a part-time member of the RUC Reserve, where he already had a few friends. They said it was great and Mervyn decided to join them. 'The comradeship was fantastic. You had your own social club. It was fantastic and there was always something to do. I'd toyed with the idea of joining the police full-time, so starting off part-time was a way of getting an insight into what it was like. I thoroughly enjoyed it. The station was on the Waterside and it wasn't like a police station, it was just like home, just like a family. That's the way everybody used it and everybody knew everybody else.'

Mervyn felt so at home in the police that five years later he decided to join the full-time RUC Reserve. He was obviously aware of the danger when serving in sensitive Republican areas like Strabane and certain parts of Derry, but the feeling that danger instilled in the men seemed to more than compensate for the risks. 'Then the comradeship and the friendship were even closer. Everybody stood by one another and you knew that whoever was supposed to be behind you was behind you – and you could stake your life on it.' Flo, as a mother, was perhaps more sensitive to the real dangers than was her son. She'd become the secretary of 'People Together', a small group of Protestants and Catholics who, not wishing to be labelled as 'Peace' people, visit the victims of violence and the families of the bereaved on all sides. Flo saw at first hand what could happen to a policeman in a bomb or shooting attack. 'I learned that hurt and bereavement are the same whether it's a Catholic or Protestant home. There's the same heartbreak, the same hurt and the same tears whether you have a son who's a Republican or a policeman.' Several of Mervyn's friends fell victim to the IRA's campaign, some injured, others killed. He was often in charge of the funeral arrangements and, pained by the grief of seeing one coffin after another being lowered into the grave, would come home and tell his parents that if anything were to happen to him, he wanted to be laid out in the corner of the sitting-room for half a day and then cremated. Arthur, wishing to make light of the unthinkable thought, used to say that when Mervyn was gone he wouldn't have a lot of say in the matter.

In 1986 Mervyn reluctantly resigned from the RUC because the pressures of his job were beginning to tell on his family. Two years later, on 22 May 1988, the IRA struck. Mervyn had been having a drink with a mate in a pub and returned to his car about five past eleven, having promised to give his friend a lift home. He noticed a bag near the front wheel of the car and flicked it away with his foot, never thinking to look under his car as a standard police security precaution since it was two years since he had left the force. 'I'll never forget it. As the car moved off, there was a big orange flash and a cloud of black dust. I remember looking at my friend and seeing him covered in blood, not realising at the time that it was mine. The next thing I remember, I was on the footpath with my elbows stuck in this wee, small drain that ran across it, trying to drag myself along – but I wasn't going anywhere. I remember this unmerciful heat.' His friend dragged him away from the blazing car and he remembers a policeman and then a soldier arriving on the scene. 'All I wanted to do was to see how my legs were as there was an awful pain in one of them. I've never been so glad to see a soldier. He slung his rifle away and then put a tourniquet on my leg and wound it very, very tight. I could hear bells, alarm bells, ringing and the pain was desperate, a burning sensation. Then all of a sudden the noise stopped, the pain left me, and I put my two hands behind my head and sort of snuggled down to go to sleep. Just then I remember the soldier – I remember the camouflage cream on his face – saying, "Keep that wee bastard awake or you'll lose him!" So I got this thing into my head that if I fell asleep, I was a "gonner". I remember fighting with the doctors as they tried to stick needles in to sedate me. I didn't want to go to sleep!' A few days later, Mervyn was told he'd have to have his right leg amputated.

Mervyn is bitter. He is not prepared to forgive and he can't forget. 'At the time, to be honest, I was full of hatred, not so much towards the person who put the bomb under the car, but against the person that sent them out to do it. Their day of judgement will come.' Every time he sees an explosion on the news, he's reminded of the blazing heat and thanks God that he, unlike hundreds of others, miraculously survived – although with the loss of a leg.

On one of my visits, Mervyn lifted himself up from his chair, searched for a video, and inserted it in the recorder. It was a recording of the news report of the car-bomb attack. He calmly and dispassionately talked me through it. The sight of the blazing inferno that was his car made me realise, in a dramatic way I'd never previously experienced, just how lucky he had been to survive. Afterwards, Flo took me aside in the kitchen and said the Mervyn had never done that before: she hoped it was a sign that he was gradually coming to terms with the terrible experience: perhaps talking about it made it easier to bear. His mother has no doubt that Mervyn will come through. 'He's shown tremendous courage. I remember him saying some months ago when he was going through sheer hell with the pain, "They've broken my body, but they will never break my spirit, because the day they do that, they'll have won."' There's no doubt that Mervyn means every word. When I asked him if he regretted having joined the RUC – because if he hadn't he probably wouldn't have been blown up – he said he didn't regret a moment. 'In fact, if I could,' he said, 'I'd go back and do it all again.' In May 1989, specialists told Mervyn he would probably have to lose part of his other leg.

To Flo and her family, Mervyn's suffering over the past fifteen months is the suffering of their fellow countrymen, Catholic and Protestant alike, over the past twenty years of the Troubles. 'Thousands of people have lost their lives and thousands of people have been maimed for life. There's no country worth shedding that amount of blood for. If anybody thinks that what they're doing is to help save Ireland, all I can say is "God help Ireland".'

As I saw the tears in her eyes and remembered all the families I had met from every side in the conflict, whatever the label – English or Irish, Nationalist or Unionist, Catholic or Protestant – I reflected that most of them would probably agree.

CHAPTER THIRTEEN

A FORGOTTEN FAMILY

Over a year ago, when I first started looking for people we might include in the television series *Families at War*, I received a letter from a woman, whom I shall call Marion Pearson, a Protestant who lived in the west of the province. It was written in a careful, neat hand, with every word in capital letters. She told me in simple, moving language how her family had suffered loss in the early years of the Troubles and of how it was still felt day after day. The image of death on the television news or the photograph that freezes tragedy on the front page of a newspaper – be they the horror of Enniskillen, or the murder of two corporals dragged from a car, stripped and shot dead, or the pictures of 'Bloody Sunday' – shock at the time but then fade in the memory. We don't want to remember. We prefer to forget. Grief mainly lingers with the loved ones of those who have been lost, regardless of the side to which they belong or the hand that has struck them down. In her letter, Marion eloquently addressed the point:

> I am proud to be associated with the security forces and my heart goes out to the mothers, wives and relations of our young soldiers from the mainland who are serving here . . . Having suffered, I feel that we, the families of the security forces, in particular the RUC, are the 'Forgotten Families' in these Troubles . . . We have lived and weathered the past twenty years with courage and dignity, living in virtual silence, not being able to express how we feel, for fear of reprisals and threats to our young families . . . Although trauma has beset my family, we are in no way bitter. My husband, William, and I have many decent Roman Catholic friends. Neither of us have any time for the politicians who are supposed to be our leaders.

I met Marion in Northern Ireland in the summer of 1988, and on several subsequent occasions with her husband William. She had long since moved away from the place where the tragedy had struck, hoping that the memory might be less painful to bear. She is a well-dressed, attractive woman, somewhere in her forties, with clear blue eyes and short dark hair. Though calm and softly spoken, you can sense the well of emotion that the painful years have taught her to control. We talked for several hours. We met and talked again. Having discussed the matter at length with her family, she said she did not want to appear in a television programme but agreed to help me with a chapter for this book if I thought it could help illuminate her feelings. But she didn't want to be identified.

Marion and her older sister June were brought up in a farming village nestling among the mountains in the west of the province. Her father ran the village paper shop and often used to do the paper round himself on a pushbike on which, given the nature of the terrain, it was necessary to do more pushing than biking. The village was a happy, mixed community in which any sectarian conflict would have been unthinkable. 'We had a happy, carefree childhood and wonderful caring parents. I didn't know the difference between Roman Catholics and Protestants when I was growing up. Most of my father's friends were Catholics and he used to drink with them in O'Callaghan's Bar. Everyone went in there.' When Marion left school at fifteen, she went to work in one of the many shirt factories in Londonderry which for years had been the main source of employment for women in the town and still were until the outbreak of the Troubles. There she met her future husband William, seven years her senior, who until they moved away had been one of the factory's most experienced cutters. William's job was to make special shirts for special people. 'Film stars and the like.' Again, as in Marion's village, sectarian problems were unheard of. 'It was great. Everybody used to mix together. Most of the girls were Catholics and many of them were my friends. We'd often go off to the cinema and dances together.'

In the fifties there were three main dances in the town on a Saturday night. Young Catholics in their teens would take their chances at the Corinthian; the older generation (although only by a decade) would trip the light fantastic to live bands at the Embassy; and the likes of Marion and June would get dressed up to impress the boys at the 'Mem' – the Memorial Hall. 'That's where everybody met their fate.' But their father was strict. Marion and June were the daughters of his second marriage and he had every intention of keeping a close eye on them. June wasn't allowed to go out on her own until she was nearly eighteen. Only then was her father prepared to let her stay the weekend with a cousin in Londonderry and go to the Saturday dance. Marion (who was five years younger) would watch her big sister get dressed up for the Mem and then catch the bus into the city. One of the reasons their father was reluctant to let his elder daughter loose on the Memorial Hall at too tender an age was that in the fifties the bulk of its male clientele were sailors from submarines fresh from NATO exercises in the North Atlantic. He was not keen that they should come up for air and light upon his daughter. To the young ladies of Londonderry, the attraction was obvious. Not only did the Royal Navy know how to have a good time, but it was a potential passport to a new world outside – in the same way that many young women took up with soldiers in their early days in the province. To the sailors and soldiers it didn't matter whether they were Catholics or Protestants as long as they were girls.

One Saturday night at the Mem in the mid-fifties June met Don, a sailor from Wolverhampton, then on submarine patrol on NATO exercises after training on board HMS *Ganges* and then serving in Korea. The relationship grew but it was some time before June told her parents about it. 'It was me who spilled the beans,' Marion laughs, 'I heard her talking to a friend about meeting Don and saying that she'd told him that she wouldn't go out with him if he wore his bell bottoms and the rest of his uniform.' When the fleet was in port, the sailors used to like to advertise the fact. 'I was very young at the time. I told June I was going to tell father. I blackmailed her!' she laughed again. Don started to write to June when the exercises were over and she eventually had to tell her father when he grew suspicious about the letters from England addressed to his daughter that landed on the doormat. The sky didn't fall in. Don came out to visit the family and they took to him at once. 'My parents grew very fond of him. He had a great personality. They thought the world of him.' William added, leaning forward from his chair by the fire, head on one side and pointing his finger, 'Both before and after he'd married June he'd come into the house and immediately make himself at home. Usually Englishmen – no offence, like – are a bit stand-offish. He had great charisma. He'd cross his great long legs and sit there drinking tea. He was good "crack". He had a great sense of humour. We really enjoyed him. He loved fishing, but he was a lousy fisherman!'

When he was on leave during Christmas 1956, Don took June over to Wolverhampton to meet his parents. She came back with an engagement ring. They decided to get married on his next leave and fixed the date for 13 August 1957. Don still had four years to do in the navy and they decided not to start a family until his service was over. Their first child, Tracy, was born a few years later. By this time Don had taken a shore job at a naval base near Plympton, but he never really found his land legs and got bored with a routine nine to five job. He thought being a policeman would be more exciting and joined the Bristol force. The family moved there but June never really settled down, finding the people aloof and not very friendly. Like so many who leave the town, she became homesick for Londonderry. In 1967 her mother died of a secondary cancer. Don and June, who now had a second child, Iain, came over for the funeral and, at the suggestion of Marion and William, who were now married, decided to return to Northern Ireland for good. They didn't need much persuading. June was longing to get back to Londonderry and Don was excited by the prospect of a transfer from the Bristol police to the RUC, where he thought the prospects of promotion were better. 'Don was delighted to come over. He loved Northern Ireland.'

His first posting could not have been more idyllic, to the seaside village of Ardglass at the southern edge of the beautiful County Down peninsula. They bought a bungalow overlooking a golf course and the sea, and in his off-duty periods Don set about cultivating the garden he loved. He used to grow beautiful roses and all his own vegetables. 'When I used to peel his potatoes, he'd say to me, "Are we having skins for dinner?" He was so proud of everything he grew in his garden.'

Don joined the RUC on the eve of the outbreak of the Troubles. Few were aware of what lay ahead; even when the violence and rioting started in 1968 and early 1969, it remained remote and distant from the majority of people in Northern Ireland, as well as in Britain. It was something that happened on a television screen: few liked to admit or face up to the fact that an unprecedented explosion of anger was erupting on streets and country lanes within the United Kingdom. Marion remembers watching the TV coverage of the Burntollet Bridge ambush, on 4 January 1969. 'I remember watching the news. I was horrified. I thought, "This can't be happening here." But when the TV went off I forgot about it. I didn't take any interest in politics. I had to cope with two young sons, with only fourteen months between them. I had my own "troubles" – raising a family.'

The violence at Burntollet Bridge, and the subsequent incursion that night of the police into the Catholic Bogside area of Londonderry, accelerated the chain of events that was to lead to the intervention of the British army eight months later. In its official report to the Government on the disturbances, the Cameron Commission wrote:

> We have to record with regret that our investigations have led us to the unhesitating conclusion that on the night of 4th/5th January [1969] a number of policemen were guilty of misconduct which involved assault and battery, malicious damage to property . . . and the use of provocative sectarian and political slogans.*

But Marion's domestic priorities understandably took precedence. Her main concern at the time was getting a house. She had waited and fought for one for four years. It is true that Catholics had problems in getting council houses at the time, but it is often forgotten that Protestants had great problems too. The fact was that there simply weren't enough houses to go round. 'We went on our bended knees to get a house. We wanted a home of our own so much. When we finally got one in 1969, we were over the moon.'

On 12 August 1969 the Troubles impinged on Marion for the very first time. The family had gone to spend a holiday with Don and June and their family in Ardglass. 'It was the last happy day we spent together as two families. That was our first night of worry.' It was a beautiful summer and the two families spent every day of the holiday on the beach, with the children building sandcastles, running in and out of the water, eating crisps and drinking lemonade. The children would retire to bed tired but happy, whilst their parents sank down to watch the news. That evening they could not believe what they saw: scenes of devastation back home in Londonderry, with exhausted policemen lying in the streets, some with blood streaming out of their heads. 'We couldn't believe our eyes. The rioting was ferocious. Bricks and paving stones were being hurled at the police. Buildings were on fire. This wasn't the place we came from. This wasn't *our* Londonderry where the people were so civil and friendly. But sadly it was. I remember Don saying, "Thank God I'm not there tonight!".'

But within hours he was. Police reinforcements were called up the length and breadth of the province. An RUC Landrover arrived and Don was asked to report for duty. Whilst he kissed the sleeping

---

* *Disturbances in Northern Ireland.* Report of the Commission appointed by the Governor of Northern Ireland. Para 177. Cmd. 532 (HMSO).

children goodbye, Marion and June rapidly made him sandwiches and rustled up flasks of tea and hot soup. The two sisters and William sat up all night drinking coffee. 'That was our first night of worry about Don being a policeman in the RUC. It wasn't worry about him getting shot [guns were barely in evidence in 1969] but about him getting an eye put out by a stone or a brick.'

Marion, William and the children were due to return to Londonderry the following day, but after a night of worry, none of them wanted to leave until they saw Don safely back. At 4.30 the Landrover arrived bringing Don home. 'His clothes, face and hands were as black as the crook. I could still smell the burning buildings. He had a large gash over his right eye where he'd been hit by a brick. I remember there was spittle on his uniform. To this day I can still remember the scorching, smoky smell. He threw himself down on the sofa, exhausted, and said, "What a bloody hell-hole you're going home to!"'

Marion remembers the troops arriving in Londonderry on 14 August 1969 but never paid much attention to it. Two days earlier the most ferocious rioting the province had yet seen erupted in the wake of the Protestant Apprentice Boys parade. The Bogsiders erected barricades, the RUC breached them, petrol bombs were thrown, and the police responded with CS gas – the first time it had ever been used in the United Kingdom. For two days the 'Battle of the Bogside' raged until the army intervened to take the pressure off the exhausted police. The historical significance of the moment was lost on most people at the time. The predominant reaction was one of relief. 'I didn't take much interest. The soldiers' arrival meant nothing to me. It wasn't people of our own persuasion who got them in. It was the Catholic people who wanted the troops. We didn't care whether they came or not.' Family matters returned again to the forefront of Marion's mind. In 1970 her father died. Don and June came over from Ardglass for the funeral. But this time Don astounded the family by announcing that he'd decided to put in for a transfer to the west of the province so they could all be nearer to the family. June in particular wanted to be closer to home. Marion and William were amazed that Don was prepared to exchange the peace and tranquillity of Ardglass for the dangerous unpredictability of the other side of Northern Ireland. Don pointed out that he wanted to make his way in the traffic branch of the RUC and the opportunities for studying traffic flows and jams in Ardglass were strictly limited. He thought he'd get far greater experience in a bigger town like Coleraine or a border town like Strabane, a few miles down the road from Londonderry, where the traffic problems were (and still can be) horrendous.

Don took his sergeant's exams and then transferred to where the jams were. He'd already had bitter experience of the hatred in Londonderry and soon found that it extended well beyond the city to the area where he lived. One day when Marion and William drove down to see him for a day out, they were upset to find that his car tyres had been slashed whilst it was standing outside the house; and on another occasion, stones had been thrown at the windows. Don brushed the incidents off as 'just minor things'. He didn't talk much about his work as he didn't want to worry June any more than was necessary as she was expecting their third child, Hayley, in May 1972. He sometimes complained of headaches but June put it down to long hours, irregular meals and smoking too much. But Marion suspected, probably correctly, that the real reason for the headaches was the tension and pressure of his job as the situation got progressively worse. 'We never expected things to develop stage by stage as they have. And we certainly never expected it to become so vicious.'

Apart from such 'minor' incidents, which acted as a nagging reminder of the nastiness beneath the surface, the deteriorating situation came home to Marion for the second time on 31 July 1972. As troops were dismantling the barricades that defended the 'No Go' areas in the Bogside and Creggan districts of Londonderry (behind which the Provisionals had grown strong), the IRA devastated the village of Claudy, nine miles away from Londonderry, with three huge car bombs. No warning arrived. The Provisional IRA denied responsibility. Six people were killed, including a nine-year-old girl. Three more subsequently died from their injuries. The first bomb, in a stolen Cortina, exploded outside McIlhinney's public house and killed a little girl as she cleaned the windows of her father's grocery store across the street. The second bomb, in a stolen mini-van, went off outside the Beaufort Hotel, leaving it in ruins and killing two workmen and a boy of sixteen. The third bomb, in a stolen mini-traveller, exploded outside the post office, hurling people across the street. 'Many of us knew the little village as it was only a few miles up the road. The loss seemed to be so near. It was heartbreaking for us all.'

Saturday 13 January was Marion's daughter's fourth birthday and she'd planned a small party. Don and June brought their children up to Londonderry for the afternoon before Don went back on duty. As he left, he told Marion not to forget to have his 'Ulster Fry' ready for him at teatime when he came back to pick up his wife and children. (An 'Ulster Fry', better known as 'a heart attack on a plate', is bacon, egg, sausage, tomato, mushrooms, fried bread, fried potatoes, soda bread and anything else that can be thrown into the fat in the pan.) 'Don loved his "Ulster Fry".' The party was a great success, although like all children's parties, especially for four-year-olds, utterly exhausting for the organisers. Don returned for his family and 'Ulster Fry' and drove them home, with Tracy and Iain laughing and waving to their aunt through the back window of the car. Don tooted his horn as he went off round the corner.

The following day, Sunday 14 January, threatened another birthday party. Iain was eight. Neither June nor Marion could face the prospect of further entertainment, this time with eight-year-olds, so June decided she'd just have a small family tea with a birthday cake which they would share with Don when he came home from duty around seven o'clock that night. June asked her sister to come over but Marion, tired after one birthday party, declined, saying that they'd get together again some time the following week.

Sunday dawned a terrible day, with a driving wind and sleet and snow. Marion felt depressed and irritable with the children. 'Maybe it was because I was tired from the day before and the children running around shouting and laughing just seemed to grate on my nerves. It was almost as if I had a sense of foreboding something was going to happen.' Miles away, in the early evening, her sister June started to shiver, which was unusual in a house that was always warm in winter with storage heaters. She turned on the three bars on the electric fire. Around that time there was a massive explosion. Both Marion and June lived too far away to hear it. Marion was lying on the sofa sleeping, having asked William to put the children to bed as she'd had enough. William was watching TV. About eight o'clock there was a knock on the door. William got up to answer. Marion remembers hearing the words, 'God, there's terrible bad news for you both tonight.' She leaped up from the sofa and rushed into the hall, knowing immediately, as if with second sense, what had happened. 'It's Don, it's Don, isn't it?' she cried. The bringer of the tragic news was her brother. 'They were just going home for their tea,' he tried to explain, 'and a bomb went off under their car.' Marion remembers reaching for her brother's hair and starting to pull it. 'Tell me he's not dead! Tell me he's not dead!' she screamed. Then she saw William and the police officer who'd come with her brother exchanging a look. That told her everything. 'I knew, I knew then that he was dead. I remember throwing myself on the floor. I just lost my head completely. The next thing I remember was a slap right across the face to try and bring me round. I went into hysterics. I screamed and I roared but I didn't faint. Someone sent for the doctor, who gave me an injection. I can still remember the children standing on the stairs, with three wee faces staring over the banister and my four-year-old, clutching her little doll, saying over and over again, "What's wrong with mummy?" They didn't know what was happening.'

An hour later Marion and William left for June's house. When they arrived, just before nine o'clock, she was sitting in a chair by the fire, apparently in a world of her own, drugged by the doctor's injections, her eyes swollen from crying. 'She'd aged ten years overnight. I felt so inadequate. My heart was breaking for her. I rushed over to her chair to hold and comfort her. She was like a zombie. Her first words were, "What kept you?" The bomb had gone off at ten past seven and it was now nearly nine o'clock. It had taken the doctor nearly an hour to calm me down. June just sat there saying, "I can't believe it. I just can't believe it." She was very calm, sedated after the injections.' Ten-year-old Tracy just wanted to go away. Eight-year-old Iain refused to leave his mother. He'd been waiting for his father to come home for his birthday tea. The cake, with eight candles, was still sitting on the dining-room table, with 'Happy Eighth Birthday' written in blue icing. 'He couldn't understand. He knew there was something wrong.'

The following day, the coffin was brought from the morgue to the house and laid in the bedroom. The two sisters, in tears, stood beside it. 'June was really breaking her heart, sobbing and crying and running her hand over the polished wood. All of a sudden she stopped and looked at me, caressing the top of the coffin with her right hand. "I suppose his head is up there," she said, startling me with the question. Common sense told me that there was no body, there was no head – just a plastic bag of blood and limbs. But I told her that's where the head was.' The car bomb had been placed directly under Don's seat and he'd taken the full force of the blast. 'She seemed to accept it and then the tears started to stream down her cheeks again. "How am I going to cope?" she cried. "How am I going to cope without him?"'

The house soon became full of people, Protestant and Catholic, who came to pay their respects. On a couple of occasions little Iain disappeared. He was finally found in the bedroom, sitting cross-legged under the coffin. 'It's something I'll remember till the day I die.'

Tracy never cried and never mentioned her father's name. 'Whenever we wanted to talk about her daddy, she didn't want to know, she just went out of the room. June used to say how she wished Tracy would cry instead of bottling it all up inside her.' The morning of Iain's birthday, brother and sister had fought like cats and dogs, with Iain taunting Tracy that she wasn't going to get any birthday cake when daddy came home that night. Tracy, provoked, hit Iain. 'Don, who never, ever, hit Tracy, scolded her and she got the blame for starting the row. She ran outside in anger. Don, who was just about to go on duty, shouted after her, "Put the kettle on and make me a cup of tea before I go out!" Tracy yelled, "No, I'm not!" Don replied, "That's the last thing I'll ask you to do for me!" And it was.' Years later, when Marion told Tracy the full story, she cried her eyes out.

Don was laid to rest alongside his parents-in-law in the village churchyard where he'd married June, overlooking the river where he'd loved to fish. After a few days people stopped calling, getting on with their own lives as the memory of Don faded. 'The police welfare people were good to her and she had one or two faithful friends, but the rest seemed to drift away and forget.' They became, like hundreds of others, a forgotten family. June was awarded £4000 for the loss of a husband and father. She became more and more depressed, finding it increasingly difficult to cope with two young children and a young baby. The family rallied round and gave her all the support they could. June gave a television interview and said she had no bitterness and that it wasn't in her heart to hate. Marion told me that if the man responsible for Don's death came in through the door, and she was told she had the right to shoot him, she couldn't do it. She said their attitude went back to the way they'd been brought up.

June developed asthma, a condition that can be triggered by extreme trauma. The attacks gradually got worse, and when she eventually died, she left three children 'as orphans due to the Troubles'. But before she died she had made a special friend who had brought some joy back into her life, a Catholic woman whom she'd met in hospital. They shared a special understanding as her brother had been killed by Protestant paramilitaries.

The family may be forgotten, but Marion can never forget. 'It's not like a normal death, where time heals wounds. You pretend everything's all right but it's not. Every atrocity you see on TV, whatever side is responsible, brings it all back, so you live with it every day.' I thought of the families of nearly 3000 victims of the

Troubles, and wondered if they all felt the same. I suspected most of them did, regardless of the side to which they belong. I wondered too if most would agree with the closing sentence of that first letter that Marion sent me:

> We used to pray that the Troubles would be over before our sons became teenagers. Now we pray that they will be over before our grandsons become teenagers. We pray for peace *soon*, *soon*.

I suspect that most of them would.

CHRONOLOGY

1607–18   Plantation of Ulster by King James I on lands confiscated from rebellious Irish chieftains. By 1618 around 40 000 Scots had emigrated to obtain land and escape religious persecution. In 1613 Derry became Londonderry, in acknowledgement of finance from City of London to defray cost of Plantation.

1652   Suppression of rebellion of dispossessed native Irish by Oliver Cromwell. Much of best land confiscated and given to new Protestant settlers and Cromwellian soldiers.

1685   By accession of King James II only 22% of Irish land left in Catholic hands.

1689   Siege of Londonderry.

1690
12 July   Protestant King William of Orange defeats the Catholic King James II at the Battle of the Boyne.

1791   First open meeting of Wolfe Tone's United Irishmen in Belfast. Resolution adopted that all Irishmen of all religious persuasions should join together to counteract English influence in Ireland.

1795   The Orange Society, forerunner of the Orange Order, founded in County Armagh, with secret oath of loyalty to the throne and the Protestant succession.

1798   Defeat of rebellion of United Irishmen in their attempt to establish Irish Republic.

1800   Act of Union between Britain and Ireland.

1803   Failed rebellion of Robert Emmet; famous speech from dock before execution.

1846   The Great Famine almost halved population of Ireland.

1858	Foundation of Irish Republican Brotherhood – 19th-century root of the Irish Republican Army.
1867	Failure of Fenian insurrection.
1868	Gladstone announces, 'My mission is to pacify Ireland'.
1886–93	Gladstone's Bills giving Home Rule to Ireland defeated by Conservatives and Unionists. Lord Randolph Churchill declares that, if Home Rule is introduced, 'Ulster will fight; Ulster will be right.'
1914	Home Rule Bill passes, but not to come into force until end of war. Ulster Volunteers arm and prepare to resist Home Rule.

1916

24–29 Apr	Easter Rising led by Patrick Pearse, who proclaims the 'Irish Republic' outside the GPO in Dublin.
May	The seven leaders of the rebellion, including Pearse and James Connolly, executed by the British.
3 Aug	Roger Casement executed.

1918	Sinn Fein wins sweeping victories in Ireland in elections to British Parliament. Their representatives refuse to take their seats and set up their own Irish Parliament, Dail Eireann. The army of the new Irish Parliament is known as the Irish Republican Army (IRA).
1920	The Anglo–Irish War (or the 'War of Independence'). Britain introduces the 'Black and Tans'.
19 July	Beginning of four nights' rioting in Derry. Nineteen killed.
Dec	British Parliament passes the Government of Ireland Act, setting up separate Parliaments for North and South.
1921	Irish representatives sign Treaty with British government granting Ireland Dominion status as the Irish Free State, and allowing 'Northern Ireland' to adhere to existing arrangement of 1920.
1922–3	Civil War between Michael Collins and supporters of the Treaty and Eamonn de Valera and its opponents, who believe the Treaty is a 'sell-out' that fails to achieve the goal of the Irish Republic because the six counties of the North are excluded from it. Pro-Treaty forces victorious; 232 people killed and around 1000 wounded. The new Free State government executes 77 of its opponents. Casualties greater than in Anglo–Irish War.

1925   Irish Free State government confirms border of Northern Ireland laid down in 1920 Act.

1931   IRA declared illegal in Free State.

1937   New Irish Constitution envisages eventual unity of Ireland.

1949   Ireland becomes the Republic of Ireland.
British government gives constitutional guarantee to Unionist government at Stormont that Northern Ireland will remain part of the United Kingdom as long as it is the wish of the majority of its people.

1956–62 IRA border campaign ends when internment introduced North and South; 6 RUC, 8 IRA and 9 Republican supporters killed. Campaign fails to gain any significant support from Nationalists in Northern Ireland.

1966
7 Mar   IRA blow up Nelson's Pillar in Dublin's O'Connell Street.

1967
29 Jan   Northern Ireland Civil Rights Association (NICRA) formed and demands: one man one vote in local elections; removal of gerrymandered boundaries (as in Derry); anti-discrimination laws; allocation of public housing on points system; repeal of Special Powers Act; disbandment of 'B Specials'.

1968
24 Aug   First civil rights march from Coalisland to Dungannon to protest about housing allocation.

5 Oct   Violence at civil rights march in Derry. 'B Specials' seen in action on world's media.

1969
4 Jan   Loyalists ambush civil rights protesters on march from Belfast to Derry at Burntollet Bridge.

5 Jan   'You are now entering Free Derry' painted on gable end after RUC incursion of Bogside and formation of local 'citizens' army'. Police action condemned in Cameron Report.

12 Aug   Violence after Apprentice Boys Parade in Derry. 'Battle of the Bogside' begins. CS gas used for first time.

| 13 Aug | Stormont government asks Home Secretary, James Callaghan, to send in British troops as RUC exhausted. |
| | Protestants start burning Catholic homes in Belfast around Bombay Street. |

14 Aug   British troops arrive in Derry.

15 Aug   British troops arrive in Belfast. Given heroes' reception by Catholics in Belfast and Derry.

16 Aug   First 'Citizens Defence Committees' formed, the nucleus of the future IRA.

9 Sept   Announcement that a 'Peace Line' will be built between the Falls and the Shankill in Belfast.

10 Oct   Hunt Report recommends disbandment of 'B Specials' and formation of new part-time force, which becomes the Ulster Defence Regiment (UDR).

11 Oct   First RUC officer shot dead by Loyalist gunman during rioting in Shankill Road.

29 Dec   Split revealed within IRA into the 'Provisional' IRA and 'Official' IRA. Failure to defend Northern Catholics from Protestant attack one of reasons for split.

1970

27 June   Gun battle at St Matthew's church in Belfast with newly formed Provisional IRA (PIRA) defending Short Strand from Protestant attack: 1 IRA man and 3 Protestants killed.

3 July   Falls Road curfew maintained for 34 hours. Three civilians killed; 1600 canisters of CS gas fired; considerable amount of arms and ammunition found.

21 Aug   Mainly Catholic Social Democratic and Labour Party (SDLP) founded, with goal of achieving Irish unity by consent not violence.

1971

6 Feb   Provisional IRA kills Gunner Robert Curtis in machine-gun attack, first British soldier to die on service in Ireland since 1920–1. Army kill first member of PIRA.

9 Mar   PIRA kill 3 young Scottish soldiers out for a drink.

22 May   Corporal Robert Bankier shot by IRA in Markets area of Belfast, the first member of the Royal Green Jackets to be killed.

8 July	Seamus Cusack and Desmond Beattie shot by army in Derry during rioting.
9 Aug	Internment. 'Lord Jim' wounded.
18 Aug	Army shoot dead Eamonn Lafferty of PIRA in Derry after he's just taken over patrolling Creggan from Shane Paul O'Doherty.
Sept	Ulster Defence Association (UDA) formed.
16 Nov	Compton Commission finds some detainees ill-treated after internment.

1972

30 Jan	'Bloody Sunday'. Paratroopers shoot dead 13 civilians during civil rights march in Derry. Shane Paul O'Doherty becomes reinvolved in PIRA.
24 Mar	HMG abolishes Stormont Parliament and introduces Direct Rule from Westminster.
28 Mar	William Craig's 'Vanguard' movement holds rally of 100 000 Loyalists at Stormont to protest introduction of Direct Rule. Lindsay Mooney attends: the Lewers brothers do not.
19 Apr	Widgery Report on Bloody Sunday published. Dismissed as 'whitewash' by Nationalists.
20 June	PIRA hunger strike in Crumlin Road gaol ends after HMG grants Special Category Status – which paramilitaries take to be 'Political Status'. Prisoners allowed to wear own clothes, freely associate with each other and be excused prison work.
27 June	PIRA announces ceasefire.
3 July	UDA establishes own 'No Go' areas to force authorities to dismantle IRA 'No Go' areas in Derry and Belfast.
7 July	PIRA's Army Council meets Secretary of State for Northern Ireland, William Whitelaw, in London.
9 July	Ceasefire ends after confrontation in Lenadoon Avenue, Belfast, over rehousing Catholics.
18 July	100th British soldier to die on service in Northern Ireland since 1969.
21 July	'Bloody Friday' in Belfast: 22 PIRA bombs kill 9 and injure 130 civilians.
31 July	Army removes 'No Go' areas in 'Operation Motorman'.

1973

8 Mar   First PIRA bombs in London: 1 person dies and 180 injured. Price sisters arrested. Publicity makes impact on Shane Paul O'Doherty.

Border poll in Northern Ireland finds 57% of electorate favour union with Britain.

17 Mar   Lindsay Mooney, 'Sergeant' in UDA, blown up by own bomb.

21 Nov   Announcement of decision to set up new government in Northern Ireland in which for first time Catholics and Protestants will share power in Cabinet as a 'Power Sharing Executive'.

6 Dec   The Sunningdale Agreement: British and Irish governments to set up a Council of Ireland as part of power-sharing agreement.

1974

13 May   Sean McKearney blown up by own bomb.

15 May   Beginning of province-wide strike organised by the Protestant Ulster Workers Council in opposition to Power Sharing Executive and Sunningdale Agreement.

28 May   New Executive resigns and political initiative collapses.

5 Oct   Guildford pub bombs: 5 killed and 54 injured.

21 Nov   Birmingham bombs: 19 killed and 154 injured.

29 Nov   Prevention of Terrorism Bill becomes law.

2 Dec   Explosion at Shane Paul O'Doherty's bomb factory in Derry. IRA volunteer Ethel Lynch killed.

10 Dec   Talks between IRA, Sinn Fein and Protestant clergymen at Feakle in Irish Republic.

20 Dec   IRA ceasefire begins, runs until middle of 1975.

1975   NI Secretary of State, Merlyn Rees, sets up 'incident centres' where NI Office officials can contact Sinn Fein.

8 May   Shane Paul O'Doherty arrested at home in Derry.

10 May   PIRA shoot dead RUC Constable Paul Gray in relatiation for arrest of Shane Paul O'Doherty.

31 July   Members of Miami Showband murdered by Ulster Volunteer Force, one of whom was member of UDR.

5 Sept   Margaret McKearney branded as 'Terror Girl' by British press.

1976

4 Jan   Loyalist gunmen murder 5 Catholics in South Armagh.

5 Jan   Republican gunmen, claiming to be members of the 'Republican Action Force', murder 10 Protestants in a minibus near Kingsmills in South Armagh, in retaliation for Loyalist killings of previous day.

1 Mar   Government begins phasing out of Special Category Status. All prisoners convicted of terrorist offences after this date are to be treated as 'ordinary' criminals and subsequently locked up in the new 'H blocks' (so called because of their shape).

5 Apr   PIRA bomb blitz in Belfast; 18-year-old Mairead Farrell arrested having planted bombs that destroy the Conway Hotel.

21 July   PIRA kill Christopher Ewart-Biggs, British Ambassador to Ireland, and Judith Cooke, a civil servant.

10 Sept   Shane Paul O'Doherty sentenced to 30 life sentences in London for letter-bomb campaign.

16 Sept   Ciaran Nugent, an IRA prisoner at the Maze near Belfast, refuses to put on prison uniform and wears blanket. The beginning of the 'blanket protest' in attempt to retrieve 'political status'.

28 Oct   Part-time UDR corporal, Stanley Adams, shot dead by PIRA. Thomas McKearney subsequently given life sentence for his murder.

1977

10 Aug   Queen's Jubilee visit to Belfast.

10 Oct   Mairead Corrigan and Betty Williams, leaders of the Peace People, awarded Nobel Peace Prize for 1976.

Autumn   Allegations that IRA (and some Loyalist) suspects are being ill-treated during RUC interrogation.

1978

17 Feb   In his local home-town paper, the *Derry Journal*, Shane Paul O'Doherty rejects violence and the Provisional IRA.
PIRA firebomb the La Mon Restaurant outside Belfast: 12 people burned to death and over 30 injured.

March   IRA prisoners' 'dirty protest' begins in Maze Prison.

1979   Shane Paul O'Doherty finally allowed to contact his victims and apologise. He is still regarded as a 'subversive' prisoner by the authorities as he maintains protests to try and achieve repatriation to a NI prison.

16 Mar   The government's Bennett Report into ill-treatment allegations during police interrogation finds prima facie evidence of abuse. The Amnesty Report goes much further and condemns abuses.

31 Mar   Airey Neave blown up by INLA car bomb as he is leaving House of Commons.

27 Aug   IRA assassinate Lord Mountbatten at Mullaghmore in County Sligo and kill 18 British soldiers at Warrenpoint.

1980
27 Oct   Thomas McKearney and 6 IRA prisoners start hunger strike.

1 Nov   Mairead Farrell and 3 IRA prisoners in Armagh gaol start hunger strike.

18 Dec   Hunger strike called off.

1981
Feb   Rev. Ian Paisley starts 'The Carson Trail'.

1 Mar   On fifth anniversary of ending of Special Category Status, IRA prisoner Bobby Sands begins hunger strike.

11 Mar   Army begins rebuilding the 'Peace Line' with bricks.

9 Apr   Hunger striker Bobby Sands elected Westminster MP for Fermanagh/South Tyrone in bye-election with 30 492 votes.

5 May   Bobby Sands dies on 66th day of hunger strike. During the summer a further 9 PIRA and INLA prisoners follow him to their deaths.

28 May   On a visit to Belfast, Prime Minister Margaret Thatcher says, 'The men of violence have chosen in recent months to play what may well be their last card.'

3 Oct   Hunger strike called off.
16 Nov   Rev. Ian Paisley's 'Third Force' makes first appearance, with over 500 men marching in Enniskillen.

1982
25 Mar   Three Royal Green Jackets shot dead in IRA ambush in Crocus Street in West Belfast.

20 July	PIRA bomb the Household Cavalry riding through Hyde Park and the Royal Green Jackets Band in Regents Park; 11 people die.
Nov–Dec	RUC's anti-terrorist unit shoot dead 3 members of IRA, 2 of INLA and a young civilian, in incidents that give rise to 'shoot to kill' allegations.
6 Dec	INLA bomb Droppin' Well pub, killing 12 soldiers and 5 civilians. Trial of 38 people named by PIRA 'supergrass' Christopher Black begins.

1983

9 June	Gerry Adams, President of Sinn Fein, elected Westminster MP for West Belfast in General Election.
25 Sept	Padraig McKearney and 37 IRA prisoners escape from Maze Prison.
13 Oct	UDR auction organised by Major 'Mary Wallace'.
17 Dec	PIRA car bomb explodes outside Harrods in London, killing 8 and injuring 80.

1984

12 Oct	PIRA bomb Grand Hotel, Brighton, during Conservative Party Conference; 5 killed.

1985

28 Feb	PIRA mortar-bomb Newry RUC station, killing 9 officers.
15 May	Sinn Fein take 59 out of 566 seats in Northern Ireland local government elections.
5 Sept	Shane Paul O'Doherty to be transferred from England to the Maze Prison, Northern Ireland.
15 Nov	Anglo–Irish Agreement signed at Hillsborough, Northern Ireland, by British and Irish Prime Ministers.

1986

31 Mar	Riots in Portadown as Loyalists attack RUC; first Loyalist to die from plastic bullet injury.
20 May	HMG reveals that there have been 368 cases of intimidation on RUC members since signing of Anglo–Irish Agreement.

5 June   John Stalker, Deputy Chief Constable of Greater Manchester Police, removed from inquiry into alleged 'shoot to kill' incidents; his place taken by Colin Sampson, Chief Constable of West Yorkshire.

2 July   Four members of UDR sentenced to life imprisonment for murder of Catholic in November 1983.

19 Sept   Mairead Farrell released from Armagh gaol.

1987

23 Mar   RUC Chief Constable, Sir John Hermon, receives Stalker/ Sampson Report.

25 Apr   Lord Justice Gibson and wife killed by PIRA car bomb whilst crossing Border.

8 May   Padraig McKearney and 7 other IRA men killed by RUC and SAS after bombing Loughgall RUC station.

1 Nov   Huge consignment of Libyan arms and ammunition, including surface-to-air missiles, discovered on board *Eksund* in French waters.

8 Nov   PIRA bomb Remembrance Day parade at Enniskillen; 11 killed and 63 injured.

1988

14 Jan   John Hume of SDLP and Gerry Adams of Sinn Fein begin series of meetings to explore possible common ground on Irish unity. Not enough found for dialogue to produce results.

25 Jan   The Attorney General, Sir Patrick Mayhew, announces that no RUC officers will be prosecuted as a result of the Stalker/ Sampson inquiry, for reasons of 'national security'.

28 Jan   In London, the Court of Appeal rejects the appeal of the 'Birmingham Six' convicted for Birmingham bombs.

6 Mar   Mairead Farrell, Sean Savage and Daniel McCann shot dead by SAS in Gibraltar.

16 Mar   At Milltown cemetery in Belfast, 3 men shot dead by lone Loyalist gunman as 3 IRA dead from Gibraltar being buried.

19 Mar   Two British soldiers, who drove into funeral procession of one of victims of Loyalist gunman's attack in Milltown cemetery, attacked, beaten by crowd and then shot dead by IRA.

22 May   Mervyn Lewers seriously injured by PIRA car bomb, two years after leaving RUC Reserve.

15 June	Six British soldiers killed by PIRA car bomb whilst taking part in Lisburn 'Fun Run'.
20 Aug	Eight young British soldiers killed in IRA bomb attack on their coach at Ballygawley, County Tyrone.
19 Oct	Home Office announces restrictions on broadcasting interviews with Sinn Fein and other Republican and Loyalist supporters of terrorism.

1989

April	Life Sentence Review Board recommends that Shane Paul O'Doherty be released on licence.
May	Derry City Football Club win the Irish 'Treble'.
19 May	Rev. Ian Paisley's DUP and Sinn Fein suffer reverses in Northern Ireland district council elections. DUP loses 33 seats (out of 109) and Sinn Fein 20 (out of 59), but Sinn Fein's overall share of vote falls by less than 1%. SDLP gain 20 seats and increase share of vote by 3%.
24 May	British and Irish governments announce conclusion of review of Anglo–Irish Agreement and reaffirm their commitment to it.
1 June	Sir John Hermon hands over command of RUC, which he has led for 9 years, to Hugh Annesley, assistant commissioner of Metropolitan Police.
1 June	Death toll in the Troubles since 1969 – 2743. This includes: RUC 171, RUC Reserve 89, Army 415, UDR 180, Civilians 1888. (NB this civilian figure includes Republican and Loyalist paramilitary dead as RUC classes PIRA, INLA, UDA, UVF etc. as 'civilians'.)

BIBLIOGRAPHY

Arthur, Max, *Northern Ireland: Soldiers Talking* (Sidgwick, new ed. pbk 1988)

Arthur, Paul, and Jeffery, Keith, *Northern Ireland since 1968* (Making Contemporary Britain, Basil Blackwell, 1988)

Barzilay, David, *The British Army in Ulster* (Century Services, Belfast, 1973)

Bell, Geoffrey, *The Protestants of Ulster* (Pluto Press, 1976)

Beresford, David, *Ten Men Dead. The Story of the 1981 Irish Hunger Strike* (Grafton, 1987)

Bew, Paul, and Patterson, Henry, *The British State and the Ulster Crisis: From Wilson to Thatcher* (Verso edns, 1985)

Bishop, Patrick, and Mallie, Eamonn, *The Provisional IRA* (William Heinemann, 1987)

Bowyer Bell, J., *The Secret Army: History of the IRA from 1916–1970* (The Academy Press, Dublin, rev. ed. 1983)

Boyle, Kevin, and Hadden, Tom, *Ireland: A Positive Proposal* (Penguin, 1985)

Boyle, Kevin, Hadden, Tom, and Hillyard, Paddy, *Law and State. The Case of Northern Ireland* (Martin Robertson, 1975)

Coogan, Tim Pat, *The IRA* (Fontana, rev. ed. 1987)

Cronin, Sean, *Irish Nationalism. A History of its Roots and Ideology* (Pluto Press, 1983)

Curtis, Liz, *Ireland. The Propaganda War* (Pluto Press, 1984)

Dillon, Martin, and Lehane, Denis, *Political Murder in Northern Ireland* (Penguin Special, 1973, o.p.)

Dudley Edwards, Ruth, *Patrick Pearse: The Triumph of Failure* (Victor Gollancz, 1977, o.p.)

Dunne, Derek, *Out of the Maze. The True Story of the Biggest Jail Escape Since the War* (Gill & Macmillan, Dublin, 1988)

Farrell, Michael, *Northern Ireland: The Orange State* (Pluto Press, 1980, o.p.)

Flackes, W. D., *Northern Ireland: A Political Directory 1968–1983* (BBC, Ariel Bks, 1983, o.p.)

Gray, Tony, *No Surrender. The Siege of Londonderry 1689* (Macdonald & Jane, 1975)

Gray, Tony, *The Orange Order* (Bodley Head, 1972, o.p.)

Hall, Michael, *Twenty Years. A Concise Chronology of Events in Northern Ireland from 1968–1988* (Island Publications, Newtownabbey, NI, 1988). I am greatly indebted to this account for my chronology.

Hamill, Desmond, *Pig in the Middle. The Army in Northern Ireland 1969–1984* (Methuen, new ed. pbk 1986)

Hezlet, Sir Arthur, *The 'B' Specials. A History of the Ulster Special Constabulary* (Pan, 1973, o.p.)

Kee, Robert, *The Green Flag. A History of Irish Nationalism* (Quartet, new ed. pbk 1976–1980)

Kitson, Frank, *Bunch of Five* (Faber & Faber, new ed. pbk 1988)

Kitson, Frank, *Low Intensity Operations. Subversion, Insurgency and Peacekeeping* (Faber & Faber, 1971, o.p.)

Longford, Lord, and McHardy, Anne, *Ulster* (Weidenfeld & Nicolson, 1981, o.p.)

Macardle, Dorothy, *The Irish Republic* (Corgi, 1968, o.p.)

O'Broin, Leon, *Revolutionary Underground. The Story of the Irish Republican Brotherhood 1858–1924* (Gill & Macmillan, Dublin, 1976, o.p.)

Stalker, John, *Stalker* (Harrap, 1988. Penguin, 1988)

Sunday Times Insight Team, *Ulster* (Penguin Special, 1972, o.p.)

Taylor, Peter, *Beating the Terrorists? Interrogation in Omagh, Gough and Castlereagh* (Penguin Special, 1980, o.p.)

Taylor, Peter, *Stalker. The Search for the Truth* (Faber & Faber, pbk 1987)

Uris, Jill and Leon, *Ireland: A Terrible Beauty: The Story of Ireland Today* (Andre Deutsch, 1976, o.p.)

Windlesham, Lord, and Rampton, Richard, *The Windlesham/Rampton Report on 'Death on the Rock'* (Faber & Faber, 1989)

INDEX